Compulsory Voting

In many democracies, voter turnout is low and getting lower. If the people choose not to govern themselves, should they be forced to do so?

For Jason Brennan, compulsory voting is unjust and a petty violation of citizens' liberty. The median nonvoter is less informed and rational, as well as more biased, than the median voter.

According to Lisa Hill, compulsory voting is a reasonable imposition on personal liberty. Hill points to the discernible benefits of compulsory voting and argues that high-turnout elections are more democratically legitimate.

The authors – both well known for their work on voting and civic engagement – debate such questions as

- Do citizens have a duty to vote, and is it an enforceable duty?
- Does compulsory voting violate citizens' liberty? If so, is this sufficient ground to oppose it? Or is it a justifiable violation? Might it instead promote liberty on the whole?
- Is low turnout a problem or a blessing?
- Does compulsory voting produce better government? Or might it instead produce worse government? Might it, in fact, have little effect overall on the quality of government?

Jason Brennan is Assistant Professor of Strategy, Economics, Ethics, and Public Policy at the McDonough School of Business and Assistant Professor of Philosophy at Georgetown University. Formerly, he was Assistant Professor of Philosophy at Brown University, where he was also Assistant Director of the Political Theory Project, an interdisciplinary research center. He received his PhD in philosophy from the University of Arizona in 2007. Brennan is the author of *Libertarianism: What Everyone Needs to Know* (2012); *The Ethics of Voting* (2011); and, with David Schmidtz, *A Brief History of Liberty* (2010).

Lisa Hill is Professor of Politics at the University of Adelaide, and formerly an ARC Senior Fellow (University of Adelaide) and a five-year Fellow in the Political Science Program, Research School of Social Sciences, Australian National University. Prior to that she was a lecturer in Government at the University of Sydney and took a D. Phil. in Politics at the University of Oxford. Her current areas of interest are political theory, history of political thought, and issues in electoral law. In 2011 Hill was elected a Fellow of the Academy of the Social Sciences of Australia. Her most recent book, co-authored with Bruce Buchan, is *An Intellectual History of Political Corruption* (2014).

Compulsory Voting

For and Against

JASON BRENNAN
Georgetown University

LISA HILL
University of Adelaide

CAMBRIDGE
UNIVERSITY PRESS

32 Avenue of the Americas, New York, NY 10013-2473, USA

Cambridge University Press is part of the University of Cambridge.

It furthers the University's mission by disseminating knowledge in the pursuit of education, learning, and research at the highest international levels of excellence.

www.cambridge.org
Information on this title: www.cambridge.org/9781107613928

First published 2014

A catalog record for this publication is available from the British Library.

Library of Congress Cataloging in Publication data
Brennan, Jason, 1979–
Compulsory voting : for and against / Jason Brennan, Lisa Hill.
pages cm
Includes bibliographical references and index.
ISBN 978-1-107-04151-6 (hardback) – ISBN 978-1-107-61392-8 (paperback)
1. Voting, Compulsory. I. Hill, Lisa, 1961– II. Title.
JF1031.B74 2014
325.6'5–dc23 2014001487

ISBN 978-1-107-04151-6 Hardback
ISBN 978-1-107-61392-8 Paperback

Contents

Acknowledgments

Jason benefited greatly from discussing these issues with his colleagues at Georgetown and elsewhere. He thanks Loren Lomasky, John Hasnas, Dennis Quinn, Peter Jaworski, Bryan Caplan, John Tomasi, David Estlund, Peter Boettke, Geoffrey Brennan, David Schmidtz, Matt Zwolinski, Kevin Vallier, Bas van der Vossen, Andrew J. Cohen, Andrew I. Cohen, Hélène Landemore, William Galston, Alfred Apps, the philosophy department at Georgia State University, and the audience and fellow panelists at the American Political Science Association 2013 Annual Meeting. Thanks especially to Lisa Hill for agreeing to work on this project.

Lisa Hill wishes to thank her research assistants, Brendan Drew, Carolyn Walsh, and especially Kelly McKinley, for their able assistance in the completion of this manuscript as well as the Australian Research Council, whose funding made its completion possible. She also thanks Jason Brennan for conceiving this project and generously suggesting it to her.

We are both grateful to editors at the *New York Times*, who helped bring us together in the first place to debate this topic, and to Robert Dreesen at Cambridge University Press for his support for this project.

PART I

MEDICINE WORSE THAN THE DISEASE?

Against Compulsory Voting

Jason Brennan

1

The Heavy Burden of Proof

1.1 Where Are We the People?

Democracy is rule by the people. But what if the people refuse to rule? Many people worry if we do not have government *by* the people, then we will not have government *for* the people – at least not for all of them.

During presidential elections in the late nineteenth century, 70–80 percent of eligible Americans voted. For whatever reason, in the twentieth century, participation rates seem to have dropped to 50–60 percent.[1] Midterm national, state, and local elections averaged a mere 40 percent.

A U.S. president has never been elected by a majority of eligible voters. In the 1964 election, 61.05 percent of voters cast their ballots for Lyndon Johnson – the largest majority any president has ever enjoyed. Yet, at the same time, because turnout was so low, Johnson was in fact elected by less than 38 percent of all voting-eligible Americans. We call Reagan's 1984 victory a "landslide," but less than a third of voting-age Americans actually voted for him. Less than a quarter of eligible Americans voted to reelect Bill Clinton in 1996. In all elections, a

[1] One classic paper attempting to explain this phenomenon is Richard Boyd, "Decline of U.S. Turnout: Structural Explanations," *American Politics Quarterly* 9 (1981): 133–59. However, note that some prominent political scientists think the official U.S. turnout rates are mistaken. See Michael P. McDonald and Samuel L. Popkin, "The Myth of the Vanishing Voter," *American Political Science Review* 95 (2001): 963–74.

minority of the voting-eligible population imposes a president on the majority.

When most people hear these numbers, they shake their heads and wring their hands. They conclude that Americans fail to take the responsibility of self-government seriously. They worry that Americans – especially young adults, of course – are complacent, apathetic, and self-centered.[2] I have heard conservative Americans complain, "Our brave troops died to protect our democratic freedoms, yet half of us can't be bothered to vote." The thought: democratic apathy means they died in vain.

Low turnout is not a distinctly American condition. Canada's rates are similarly low. Swiss national election rates are significantly lower.

Many pundits, politicians, philosophers, and political theorists believe low turnout is a problem. Democracy is dying. Low turnout shows we have low civic virtue. Low turnout means worse government.

Suppose they are right. If so, there seems to be a simple solution. If the people will not choose to govern themselves, we could just *force* them to do so.

I think that would be a terrible idea.

1.2 Against Compulsory Voting

I argue that we should not endorse compulsory voting. A fortiori, we should oppose it. Those countries that currently practice compulsory voting are obligated to eliminate it.

In this introductory chapter, I establish that there is a moral presumption against compulsory voting. I argue we should presume compulsory voting is unjust until someone adduces a compelling justification for the practice. I also establish that the bar for justifying compulsory voting is high. It is not enough to *speculate* that compulsory voting might produce good consequences. It is not enough to offer evidence that merely suggests it would produce good consequences. Even

[2] They are probably mistaken. Instead, it appears that young people are civically engaged rather than apathetic. However, they engage through volunteering and other means rather than by voting. See Cliff Zukin, Scott Keeter, Molly Adolina, Krista Jenkins, and Michael X. Delli Carpini, *A New Engagement?* (New York: Oxford University Press, 2006).

proving that compulsory voting does produce good consequences is not enough. To successfully defend compulsory voting, one must show that the purported good consequences are significant, that they are the right kind of consequences to produce through government coercion, and also that there are no superior alternative ways to produce those consequences. Justifying compulsory voting is no easy task.

Next, in Chapters 2 and 3, I argue that so far there is no compelling justification for compulsory voting. Some arguments for compulsory voting rely on mistaken or unproven empirical speculation. Others rely on flawed moral premises. In other cases, there are viable non-coercive (or less coercive) alternative means of getting the supposed benefits of compulsory voting.

Because compulsory voting is presumed unjust, to show that there is no good case for compulsory voting is sufficient to show that we must oppose it. Thus, by the end of Chapter 3, I will have done sufficient work to justify opposition to compulsory voting.

However, in my final chapter, I go even further. I argue that there is also a strong independent argument against compulsory voting. Making all citizens vote is like forcing the drunk to drive. It endangers us all.

So, in short, Chapters 1–3 show compulsory voting is a bad idea because it is not a good idea. Chapter 4 argues compulsory voting is a bad idea because it is a bad idea.

1.3 Compulsory Voting "Works," but So What?

We can learn what it takes to make a good argument for compulsory voting by seeing what is wrong with some bad arguments. Here is one simple but flawed argument:

The Turnout Argument

1. Compulsory voting produces high turnout.
2. If compulsory voting produces high turnout, then compulsory voting is justified.
3. Therefore, compulsory voting is justified.

This argument has too many controversial moral assumptions built in.

Premise 1 is relatively uncontroversial, provided we confine our discussion to well-developed Western democracies. In the most straightforward sense, compulsory voting *works*, at least in well-developed Western democracies.[3] For instance, back in the 1920s, when voting was voluntary, only about half of Australians tended to vote. Australia introduced compulsory voting, and as a result, voter turnout rose. If a well-developed Western democracy instantiated compulsory voting, it would probably get high turnout as a result.

However, premise 2 is implausible on its own. Just because compulsory voting makes people vote, it does not thereby follow that compulsory voting is good or just. The mere fact that compelling people to do something produces more of that thing does not show we should compel them to do it. We need a real argument. We need a real explanation of why it is important to get more of that thing. Over the next few chapters, we will see a few such purported explanations. None of them succeed, as far as I can tell.

1.4 Who Holds the Burden of Proof?

In one sense, I am at a disadvantage in this debate. If I want to convince people that they should not support compulsory voting, I must consider and rebut a wide range of possible arguments supporters might adduce.[4] I try to do this in Chapters 2 and 3. However, someone might always produce a new argument I failed to consider.

At the same time, I hold an advantage. The two sides of this debate do not begin on equal footing. Instead, the side that supports

[3] Sarah Birch, *Full Participation: A Comparative Study of Compulsory Voting* (New York: United Nations University Press, 2009): 79–98, shows that compulsory voting has a weaker or insignificant ability to increase participation in many second- or third-world democracies.

[4] A. John Simmons, in his debate with Christopher Wellman over whether there is a duty to obey the law, makes a similar point. On one hand, Wellman has the burden of proof. We get to assume that there is no duty to obey the law until we are shown otherwise. On the other hand, Simmons has to consider and rebut a wide range of possible arguments for a duty to obey the law, whereas Wellman need only produce one decent argument. See Christopher Heath Wellman and A. John Simmons, *Is There a Duty to Obey the Law?* (New York: Cambridge University Press, 2005). See also Michael Huemer, *The Problem of Political Authority: An Examination of the Right to Coerce and the Duty to Obey* (New York: Macmillan, 2012), for a similar point.

compulsion bears the *burden of proof*. Those who claim governments should compel citizens to vote bear the burden of proving this claim. Those who wish to compel their fellow citizens to vote must produce a compelling justification for this compulsion. Otherwise, by default, we should not support compulsory voting.

When one side has the burden of proof, it has to win the debate. The other side only needs not to lose. It "wins" by default. Because the pro-compulsion side bears the burden of proof, if, upon reasoned reflection, the balance of the arguments for and against compulsory voting leaves you feeling largely agnostic or undecided, then, for that very reason, you must oppose compulsory voting. If, after careful reflection, you are not sure whether compulsory voting is justified, then you must oppose it.

The pro-compulsion side has the burden of proof for two reasons. First, it asserts the positive. Second, it advocates compulsion. Let us examine each of these in turn.

1.5 The Burden of Proof: The Logic of Argumentation

My college housemate, Linea, claimed to be a witch with magic powers. Now, I never believed Linea was actually a witch. To justify my skepticism, I did not have to prove she was lying or delusional. Rather, my skepticism was justified because she never demonstrated she had any magic powers.

Suppose a researcher claims acupuncture cures cancer. We are justified in being skeptical until we acquire compelling evidence that acupuncture really does cure cancer. Now, suppose the researcher shows me some data that appears to support the claim that acupuncture causes cancer. However, suppose I show that she made some mistakes in her calculations, and thus her results are not statistically significant. This would be enough to invalidate her argument and justify my continuing skepticism. I would not need to prove definitively that acupuncture does not cure cancer.

In general, in any controversial debate, the side that asserts the positive claim bears the burden of proof. No one has a standing intellectual duty to prove a negative. Rather, those who assert that a controversial positive claim is true bear the intellectual obligation to establish its truth.

So it goes with philosophical arguments as well. Sure, in a debate between a Kantian and a utilitarian over the best moral theory, the two begin on equal footing. Each of them defends a controversial moral theory. But our debate in this book is not that kind of debate. Rather, this is more like a debate in which one person defends Kantianism, while the other merely defends skepticism about Kantianism. In that case, the Kantian bears the burden of proof. The skeptic need not prove, definitively, that Kantianism is false. The skeptic need only poke holes in the Kantian's argument.

Lisa Hill, William Galston, Bart Engelen, and other supporters of compulsory voting assert that the state should force citizens to vote. They thus assert a controversial positive claim. They thus bear the burden of proof. To justify my skepticism, I do not thereby have to prove definitively that compulsory voting violates citizens' rights, that the state should not compel citizens to vote, that compulsory voting would be a disaster, that compulsory voting fails to produce good results, or the like. I need only poke holes in their arguments or find fault with their reasons.

Suppose you do a literature search, looking up published empirical research on the consequences of compulsory voting. You find that, say, five papers conclude compulsory voting produces certain good consequences, but five papers (of equal merit, as far as you can tell) claim it does not; this *helps* my argument but hurts the pro-compulsion side.

By default, we are justified in failing to advocate compulsory voting until they give us compelling reasons to advocate it. If we do not have sufficiently good reasons to accept compulsory voting, then we should not endorse it.

1.6 The Burden of Proof: The Morality of Compulsion

There is a second reason why the pro-compulsion side bears the burden of proof. This second reason shows us why, in the absence of a strong argument for compulsory voting, we must not only *fail to advocate* compulsory voting but must actively *oppose* it. This second reason shows us why, in the absence of a compelling justification for compulsory voting, we must presume it to be *unjust*.

Compulsory voting is, after all, compulsory. Advocates of compulsory voting want governments to coerce people into voting. In commonsense morality, we presume coercion – including government coercion – is wrong, until shown otherwise. We presume it is wrong for a state to intrude into citizens' lives or force them to perform a service. We presume it is unjust for a state to restrict citizens' liberties. In general, compulsion has to be justified; the lack of compulsion does not.

As an analogy, imagine we were debating about whether to go to war. The pro-war side would have the burden of proof. Wars are presumed illegitimate. In any debate about going to war, the antiwar side does not need to prove that the proposed war is bad. Rather, the pro-war side has to prove that the proposed war is just. Otherwise, the antiwar side wins by default. A good way of putting this is that unless there is good reason to go to war, we automatically have good reasons not to go to war. The antiwar side only acquires a burden of showing that the war is bad once the pro-war side starts to make a strong case on behalf of the war. So it goes with compulsory voting as well.

Of course, wars are horrific affairs. Although I think compulsory voting is unjust, it is not nearly as unjust as a typical unjust war. But that does not undermine my point. To see why, consider a silly example. Suppose we are considering whether the government should criminalize booger eating by making booger eaters pay a $20 fine. Now, hardly anyone over age five wants to eat boogers.[5] Forcing booger eaters to pay a small fine would be only a minor injustice. Yet, if this law were really in consideration, the pro-criminalization side would still bear a heavy burden of proof. The anti-criminalization side need not prove that eating boogers is healthy, that criminalization would cause more harm than good, that laws against booger eating are "undemocratic," or that citizens have some sort of natural right to eat boogers. Rather, the anti-criminalization side gets to presume that criminalization is wrong just because it coercively intrudes into people's lives. Government coercion, no matter how petty, is presumed unjust until shown otherwise. So it goes with compulsory voting.

One might object that the presumption against coercion is just a *libertarian* position. That would be a problem, if true. Libertarianism is

[5] Actually, I had a difficult time finding hard numbers for this. But see J. W. Jefferson and T. D. Thompson, "Rhinotillexomania: Psychiatric Disorder or Habit," *Journal of Clinical Psychology* 56 (1995): 56–9.

a controversial political philosophy.[6] It claims citizens have expansive and stringent rights against interference. However, the presumption against coercion is not unique to libertarians. If the presumption against coercion is to be identified with a background ideology, that ideology is liberalism in general. Many of the advocates of compulsory voting claim themselves to be liberals.

All liberals share the view that there is a strong presumption in favor of liberty and a strong presumption against government coercion. Indeed, this may be the defining feature of liberalism. As Gerald Gaus explains,

> The liberal tradition in political philosophy maintains that each person is free to do as he wishes until some justification is offered for limiting his liberty.... As liberals see it, we necessarily claim liberty to act as we see fit unless reason can be provided for interfering.... A person is under no standing obligation to justify his actions.... Interference with another's action requires justification; unjustified interference is unjust.[7]

Liberals – including libertarians Robert Nozick and Eric Mack, classical liberals John Stuart Mill, Gerald Gaus, and David Schmidtz, and left-liberals such as John Rawls and Joel Feinberg – argue there is a strong presumption in favor of liberty.[8] The presumption of liberty holds that, by default, people should be free to live as they see best, without having to ask permission from or justify themselves to other people. By default, *all* restrictions on liberty are presumed wrong and unjust until shown otherwise.

This liberal presumption against coercion is not itself special to liberalism, it comes from, or at least is now part of, commonsense moral thinking. By default, common sense holds that I may not slap you, kick you, take your money, or kill you. Common sense holds that, by

[6] Though approximately one-fifth to one-third of Americans are broadly libertarian. See Jason Brennan, *Libertarianism: What Everyone Needs to Know* (New York: Oxford University Press, 2012): 171–2.

[7] Gerald Gaus, *Contemporary Theories of Liberalism* (Thousand Oaks, CA: Sage, 2004): 207.

[8] For left-liberal articulations and defenses of the presumption of liberty, see Joel Feinberg, *Social Philosophy* (Englewood Cliffs, NJ: Prentice-Hall, 1979): 18–20; Joel Feinberg, *Harm to Others* (New York: Oxford University Press, 1984): 9; John Rawls, *Justice as Fairness: A Restatement* (Cambridge, MA: Harvard University Press, 2001): 44, 112; Stanley Benn, *A Theory of Freedom* (New York: Cambridge University Press, 1988): 87.

default, I may not force you to mow my lawn, draw me a picture, sing me a song – nor may I force you to write checkmarks next to names on a list. Common sense also holds that groups of people – even the majority of your fellow citizens – may not force you to do these things just because they feel like it, even if they really want to, and even though they are convinced it would be good to do so. Rather, it is part of commonsense morality that coercion can be justified only in special circumstances. Even democratic governments may not coerce people without a compelling justification.

1.7 Strong Doubt Kills Compulsory Voting

Because compulsion is presumed wrong, this makes it easier to *object* to compulsion than to defend it. There is an asymmetry in the strength of the evidence that each side needs to produce. For instance, suppose proponents of compulsory voting produce evidence that suggests, but does not conclusively show, that compulsion would produce desirable effects. The pro-compulsion side actually wants to use compulsion against citizens. It actually wants governments to force citizens to vote. This kind of argument is not good enough.

In contrast, in Chapter 4, I produce empirical evidence that strongly suggests, but does not conclusively prove, that compulsory voting would produce lower-quality government. Because I take the anti-compulsion side, I have a much weaker argumentative burden than the pro-compulsion side. There is an asymmetry between what it takes to justify coercion versus what it takes to invalidate coercion. Arguments in favor of coercion must be compelling; arguments against the exercise of power need only cast strong doubt.

By analogy, think of a criminal trial. The government bears the burden of proof in criminal prosecutions. After all, it proposes to harm a potentially innocent person. For the government to be justified in doing so, it must prove beyond a reasonable doubt that the defendant really is guilty and really is an appropriate target for such deprivations. The prosecution cannot just speculate that the defendant committed the crime. It must nail down its case.

The defense needs only to establish some reasonable doubt to win. It does not have to prove that the defendant is innocent; it must only poke holes in the prosecution's case. The defense is free to produce speculative arguments that, say, someone else could have committed the crime as a means of casting doubt. If it becomes reasonable to *suspect* someone else committed the crime, then the government must not convict the defendant.

So it goes with this debate. I argue later in the book that compulsory voting would be harmful and produce lower-quality government. I might be wrong. But I am free to hypothesize in a way the pro-compulsion side is not. "Given this evidence, there's a decent chance this will make things better, but I'm not sure" is a weak argument for compulsion. "Given this evidence, there's a decent chance this will make things worse, but I'm not sure" is a moderately strong argument against compulsion.

1.8 The "Right Not to Vote" as a Red Herring

Defenders of compulsory voting often express skepticism about whether citizens have a "right not to vote" or a "right to abstain." As Heather Lardy (who rejects any such rights) explains, "Claims about rights have a privileged position in political debates ... an authoritative aura which increases the burden of explanation and justification borne by the advocates of the challenged measures."[9] Thus Lardy claims that if skeptics of compulsory voting think citizens possess a right not to vote (akin to the right of free speech or the right of freedom of conscience), then they must produce a compelling argument that such a right exists. Considering the philosophical contortions that, for example, Rawls or Mill have to go through just to establish a right to free speech, it seems it would be even more difficult to establish that there is a specific liberty to abstain from voting.[10]

However, this argumentative strategy illicitly attempts to shift the burden of proof away from the defender of compulsory voting and onto the skeptic. Whether or not there is a "right not to vote" is a red herring. Skeptics do not have to establish that all citizens possess a specific right not to vote. We just need to point out that there is a strong moral presumption against coercion. Until we are shown otherwise,

[9] Heather Lardy, "Is There a Right Not to Vote?," *Oxford Journal of Legal Studies* 24 (2) (2004): 303–21.

[10] Rawls, *Justice as Fairness*: 18–24, 92–4, 111–13; John Stuart Mill, *On Liberty* (Indianapolis: Hackett, 1981), chap. 2.

we presume every person is at liberty to do as he pleases and spend his time as he pleases, provided he does not trample on others' rights.

Or, in a similar vein, Bart Engelen says, "There is nothing inherently undemocratic about compelling citizens to do something, which not all of them want to do voluntarily."[11] Engelen subtly attempts to shift the burden of proof. He makes it seem as though skeptics are burdened with showing that compulsory voting is "undemocratic." But Engelen's objection is beside the point. I think compulsory voting is unjustified, but I would not claim that it is unjustified *because* it is undemocratic. On the contrary, I will readily admit that compulsory voting is consistent with democracy. I argue it is unjustified because coercion is presumed unjust until shown otherwise, and no one can show otherwise. I also claim it is unjustified because it will lower the quality of government.

1.9 Good Consequences Are Not Enough

Some of the arguments on behalf of compulsory voting argue that it would produce various sorts of good consequences. In the next two chapters, I examine these different arguments at length. However, first, I want to explain that proving that compulsion would produce good consequences is not enough to justify compulsion.

Consider that only a small percentage of Americans choose to attend operas, Bach concerts, or Shakespearean plays. That is really too bad. Imagine how we could improve American culture if Americans would only watch *Tosca* instead of *The Bachelor*. Experiencing high culture could even improve democracy. Imagine what would happen if we could get Americans to read and reflect upon *Antigone, Coriolanus, Babbitt*, or *1984*.

Democratic governments could make culture compulsory. They could sponsor performances of *Turandot* and punish citizens who fail to attend. Governments could penalize citizens who do not attend an art museum at least once per year. And so on. To preserve freedom of choice, governments could even let citizens decide for themselves what high culture to consume, provided the citizens consume enough of it.

[11] Bart Engelen, "Why Compulsory Voting Can Enhance Democracy," *Acta Analytica* 42 (2007): 23–39.

Most people would balk at this suggestion, even if it actually succeeded in getting Americans to appreciate high culture more. Hardly anyone advocates compulsory culture (or, more precisely, they advocate compulsory culture for public school children but not for full adults). Yet many people advocate compulsory voting. Many more are at least sympathetic to the idea of compulsory voting if they do not quite yet advocate it. Yet what is the difference, if any, between compulsory voting and compulsory culture? Why would it be permissible for governments to compel citizens to vote but not to watch an opera? If you advocate compulsory voting because you think it generates good consequences, you need to show us these are the right kinds of consequences, the kinds it is permissible to compel.

Social scientists also consistently find that regular church attendance makes people happier, or at least that regular church-goers tend to be happier than non-church-goers.[12] Any humanitarian wants people to be happier. The U.S. Constitution even says the federal government is supposed to "promote the general Welfare." Yet none of this would justify the state in forcing people to go to a church, even one of their own choosing, even if there were no First Amendment, and even if the state decided to count atheist and agnostic clubs as "churches." It would not even justify the state incentivizing church attendance or marriage by making atheists pay a $20 fine.

Social scientists consistently found that unemployment causes unhappiness.[13] Yet this would not by itself justify governments in forcing the unemployed to work (even, for instance, at government-

[12] For example, see Michael Argyle, *The Psychology of Happiness* (London: Routledge, 2002). The Pew Research Center, using data from the General Social Survey, reports that regular church attendees are about twice as likely to report being very happy than those who never or seldom attend church. See Pew Research Center, "Are We Happy Yet" (February 13, 2006); available at: http://www.pewsocialtrends.org/2006/02/13/are-we-happy-yet. That religious service attendance is strongly correlated with happiness is well known, but researchers dispute why religious attendance seems to make people happier.

[13] For example, see Andrew E. Clark and Andrew J. Oswald, "Unhappiness and Unemployment," *The Economic Journal* 104 (1994): 648–59; Lilliana Winkelmann and Rainer Winkelmann, "Why Are the Unemployed So Unhappy?," *Economica* 65 (1998): 1–15; M. Argyle, "Causes and Correlates of Happiness," in D. Kahneman, E. Diener, and N. Schwarz (eds.), *Well-Being: The Foundations of Hedonic Psychology* (New York: Sage, 1999): 353–73; Clark and Oswald, "Unhappiness and Unemployment."

YBP Library Services

BRENNAN, JASON, 1979-

COMPULSORY VOTING: FOR AND AGAINST.

Paper 231 P.

NEW YORK: CAMBRIDGE UNIV PRESS, 2014

AUTH: GEORGETOWN UNIVERSITY.

LCCN 2014001487

ISBN 1107613922 **Library PO#** SLIP ORDERS

6207 UNIV OF TEXAS/SAN ANTONIO

App. Date 11/26/14 PAD.APR 6108-09

List 29.99 USD

Disc 17.0%

Net 24.89 USD

SUBJ: VOTING, COMPULSORY.

CLASS JF1031 DEWEY# 325.65 LEVEL ADV-AC

supplied jobs) or making the unemployed pay a small tax, even if the tax actually caused the unemployed to find jobs.

Social scientists have also shown that getting sufficient sleep makes people happier.[14] Yet this would not justify the state in forcing us to get more sleep. It would not even justify the state in making those of us who get too little sleep to pay a small fine, even if this actually made us sleep more.

Americans who live in sunny areas tend to be happier than those who live in rainy areas. Yet that would not justify the state in making citizens pay a small tax penalty for choosing to live with bad weather, even if this actually made them move to happier climates.

Or consider that from a sociological standpoint, marriage is good. Even when we control for income and other demographic factors, children raised in homes with two married, biological parents do better on a wide range of measures than children raised by divorced, never-married but cohabitating, or single parents. They do better in school, have better emotional and physical health, and are less likely to be delinquent, aggressive, or criminal.[15] Yet it is certainly not clear that even this would justify the state in compelling parents to marry or making

[14] Daniel Kahneman, Alan B. Krueger, David A. Schkade, Norbert Schwarz, and Arthur A. Stone, "A Survey Method for Characterizing Daily Life Experience: The Day Reconstruction Method," *Science* 306 (2004): 1776–80.

[15] See, e.g., Paul Amato and Keith Bruce, "Parental Divorce and the Well-Being of Children: A Meta-Analysis," *Psychological Bulletin* 110 (1991): 26–46; Paula Fomby and Andrew J. Cherlin, "Family Instability and Child Well-Being," *American Sociological Review* 72 (2007): 181–204; Wendy D. Manning and Kathleen Lamb, "Adolescent Well-Being in Cohabitating, Married, and Single-Parent Families," *Journal of Marriage and Family* 65 (2003): 876–93; Sara McLanahan and Gary Sandefur, *Growing Up with a Single Parent* (Cambridge, MA: Harvard University Press, 1994); Susan Mayer, *What Money Can't Buy: Family Income and Children's Life Chances* (Cambridge, MA: Harvard University Press, 1997); Stacey Aronson and Aletha C. Huston, "The Mother-Infant Relationship in Single, Cohabitating, and Married Families: A Case for Marriage?" *Journal of Family Psychology* 18 (2004): 5–18; Susan L. Brown, "Family Structure and Child Well-Being: The Significance of Parental Cohabitation," *Journal of Marriage and the Family* 66 (2004): 351–67; Susan L. Brown, "Family Structure Transitions and Adolescent Well-Being," *Demography* 43 (2006): 447–61; Susan L. Brown and Wendy D. Manning, "Family Boundary Ambiguity and the Measurement of Family Structure," *Demography* 46 (2009): 85–101; Jacinta Bronte-Tinkew, Kristin A. Moore, and Jennifer Carrano, "The Influence of Father Involvement in Youth Risk Behaviors among Adolescents," *Social Science Research* 35 (2006): 181–209; Shannon E. Cavenagh and Aletha C. Huston, "Family Instability and Children's Early Problem Behavior," *Social Forces* 85 (2006): 551–80; Marcia J. Carlson, "Family Structure, Father Involvement, and

single or unmarried parents pay a tax penalty, even if such measures actually made people stay married for their children's benefit.

The lesson? To show coercing people would produce good consequences is not enough by itself to justify coercion. It would be desirable for people to exercise more, to read more, to be friendlier, and to do a wide range of things, yet none of this shows we may compel other people to do these things.

Thus, even if compulsory voting were shown to produce good consequences, this would not, by itself, show that it is justified. We would need to show that compulsory voting produces the right kind of consequences, consequences that the state has the right to force citizens to produce.

1.10 How Compulsory is Compulsory Voting?

There are stronger and weaker possible ways to instantiate compulsory voting. Some forms of compulsory voting are more compulsory than others. Consider the following issues:

1. *Are citizens forced to vote or just penalized for abstention?* We could imagine a system in which governments literally force all citizens to vote, making them perform the task of voting at gunpoint if need be. In this system, resistance is futile. Everyone eventually relents and votes.

Of course, no one actually advocates this radical kind of compulsory voting. Instead, most governments with compulsory voting just penalize citizens for failing to vote.

2. *Are citizens actually forced to support a candidate?* Governments could require citizens to cast a vote in favor of a candidate or party in

Adolescent Outcomes," *Journal of Marriage and the Family* 68 (2006): 137–54; A. Sourander, H. Elonheimo, S. Niemela, A. M. Nuutila, H. Helenius, L. Sillanmaki, J. Piha, T. Tamminen, K. Kumpulainen, I. Moilenen, and F. Almqvist, "Childhood Predictors of Male Criminality: A Prospective Population-Based Follow-Up Study from Age 8 to Late Adolescence," *Journal of the American Academy of Child and Adolescent Psychiatry* 45 (2006): 578–86. Note that when I say "two biological parents," I mean to compare biological parents with foster or stepparents. However, these studies do not examine children raised by homosexual partners. For a study on whether these correlations result from nature or nurture, see Thomas G. O'Connor, Avshalam Caspi, John D. DeFries, and Robert Plomin, "Are Associations between Parental Divorce and Children's Adjustment Genetically Mediated? An Adoption Study," *Developmental Psychology* 36 (2000): 429–37.

each open office. Or a government might not require citizens to actually support any candidate or party. Instead, governments might just require that citizens submit a ballot.

In this case, citizens remain free to spoil the ballot (e.g., by writing in "Mickey Mouse") or to submit a blank ballot. In Australia, citizens are de facto free to spoil their ballots or leave them blank. Thus Australians are not literally made to endorse candidates.

In order to ensure that citizens are not forced to support candidates they disapprove of, a government might put a box marked "None of the above" or "I support no one" on each ballot. Citizens are required to submit a ballot, but they are free to mark this box. Thus a supporter of compulsion might say, even the most conscientious anarchist can rest assured that he is not partially responsible for empowering government leaders.

3. *What kind of criminal offense is nonvoting?* In the United States, criminal offenses often come in different classes: infractions, misdemeanors, and felonies. Infractions carry the least degree of stigma, felonies carry the most, and misdemeanors fall somewhere in the middle. In many systems of compulsory voting, failure to vote counts as a minor misdemeanor or an infraction, akin to getting a parking or speeding ticket.

Technically, infractions are not properly called criminal offenses because infractions do not appear on a citizen's Department of Justice criminal record and cannot be punished by jail time. When protesting infractions, citizens do not have a legal right to a jury trial or a right to an attorney.

We could imagine political systems in which abstention is treated as a felony. As a matter of fact, proponents of compulsory voting usually want to treat nonvoting as an infraction or minor misdemeanor.

4. *In what way is voting enforced or nonvoting punished?* We could imagine governments that torture, execute, exile, or jail citizens for nonvoting. We could imagine governments that deprive nonvoting citizens of some of their civil liberties (in fact, some countries do just that).

For instance, I have heard many people assert that people who do not vote have no right to complain. We could imagine that the government takes this literally and forbids citizens from expressing any political opinions unless they voted in the last election. Didn't vote in the last election? Then you can't write books or blogs.

In Bolivia, citizens who fail to vote are barred from holding public employment, from conducting many bank transactions, and from getting a passport for ninety days.[16] Thus Bolivia deprives its citizens of their civil liberties – including the right of exit – unless they vote. In Brazil, nonvoters are barred from receiving state-funded education.

On the other hand, a government with compulsory voting could make abstainers pay a small fine. As of 2012, Australians who fail to vote pay a $20 fine. If a citizen takes her case to court and loses, she pays $50.[17] Repeat offenders pay increasing penalties.

Instead of issuing fines, a government could censure, rebuke, or ridicule nonvoters. It could publish their names on a public blacklist or wall of shame. It could run television ads making fun of nonvoters by name: "Meet Jason Brennan, scumbag citizen." We might not want to classify these kinds of penalties as *compulsory* or coercive per se. Having the government publically censure you is more onerous than paying a small fine, but it does not involve any violence or threat of violence.

5. *Can citizens opt out?* Governments with compulsory voting can choose whether or not to make exceptions to the law. For instance, a government might allow citizens to abstain if they are experiencing certain hardships, such as bad health. A government might allow citizens to abstain if they are living in a foreign country. A government might allow citizens to abstain after they reach a certain age. In Ecuador, for instance, citizens over age sixty-five may choose not to vote without incurring any penalties. A government might allow citizens to opt out of voting if they conscientiously object to the practice. Or a government could require citizens to vote (or cast a ballot), no matter what. In fact, most governments with compulsory voting have at least some conditions under which abstainers can escape punishment.

A defender of compulsory voting might be tempted to claim that so long as government allows conscientious objectors to opt out, then compulsory voting is not *really* compulsory. But that cannot be right. That would be like saying the military draft is not really compulsory because it allows for conscientious objection. If

[16] Birch, *Full Participation*: 9.

[17] Australian Electoral Commission, *Frequently Asked Questions* (2013); available at: http://www.aec.gov.au/faqs/voting_australia.htm#not-vote.

a government says to citizens, "We will punish you for abstaining, unless you jump through the following legal hoops," it is still coercing citizens. Instead of compelling them to vote, it is compelling them either to vote or jump through hoops to become conscientious objectors. Compelling a person to jump through hoops to avoid compulsion is still compulsion.

In summary, compulsory voting is not just one thing. As a matter of fact, most proponents of compulsory voting advocate the less restrictive and harsh versions of it. They want abstention to be a minor infraction carrying a small financial penalty, not a felony carrying a penalty of jail time. Few of them support Bolivia's harsh penalties. They want citizens to have some legal means to opt out of voting, although they also want citizens to have to jump through some legal hoops before they are permitted to opt out. For this reason, they have less of an argumentative burden than if they advocated the harsher versions.

However, note that defenders of compulsory voting should advocate a level of coercion that befits their arguments. The more severe the purported consequences of mass abstention, the more compulsion one should advocate for in order to prevent these bad consequences. So, for instance, imagine some fanatic believed that if even one person abstains, everyone would immediately die in severe pain. In that case, the fanatic should not advocate a mere fine – he should advocate having the government do whatever it takes to ensure everyone actually votes.

1.11 Noncoercive Alternatives Kill the Case for Compulsory Voting

William Galston agrees that compulsory voting infringes citizens' liberty. He agrees that compulsory voting really is coercive. However, he says, compulsory voting is only a *small* or *trivial* infringement of liberty. Compulsory voting requires little from citizens.[18] Voting takes a half hour every few years. Compulsory voting is less onerous than jury duty, and hardly anyone thinks compulsory jury duty is unjustifiable. Let's not exaggerate the degree of compulsion, he says.

[18] William Galston, "Telling Americans to Vote, or Else," *New York Times*, November 6, 2011, SR9.

For the sake of argument, let us grant Galston that forcing citizens to vote is only a small infringement of liberty. But even the pettiest violations are hard to justify.

Now that we have a good handle on the burden of proof and the difficulty of justifying compulsion, let us walk through what it would take to justify a hypothetical law. Suppose that – for no good reason – Congress passed the following law:

The Red Scarf Mandate

Congress shall provide a red scarf to each citizen. Each citizen must wear this red scarf for a total of fifteen minutes per year. The citizen may choose the time most convenient to her to wear the scarf.

The Red Scarf Mandate is a petty, minor violation of liberty. It asks citizens to do little. It imposes only the most minor inconvenience.

However, the Red Scarf Mandate is, to put it bluntly, a stupid law. If my fellow citizens passed this law out of nothing more than caprice, I would rightfully hold them in contempt. They would lack moral permission to enforce the law, and citizens would have no obligation to obey it.

In principle, though, the Red Scarf Mandate could be justified, but we need to find the right justification. Now, suppose Congress offered the following justification for the Red Scarf Mandate:

Human psychology is strange. It turns out, empirically, that if we force all citizens to wear a red scarf once a year for fifteen minutes, this will cause them to appreciate art more. As a result, we will see a small artistic renaissance.

Imagine Congress is right. Imagine it could produce overwhelming evidence that forcing people to wear red scarves does indeed produce more and better art.

Yet, as we discussed, citizens can reasonably say, "So what?" Just because art is valuable, it does not follow that we can make citizens work to promote it. People are free to act indifferently toward many of the things they ought to value and promote. Some citizens reasonably (although, we are supposing, wrongly) think producing better art is not worth even fifteen minutes of their time. Others agree that producing better art is worth fifteen minutes of their time, but they reasonably object to being *made* to do it by Congress. I, for one, would happily wear a red scarf to promote art. However, if you tried to force me to wear it, I'd resist.

Now, suppose instead Congress offered this justification for the Red Scarf Mandate:

The Red Scarves Stop Crime Effect

Human psychology is strange. It turns out empirically that if we force all citizens to wear a red scarf for fifteen minutes per year, violent crime will vanish. No one will commit any violent crimes, period.

Suppose the Red Scarves Stop Crime Effect were real – for whatever reason, making people wear red scarves for a short time really does stop all crime. Suppose many people dislike the Red Scarf Mandate, but the law has no other deleterious effects. At this point, only the most hardcore libertarians or anarchists would object to the Red Scarf Mandate.[19] Perhaps they are right to do so. However, for the sake of argument, I will assume that if wearing red scarves ended violent crime, this would be strong prima facie grounds for justifying the Red Scarf Mandate. Yet even *this* would not *yet* be enough to justify the Red Scarf Mandate.

To see why not, imagine the following silly phenomenon also turned out to be real:

The Bunny Flag Phenomenon

Human psychology is strange. It also turns out empirically that we can make crime disappear by putting a bunny on our national flag.

If this Bunny Flag Phenomenon were real, then this would kill the case for the Red Scarf Mandate. We are imagining that flying a bunny flag and forcing people to wear red scarves are equally good at ending violent crime. But, if so, flying the bunny flag and forcing people to wear red scarves would not be equally morally acceptable. Instead, it would be wrong for the government to coerce people into wearing scarves when it can instead solve the problem of violent crime without any coercion.

[19] Robert Nozick might argue that rights are side constraints, not goals. This mandate violates rights in order to minimize rights violations. For that reason, it is wrong. Robert Nozick, *Anarchy, State, and Utopia* (New York: Basic Books, 1974): 29–38.

To take another example: many people believe right now that it is permissible for the government to force all of us to get vaccines. However, suppose it turned out that flying the bunny flag also cured all disease. In that case, it would be wrong to coerce people into enduring painful shots when we could solve the problem without using coercion.

Galston claims it is justifiable to compel citizens to serve on juries. The point of jury duty is not to get citizens to participate. Instead, it is just to ensure that we have a fair criminal justice system. However, suppose we discovered some alternative way to try criminal offenses that was equally as fair to defendants, was equally protective of citizens' rightful liberty, was not expensive, was not unjust for other reasons, and did not require compulsion. For instance, suppose we established empirically that judge systems work as well as jury systems. That would be sufficient to invalidate compulsory jury duty.

There may be goals so important that governments may coerce citizens to achieve those goals. However, coercion cannot usually be justified when there are other equally good, unobjectionable, noncoercive ways to achieve those goals.

Compulsion against innocent citizens is presumed wrong. If we can get the purported benefits of compulsion through alternative, noncompulsory means, and if there is no other serious objection to these alternative means, then this will tend to show compulsion is illegitimate.

The caveat about there being no other serious objection is important. So, for example, if it were fantastically expensive to produce bunny flags, then the Red Scarf Mandate might be justified instead. Or suppose it turned out that the government could end all crime without any compulsion but only by publically ridiculing homosexuals and Native Americans. This would be even more objectionable than the Red Scarf Mandate.

Many arguments for compulsory voting are weak unless one can rule out other noncoercive (or less coercive) means of achieving the same goals. Because proponents of compulsory voting actually propose to have the government coerce us, they bear a moral responsibility to investigate these other means.

Some political scientists believe we might be able to increase turnout by making elections more competitive, by changing vote rules, by reducing the number of elections, or by having publicly financed elections. Proponents of compulsory voting need to show that these political scientists are wrong.

In Chapter 2, I will offer the following alternative to compulsory voting:

> *Voter lotteries*: Governments randomly select 20,000 citizens from all adults. These citizens – and these citizens only – are imbued with the power to vote and are each given $1,000 to reward them for voting. They are not forced to vote. Or they are asked but not forced to sign a contract that commits them to voting. If they voluntarily sign but breach their contract, they may be punished for breach of contract.

Voter lotteries are a superior, noncoercive alternative to compulsory voting. I will argue that even the very best arguments for compulsory voting fail to justify compulsory voting. At best, they justify voting lotteries.

1.12 Summary So Far

The well is poisoned. My goal is this chapter is just to make you suspicious of compulsory voting. I am trying to ground a disposition of skepticism toward arguments for compulsory voting. In the next two chapters, we will examine and undermine a wide variety of such arguments.

I have established that there is strong presumption against compulsory voting, even against the relatively wimpy and nonpunitive forms that proponents actually support. Proponents have the burden of proof. They are like prosecutors who must defend their position, if not beyond all reasonable doubt, at least against any strong doubts. In contrast, I can undermine their case with far weaker evidence because I play the role of the defense. (If the weight of the evidence is ambiguous, that's good for me and bad for the other side.) Proponents cannot just cite the good consequences of compulsory voting (if there even are any) because good consequences are not always enough to justify the presumption against coercion. Finally, they remain vulnerable to alternative proposals that generate the same good consequences without (or with less) compulsion.

Despite these serious disadvantages, the pro-compulsion side has one major advantage in this debate. People love democracy. Despite the fact that many people do not vote, most people have developed a quasi-religious reverence for democracy and for the act of voting. They feel deep down in their hearts, for reasons they cannot quite articulate, that it would be best if everyone voted. They will thus tend to feel in their hearts that compulsion is good and just, even if they have no good arguments for this view. Many people *want* to be convinced that compulsory voting is just. Political psychology says that when thinking about political matters, most of us are plagued by a host of biases, especially confirmation bias and motivated reasoning.[20] I remind readers that they have an intellectual duty to resist these biases.

[20] See Jason Brennan, *The Ethics of Voting* (paperback edition with new afterword by the author) (Princeton, NJ: Princeton University Press, 2012): 160–84; Drew Westen, *The Political Brain* (New York: Public Affairs Press, 2008); Jonathan Haidt, *The Righteous Mind* (New York: Vintage, 2013).

2

Democratic Legitimacy and the Consequences of Compulsion

In this chapter, I examine and undermine two sets of arguments for compulsory voting. The first set of arguments concerns ideas about democratic legitimacy. The second set of arguments claims compulsory voting would produce good consequences.

The connection between these two sets of arguments is psychological. While none of the arguments I examine here are sound, the arguments in the first set are particularly flawed. However, many laypeople, journalists, politicians, and even some political theorists find this first set of arguments appealing. But they find these arguments appealing because they are confused. Arguments in the first set are really just confused, badly articulated versions of the arguments in the second set. For instance, some people say compulsory voting is necessary to ensure democratic legitimacy. However, probably no one who says that actually means that democracies without compulsory voting are illegitimate. Instead, she probably just intends to say that compulsory voting would make democracy more responsive to the needs of the poor.

2.1 Compulsory Voting and Government by Consent

Alfred Apps, former president of Canada's Liberal Party, and I once debated compulsory voting. Apps probably supports compulsory voting because he believes it would benefit the Liberal Party.[1] (However, during the debate, Apps admitted he had not read any empirical research on compulsory voting. In fact, the best available evidence indicates it does not help small parties.[2]) But Apps is a cunning politician. He cannot say, "I advocate compulsory voting because I believe it would help *me*." So, instead, he offered the following argument, an argument I have heard many others make as well:

The Consent Argument

1. Democracy should be based on the consent of the people.
2. Citizens show consent by voting.
3. Therefore, a democracy without high electoral turnout rules without consent.
4. Therefore, we should compel people to vote.

Democracy should be consensual, it says, and voting counts as consent. If people will not consent on their own, we must *force* people to perform the act that signifies consent. If people will not consent voluntarily, the government should force them to consent. But that is an absurdity. That is like saying that marriages should be consensual, and so we should force people to consent to marriage. If you have to force people to vote to signify consent, then voting does not in fact signify consent

The argument not only is self-contradictory but also rests on a problematic theory of democratic legitimacy. Nonphilosophers often say that democracy is legitimate because it enjoys the consent of the governed. They say all people get a say and a share of power, and by voting (or choosing to abstain), they consent to the outcome of an election.

This sounds like a nice theory, but pretty much every philosopher thinks it is false. Most philosophers, regardless of their political views, agree: no government, democratic or otherwise, rests on the actual consent of the governed. If you sincerely believe government

[1] See Apps' May 2, 2011, speech to the Empire Club of Canada, available at: http://pdopav2.blogspot.com/2011/06/alfred-apps-speech-empire-club-of.html (last accessed October 5, 2012). As of August 20, 2013, the author appears to have made this blog open by invitation only. Please e-mail me at jb896@georgetown.edu for an archived copy of his transcript.

[2] Birch, *Full Participation*: 121–3, 140.

is legitimate only if it rests on consent, then you have to be an anarchist.

Here I'll just summarize why philosophers think the consent theory fails to justify government legitimacy: government imposes rules on us whether we like it or not. There was no ceremony, event, or time at which I freely chose to accept the U.S. government's authority. I never signed a social contract. Governments do not care whether you consent – they will impose their rules on you anyway. If you actively dissent, they impose the rules anyway.

What's more, governments control all the habitable land, so we have no reasonable way to escape government rule. At most, a small minority of us can choose *which* government will rule us. That does not signify real consent. Imagine a group of men said to a woman, "You must marry one of us or die, but we will let you chose whom you marry." When she picks a husband, she does not consent to being married. She has no choice.[3]

Laypeople tend to think that voting expresses consent. Political philosophers regard this as, well, silly. Christopher Wellman mocks the idea:

> To say a citizen is bound to a law since she voted ... is like saying that a person has consented to being shot since she expressed a preference that her abductor shoot her rather than stab her! ... Just as the abductee will be killed no matter how she responds (and even if she does not answer the abductor's questions), the citizen will be subjected to coercive laws no matter how she votes (and even if she does not vote).[4]

Our relationship to government is not at all like a consensual relationship. So the Consent Argument doesn't get off the ground. The Consent Argument only feels like a good argument to most of us because our civics and history teachers, themselves innocent of introductory political philosophy, taught us all this back in sixth grade.

Anyone advancing the Consent Argument is probably just confused. Perhaps what Apps really wanted to say, but did not quite have the

[3] For a further refutation of consent theories of political legitimacy, see Huemer, *The Problem of Political Authority*: 20–58; Wellman and Simmons, *Is There a Duty to Obey the Law?*: 116–18; Lysander Spooner, *No Treason: The Constitution of No Authority* (New York: Free Patriot Press, 2012).

[4] Christopher Heath Wellman, *A Theory of Secession* (New York: Cambridge University Press, 2005): 9.

acumen to articulate, was that we need compulsory voting to ensure democratic governments represent *all* the people. We will get to this better argument soon.

2.2 Compulsory Voting and Democratic Legitimacy

Most people think there is some nebulous, hard-to-articulate connection between voting and legitimacy.[5] This leads them to argue as follows[6]:

The Legitimacy Argument

1. Democratic governments are illegitimate unless there is high voter turnout.
2. Governments should be legitimate.
3. There will not be high turnout unless there is compulsory voting.
4. Therefore, democratic governments may impose compulsory voting.

Like the consent argument, this argument is also deeply flawed.

First, the argument is not potentially convincing to those who do not already agree. We need a compelling subargument proving premise 1. Why should we believe that democratic governments require high turnout in order to be legitimate?

Answering that question is harder than it seems. Philosophers and political theorists have spent 2,400 years debating what, if anything, makes governments legitimate. They have explored a wide range of possible theories of political legitimacy. People who advance the Legitimacy Argument seem to disregard or be unaware of this extensive literature on political legitimacy. *The Stanford Encyclopedia of Philosophy* – the authoritative reference in philosophy – contains a review article on political legitimacy. That article does not mention

[5] The word *legitimacy* has at least two meanings in normative political thinking. Philosophers tend to use the word *legitimacy* to mean something like the right to coerce or the right to create and enforce laws. A government is legitimate just in case it has permission to use violence to enforce its rules. Political theorists (people who do political philosophy but work in political science departments) and political scientists tend to use the word *legitimacy* to mean something more like stability or the *perceived* right to rule. So a political scientist might say that a Nazi regime enjoyed widespread legitimacy, but by this she means not that the Nazi regime had the right to exist but that it was stable and that citizens regarded it as having the right to exist.

[6] Birch considers but does not endorse this argument (*Full Participation*: 45).

or discuss premise 1 of the Legitimacy Argument.[7] The "high turnout is a precondition of legitimacy" theory is simply not among the theories political philosophers entertain. One never hears anyone claim high turnout is necessary for political legitimacy, *except* in discussions of compulsory voting. So premise 1 appears to assume a highly controversial theory of political legitimacy, a theory that has no purchase in political philosophy. We should thus be a touch suspicious of premise 1.

Let's toss this worry aside and consider some of the other flaws with the argument. We need to clarify what the terms *legitimate* and *illegitimate* mean.[8] These are technical terms in philosophy, so someone advancing this argument will need to make sure he means what he thinks he means. By definition, a government is legitimate just in case it is permissible for that government to stand, to create rules, and to enforce those rules coercively. In short, *legitimacy* refers to the moral permission to coerce.[9] If a government is illegitimate, then, by definition, that government may not stand, may not create rules, and may not enforce its rules.

No one really believes legitimacy literally depends on high turnout. Consider what that would imply. Canada had 61.4 percent turnout in the 2011 federal elections. Apparently, most commentators – such as Alfred Apps – believe this does not qualify as high turnout. Now, if the Legitimacy Argument were sound, it would follow that Canada's current government is illegitimate and that pretty much all past Canadian governments were illegitimate. This would, in turn, mean that the Canadian government should not exist, has no right to collect taxes, may not enforce laws against murder or theft, may not issues regulations or laws, may not make treaties, and so on. It would imply that almost everything the Canadian government does

[7] Fabienne Peter, "Political Legitimacy," in Edward N. Zalta (ed.), *The Stanford Encyclopedia of Philosophy* (Summer 2010 Ed.); available at: http://plato.stanford.edu/ entries/legitimacy/.

[8] Following Max Weber, political scientists and theorists sometimes use *legitimate* to mean *popular*, but they will then equivocate between the philosophical and Weberian meaning of the terms. To be charitable, I ignore this issue in the main text.

[9] David Estlund, *Democratic Authority: A Philosophical Framework* (Princeton, NJ: Princeton University Press, 2008): 2. In earlier political philosophy, the terms were used in sloppy or nonuniform ways. However, in the last ten years or so, it has become the convention to use the terms exactly as I define them here.

is morally impermissible. Aside from a few anarchists, does anyone actually think that?

This argument has an amusing implication. Suppose the U.S. or Canadian federal governments imposed compulsory voting in order to combat low turnout. According to the Legitimacy Argument, because these governments have low turnout, they are illegitimate. Thus, if they were to pass compulsory-voting laws, these laws would, by hypothesis, also be illegitimate! The Legitimacy Argument implies that compulsory voting-laws are legitimate only when they are passed and enforced by governments that already have and continue to have high turnout.

Anyone who finds the Legitimacy Argument attractive is probably just confused. She is probably just trying to come up with a better argument, such as one of the arguments I consider later. The person probably means that government would be better in some way if only there were high turnout. Or perhaps the person means that there would be stability, social solidarity, and greater trust in government with high turnout.

2.3 Making Government "More Democratic"

Before turning to the better arguments for compulsory voting, let us examine one more popular but silly argument:

The More Democratic Argument

1. It is more democratic if everyone votes than if only part of the population votes.
2. We should do whatever is more democratic.
3. Therefore, we should force everyone to vote.

In short: compulsory voting makes democracy more democratic. Therefore, it is good.

People often lazily equate *democratic* with *good*. But that's a mistake. *Democracy* refers to a range of related ways of distributing political power. Democracy is a method for determining when and how a government will coerce people. *Democracy* is not a synonym for the word *good*.

Contrary to premise 2, there is no moral imperative to maximize "democraticness." Suppose I said, "We should have a 100,000-member

Congress. Every law should be put to a reapproval vote every two weeks. We should have elections for office every two weeks. All these things will make democracy more democratic!" These proposals would in some sense make our democracy more democratic, but that does not make them good proposals.

Democracy is really just a way of allocating political power and making political decisions. A political system is democratic just in case all citizens have an equal share of fundamental political power. As Thomas Christiano elaborates, the term *democracy* "refers very generally to a method of group decision making characterized by a kind of equality among the participants at an essential stage of the collective decision making."[10] David Estlund says *democracy* is the "actual collective authorization of laws and policies by the people subject to them."[11]

There are many different ways to realize or instantiate democracy. We can have representative or direct democracy. We can use first-past-the-fence voting, Condorcet voting, or proportional representation. We can use deliberative polling or voting lotteries. We can staff offices by sortition rather than by voting. We can have unicameral or multicameral assemblies. We can have multiple or single branches of government. We can have more or less centralized government. We can have different assembles and ministries responsible for different linguistic communities (as in Belgium) or not. We can have a written constitution or not. We can have more or less limited government. We can have mandatory or voluntary voting. And so on. Some ways of realizing or instantiating democracy are better – producing more stability, efficiency, and justice – than others, but all these ways of instantiating democracy are equally *democratic*.

The More Democratic Argument fails. It appeals to a wishy-washy value of "being more democratic," whatever that means. Again, anyone who advances this argument is probably confused. The person probably intends to make one of the better arguments I consider below.

[10] Thomas Christiano, "Democracy," in Edward N. Zalta (ed.), *The Stanford Encyclopedia of Philosophy* (Fall 2008 Ed.); available at: http://plato.stanford.edu/archives/fall2008/entries/democracy/.

[11] Estlund, *Democratic Authority*: 38.

2.4 Compulsory Voting and Representativeness

The last three arguments for compulsory voting were dismal failures. I turn now to considering better arguments.

2.4.1 *The Argument*

Politicians need to curry favor from voters. Yet, if some people choose not to vote, then perhaps politicians might feel free to ignore them or even to exploit them. So one appealing argument contends that compulsory voting is necessary to ensure that democracies properly represent everyone. A just democracy should not arbitrarily favor some citizens over others.

Of course, for an individual voter, it makes no difference whether he votes or abstains. It is not as though the government will help you just in case you vote or ignore you just in case you abstain. As individuals, our single votes do not influence whether our elected leaders decide to help us, ignore us, or hurt us.[12] An individual's vote has an effect on political outcomes only if he changes the outcome of the election. Casting a vote is like playing the lottery – there is some small chance there will be a tie and that your vote will decisively break that tie. When political scientists and economists estimate the probability than any one voter will be decisive, they usually conclude that the probability you will break a tie is small.[13] Some think your chances are *vanishingly* small – they say you are more likely to win Powerball a few times in a row than break a tie.[14] The most optimistic estimates

[12] Some might claim that even if individual votes have almost no chance of changing the outcome of an election, individual votes can at least influence the mandate a candidate enjoys. However, the idea of mandate is just a popular myth. Hans Noel, in a review article, goes so far as to say that one thing political scientists know that laypeople do not is that "there is no such thing as a mandate." See Hans Noel, "Ten Things Political Scientists Know that You Don't," *The Forum* 8 (2010): 1–19. See also L. J. Grossback, D. A. M. Peterson, and J. A. Stimson, *Mandate Politics* (New York: Cambridge University Press, 2006); L. J. Grossback, D. A. M. Peterson, and J. A. Stimson, "Electoral Mandates in American Politics," *British Journal of Political Science* 37 (2007): 711–30. In fact, the U.S. Advanced Placement Government Exam sometimes asks students to answer the question, "Why are political scientists skeptical of the mandate theory of elections?"

[13] See Geoffrey Brennan and Loren Lomasky, *Democracy and Decision* (New York: Cambridge University Press, 2003): 56–7, 119.

[14] Steven Landsburg, "Don't Vote. It Makes More Sense to Play the Lottery Instead," *Slate* (September 29, 2004); available at: http://www.slate.com/articles/arts/ everyday_Economics/2004/09/dont_vote.html.

say you can have as high as a 1 in 10 million chance of breaking a tie, but only if you live in New Mexico, New Hampshire, Virginia, or Colorado and only if you vote Republican or Democrat.[15]

One might object that even if you have little chance of changing the outcome of an election, by voting, you can at least change the margin of victory (or loss) and then help determine whether a candidate enjoys a mandate.[16] However, the idea that candidates enjoy mandates that increase their political effectiveness is just a popular myth, roundly rejected by empirically minded political scientists.[17]

Back to the argument: 43 percent of eligible voters abstained in the 2008 U.S. presidential election. Should those 43 percent of voters be scared that Obama will ignore them? This depends in part on *who* composes that 43 percent. Imagine that the 43 percent of voters were just a random cross section of American voters. In that case, the group of people who did not vote would be a mirror image of the people who did vote. As a group, abstainers and voters would have identical political views, knowledge, and attitudes and mirror each other's demographic and socioeconomic categories. In that case, the minority who did not vote would have little to worry about. Had they all voted, the outcome of the election would have been exactly the same. In terms of whether government is representative of the people, mass abstention makes a difference only if there are *trends* in who abstains.

In fact, there are such trends. Voters and abstainers are systematically different. The old are more likely to vote than the young. Men are more likely to vote than women. In many countries, ethnic majorities are more likely to vote than ethnic minorities.[18] More

[15] See Andrew Gelman, Nate Silver, and Aaron Edlin, "What Is the Probability that Your Vote Will Make a Difference," *Economic Inquiry* 50 (2012): 321–6.

[16] See, for example, Gerry Mackie, "Why It's Rational to Vote" (University of California, San Diego, 2009), unpublished manuscript.

[17] See, for instance, R. A. Dahl, "The Myth of the Presidential Mandate," *Political Science Quarterly* 105 (1990): 355–72; Hans Noel, "Ten Things Political Scientists Know," *The Forum*, 3, article 12.

[18] In the United States, African Americans typically have a lower overall turnout than whites. However, there is some evidence that once we control for socioeconomic status and other factors that influence voting turnout, African Americans actually vote in higher rates than whites. For instance, African Americans vote less than whites because they are more likely to be poor, not because they are African American. However, this probably does not matter for the purposes of the Representativeness Argument. See Jan E. Leighley and Jonathan Nagler, "Individual and Systematic Influences on Voter Turnout: 1984," *Journal of Politics* 54 (1992): 718–40.

highly educated people are more likely to vote than less highly educated people. Married people are more likely to vote than nonmarried people.[19] Political partisans are more likely to vote than true independents. In short, under voluntary voting, the voting public – the citizens who actually vote – are not fully representative of the voting-*eligible* public.

All this leads to what I call the *Representativeness Argument*:

The Representativeness Argument

1. Voters tend to vote for their self-interest.
2. Politicians tend to give large voting blocs what they ask for.
3. When voting is voluntary, the poor, minorities, the uneducated, and young people vote less than the rich, whites, the educated, and older people.
4. If so, then under voluntary voting, government will tend to promote the interest of the rich, of whites, and of the old over the interests of the poor, of minorities, and of the young.
5. Under compulsory voting, almost every demographic and socioeconomic group votes at equally high rates.
6. Thus, under compulsory voting, government will promote everyone's interests.
7. Therefore, compulsory voting produces more representative government.
8. If compulsory voting produces more representative government than voluntary voting, then compulsory voting is justified.
9. Therefore, compulsory voting is justified.

As William Galston summarizes the argument:

> The second argument for mandatory voting is democratic. Ideally, a democracy will take into account the interests and views of all citizens. But if some regularly vote while others don't, officials are likely to give greater weight to participants. This might not matter much if nonparticipants were evenly distributed through the population. But political scientists have long known that they aren't. People with lower levels of income and education are less likely to vote, as are young adults and recent first-generation immigrants.[20]

[19] For a review of the empirical literature establishing the claims of this paragraph, see Jocelyn Evans, *Voters and Voting: An Introduction* (Thousand Oaks, CA: Sage, 2004): 152–6.

[20] Galston, "Telling Americans to Vote": SR9.

In short: the strong and advantaged vote more than the weak and disadvantaged. It seems reasonable to speculate that forcing the weak and disadvantaged to vote will protect them from selfish rich voters. It thus seems reasonable to speculate that compulsory voting will produce fairer and more equitable government.

This is probably the most popular argument for compulsory voting. Nevertheless, this argument is deeply flawed.

Before moving on to more damaging criticisms, note this argument gets off the ground only if the disadvantaged are a sizable bloc. If the disadvantaged group is a small minority, forcing them to vote probably will not do them any good. Even under compulsory voting, presidential candidates and most gubernatorial candidates can afford to just ignore the Native American vote.

2.4.2 *Representativeness without Compulsion: Voter Lotteries*

For the sake of argument, let's assume that premises 1–7 are true (later I show that many of the premises are in fact false). Assume that voluntary-voting systems really do expose poor young minorities to abuse, neglect, or exploitation. Assume compulsory voting really would rescue them and would ensure that democracies promote their interests.

Even if so, this would not justify compulsory voting. We have noncoercive alternatives to compulsory voting that would achieve these same goals.

As discussed earlier, voluntary abstention would not be a problem if the 43 percent of citizens who abstain were just like the 57 percent who vote. The Representativeness Argument gets off the ground only if the people who abstain are systematically different from the people who vote. The complaint is that the 57 percent who vote will vote in ways that fail to represent the other 43 percent (or, at least, significant portions of that 43 percent).

Premise 8 says that if compulsory voting produces more representative government than voluntary voting, then compulsory voting is justified. Not so. Recall from Chapter 1 that coercion is presumed unjustified unless there is a compelling case for it. And one of the easiest ways to kill a case for coercion is to show that you can generate the supposed benefits of coercion through noncoercive means. There is in fact a less expansive, more reliable, equally democratic, *more representative*, noncoercive alternative to compulsory voting. We can use a *voting lottery*.[21]

In a voting lottery, all citizens have the same equal fundamental political status. While in universal suffrage every citizen has one equal vote, in a voting lottery every citizen has *equal eligibility* to vote. Elections proceed normally, with candidates working to gain support from voting-lottery-eligible citizens. Shortly before the election, the system selects a predetermined number of citizens at random. These citizens – and these citizens only – become *electors*, imbued with the power to vote. To ensure turnout, the government pays each elector a substantial sum to vote.[22] They are not forced to vote. We might perhaps ask them to sign a contract committing them to voting (in exchange for the payment) and then allow them to be punished for breach of contract if they renege. This involves compulsion, but only compulsion to which citizens genuinely consent.

For instance, in a U.S. presidential election, we could select 20,000 citizens randomly from all eligible voters. We pay them $1,000 each to vote. They and they alone decide the election. In a local election, we might select a much smaller number of local citizens and pay them significantly less.

This is just one way to instantiate a voting lottery. The exact details are not important. The important idea is that we select a small, but not too small, subset of the population, give them the right to vote, and then pay them to vote. Note that we could also have voting lotteries for any set of elections where we are worried that disadvantaged citizens are not voting proportionately.

Because the 20,000 citizens are selected at random, they will be representative of the country at large. In terms of their demographics, socioeconomic status, political opinions, and so on, the 20,000 will be a mirror image of all eligible voters in the United States.

Of course, there remains the problem of *random sampling error*, that is, that the 20,000 citizens will not be *perfectly* representative of all eligible voters in the country. Yet, the greater the number of electors, the smaller is the margin of error. Let's do some statistics. The United

[21] For example, see Claudio Lopez Guerra, "The Enfranchisement Lottery," *Politics, Philosophy, and Economics* 26 (2010): 211–33.

[22] We might require employers to give electors a day off to vote as well. However, this trades compulsion against citizens as voters for compulsion against employers.

States has about 207 million eligible voters. Thus 20,000 electors produce a statistical confidence level of 99 percent, at a confidence interval of 0.9, with a margin of error of only 0.69. So the lottery would be extremely accurate.

You may be familiar with Gallup and Rasmussen polls, which attempt to predict the outcomes of elections ahead of time. These polls use a sample set of only 1,500 or so citizens to try to gauge the voting behavior of the citizenry at large. The polls are quite accurate. But the voting lottery is far more accurate than these polls, with a far lower margin of error at a higher confidence level.

Voting lotteries are not just as equally representative as compulsory voting. At current levels of technology, they may even be *more* accurate – *more* representative – than compulsory voting. It often surprises the public to hear this, but vote counting in real elections is not perfectly accurate. Every vote-counting technology or method has a significant margin of error. Political scientist David Kimball estimates that the residual vote rate (one kind of error rate) in presidential elections tends to be between 1 and 2 percent.[23] One average, hand counting of ballots results in a 2 percent error rate.[24] In general, if the Democratic and Republican candidates in a U.S. presidential election are within 1 percentage point on the popular vote, you should treat the result as a statistical tie. In general, the more votes that must be counted, the greater is the margin of error. Thus, if we want the voting population to be representative of the voting-eligible population, a voting lottery may be superior to compulsory voting.

Also, in the United States, the Electoral College makes it so some people's votes count for less than others. A Virginian vote is more likely to decide a presidential election than an Oregonian vote. A voting lottery eliminates this bias.

[23] The *residual vote rate* is the percent of votes that were cast but not counted for one reason or another. See David C. Kimball, "Summary Table on Voting Technology and Residual Vote Rates" (St Louis: University of Missouri, December 14, 2005); available at: http://www.umsl.edu/~kimballd/rtables.pdf. See also Martha Kropf and David C. Kimball, *Helping America Vote: The Limits of Election Reform* (London: Routledge, 2011): 37–44; Stephen Ansolabehere and Charles Stewart III, "Residual Votes Attributable to Technology," *Journal of Politics* 67 (2005): 365–89.

[24] Stephen N. Goggin, Michael D. Byrne, and Juan E. Gilbert, "Post-Election Auditing: Effects of Procedure and Ballot Type on Manual Counting Accuracy, Efficiency, and Auditor Satisfaction and Confidence," *Election Law Journal* 11 (2012): 36–51.

Note that even under compulsory-voting systems, a significant portion of the population still abstains from voting. In Australia, typically 5–7 percent of registered voters do not vote. The 93 percent of voters who do vote are not perfectly representative of all eligible voters. Poor minorities are still less likely to vote than rich whites. Also, Australia's much-lauded 93 percent turnout is *misleading*. In the 2011 parliamentary elections, 13.1 million citizens voted out of a voting-age population of 16.2 million. In fact, only about 81 percent of eligible voters in Australia vote; 93 percent of *registered* voters vote, but over 10 percent of the population does not register to vote.[25]

Voter lotteries have other advantages over compulsory voting. Voter lotteries are less expensive, even if we pay electors to vote. For a federal election, the voting lottery would cost $20 million in electors' fees. Add administrative expenses, such as expenses for conducting the lottery, counting votes, and so on. Suppose the voting lottery is extremely expensive to conduct – suppose it would cost $50 million total. That may seem like a lot. It's not. In contrast, the administrative costs of the 2000 U.S. federal election were about $1 billion, according to Caltech and MIT's Voter Technology Project.[26]

Voter lotteries not only cost state and local governments less money, but they cost citizens less time. Suppose we force all 207 million eligible American citizens to vote. Suppose compulsory voting advocates get their dream outcome – suppose *everyone* votes. Now suppose voting takes each citizen on average one hour, including time spent driving or walking back and forth to the polling station. Compulsory voting would thus cost 207 million hours of our time. This is equivalent to 300 full average American lifetimes spent voting. It is equivalent to 5 million American work weeks spent voting. This time has an opportunity cost. What other valuable things could Americans do in this time? In contrast, the voting lottery takes far less time.

Some people, especially those unfamiliar with democratic theory or with the real-world history of different democracies, might object that a voting lottery is not *democratic*. But this objection rests on a

[25] See the tables available at the International Institute for Democracy and Electoral Assistance; available at: http://www.idea.int.

[26] Caltech/MIT Voting Project, "Voting: What Is, and What Could Be" (Caltech/MIT, July 2001): 13; available at: http://www.vote.caltech.edu/sites/default/files/voting_what_is_what_could_be.pdf.

contentious and parochial view of democracy. In the United States, we are accustomed to representative democracy, first-past-the-post majority voting rules, and "one person, one vote." But "one person, one vote" is neither necessary nor sufficient for a political system to count as democratic.[27] The way we do democracy in the United States is just one way among many. In fact, democratic Athens used to use lotteries not just to determine who might vote on particular issues but also even to staff offices. A political system is democratic just to the extent that all citizens have an equal share of fundamental political power. In a voting lottery, all citizens have the same fundamental political status and the same fundamental degree of political power.

Unlike compulsory voting, voting lotteries are not coercive. As we discussed in Chapter 1, compulsory voting is presumed unjust and illegitimate unless there is a compelling justification. The Representativeness Argument claims we should use compulsory voting to ensure that government properly represents all eligible voters. Voter lotteries do an even better job ensuring representativeness but do not involve coercion. They are thus morally superior.

All this is *fatal* to the Representativeness Argument. At this point, I have already done enough to show that the argument fails. However, I plan to keep kicking this dead horse. The Representativeness Argument has other serious flaws as well. It rests on other mistaken premises. When we see why these other premises are mistaken, we will find even more reasons to oppose compulsory voting.

2.4.3 *Must We Protect Nonvoters from Voters?*

Premise 1 of the Representativeness Argument claims that voters vote selfishly. This is one reason why the argument seems plausible. Under voluntary voting, the voting public (the subset of eligible citizens who choose to vote) skews rich, educated, white, and male. This public will thus tend to vote in ways that benefit rich, educated, white males

[27] For more on why lotteries are democratic, see Ben Saunders, "Democracy, Political Equality, and Majority Rule," *Ethics* 121 (2010): 148–77; Ben Saunders, "The Equality of Lotteries," *Philosophy* 83 (2008): 359–72. See also Harry Brighouse and Marc Fleurbaey, "Democracy and Proportionality," *Journal of Political Philosophy* 18 (2010): 137–55, for an argument that democracy sometimes *requires* unequal votes. Brighouse and Fleurbaey argue that citizens who have a greater stake in a decision should have greater decision-making power.

rather than the benefit of all. It seems reasonable to speculate that forcing the poor to vote will protect them from selfish rich voters. It thus seems reasonable to speculate the compulsory voting will produce fairer and equitable government.

However, while it is reasonable to speculate that compulsory voting will protect the weak and downtrodden, at some point, we have to stop speculating. At some point, we have to go and check our empirical assumptions. When we do that, the Representativeness Argument for compulsory voting collapses.

Common sense holds that voters vote selfishly. But common sense is flat out wrong. Political scientists have conducted numerous empirical studies of voter behavior using a wide variety of methods. They overwhelmingly conclude that voters do *not* vote selfishly.[28] As Bryan

[28] Carolyn Funk, "The Dual Influence of Self-Interest and Societal Interest in Public Opinion," *Political Research Quarterly* 53 (2000): 37–62; Carolyn Funk and Patricia Garcia-Monet, "The Relationship between Personal and National Concerns in Public Perceptions of the Economy," *Political Research Quarterly* 50 (1997): 317–42; Dale Miller, "The Norm of Self-Interest," *American Psychologist* 54 (1999): 1053–60; Diana Mutz and Jeffrey Mondak, "Dimensions of Sociotropic Behavior: Group-Based Judgments of Fairness and Well-Being," *American Journal of Political Science* 41 (1997): 284–308; Timothy Feddersen, Sean Gailmard, and Alvaro Sandroni, "A Bias toward Unselfishness in Large Elections: Theory and Experimental Evidence." *American Political Science Review* 103 (2009): 175–92; Brennan and Lomasky, *Democracy and Decision*: 108–14; Donald Green and Ian Shapiro, *Pathologies of Rational Choice Theory* (New Haven, CT: Yale University Press, 1994); Gregory Markus, "The Impact of Personal and National Economic Conditions on the Presidential Vote: A Pooled Cross-Sectional Analysis," *American Journal of Political Science* 32 (1988): 137–54; Pamela Conover, Stanley Feldman, and Kathleen Knight, "The Personal and Political Underpinnings of Economic Forecasts," *American Journal of Political Science* 31 (1987): 559–83; Donald Kinder and Roderick Kiewiet, "Economic Discontent and Political Behavior: The Role of Personal Grievances and Collective Economic Judgments in Congressional Voting," *American Journal of Political Science* 23 (1979): 495–527; Leonie Huddy, Jeffrey Jones, and Richard Chard, "Compassion vs. Self-Interest: Support for Old-Age Programs among the Non-Elderly," *Political Psychology* 22 (2001): 443–72; Laurie Rhodebeck, "The Politics of Greed? Political Preferences among the Elderly," *Journal of Politics* 55 (1993): 342–64; Michael Ponza, Greg Duncan, Mary Corcoran, and Fred Groskind, "The Guns of Autumn? Age Differences in Support for Income Transfers to the Young and Old," *Public Opinion Quarterly* 52 (1988): 441–66; David O. Sears and Carolyn L. Funk, "Self-Interest in Americans' Political Opinions," in Jane Mansbridge (ed.), *Beyond Self-Interest* (Chicago: University of Chicago Press, 1990): 147–70; Bryan Caplan, *The Myth of the Rational Voter* (Princeton, NJ: Princeton University Press, 1997); Thomas Holbrook and James Garand, "Homo Economicus? Economic Information and Economic Voting," *Political Research Quarterly* 49 (1996): 351–75; Diana Mutz, "Mass Media and the Depoliticization

Caplan summarizes: "[P]olitical scientists have subjected the SIVH [self-interested voter hypothesis] to extensive and diverse empirical tests. Their results are impressively uniform. The SIVH fails."[29] For instance, poor people oppose the estate tax as much as the rich. Young people support old-age insurance as much as the old. For a long time, men supported abortion *more* than women. As people get wealthier, they are only weakly more likely to be Republican rather than Democrat. (In fact, in the 2008 presidential election, voters earning over $200,000 a year supported Obama more than McCain.) And so on.

Instead, voters tend to vote for what they believe (perhaps incorrectly) to be in the national interest. Voters vote for what they regard as the common good. Most voters try to promote everyone's interests, not just their own. In technical terms, voters are (in general) nationalist and sociotropic.

If you have not read the empirical literature on voter motivation, this will seem surprising, even unbelievable. You might reasonably ask, "Why are people so altruistic in the voting booth but so selfish elsewhere?" Consider: As a voter, you have a vanishingly small chance of changing the outcome of the election. If you were a sociopath who just wanted to promote your own interests, you would never bother to vote. From a selfish standpoint, the cost of casting a vote always exceeds the expected benefit.[30] So it is not surprising that voters are not selfish. If people bother to vote, it will be to express their values and sense of justice.

of Personal Experience," *American Journal of Political Science* 36 (1992): 483–508; Diana Mutz, "Direct and Indirect Routes to Politicizing Personal Experience: Does Knowledge Make a Difference?" *Public Opinion Quarterly* 57 (1993): 483–502; Jane Mansbridge, *Beyond Self-Interest* (Chicago: University of Chicago Press, 1990); Jack Citrin and Donald Green, "The Self-Interest Motive in American Public Opinion," *Research in Micropolitics* 3 (1990): 1–28; David Sears, Richard Lau, Tom Tyler, and Harris Allen, "Self-Interest vs. Symbolic Politics in Policy Attitudes and Presidential Voting," *American Political Science Review* 74 (1980): 670–84; David Sears and Richard Lau, "Inducing Apparently Self-Interested Political Preferences," *American Journal of Political Science* 27 (1983): 223–52; David Sears, Carl Hensler, and Leslie Speer, "Whites' Opposition to 'Busing': Self-Interest or Symbolic Politics?" *American Political Science Review* 73 (1979): 369–84.

[29] Caplan, *Myth of the Rational Voter*: 149.

[30] For more on this, see Brennan, *Ethics of Voting*: 19, 162–3. Most voters do not know what their exact probability of being decisive is. However, the evidence indicates that they know in some way that their individual votes make little difference.

In short, premise 1 of the Representativeness Argument is false. So proponents of compulsory voting want to force people to vote in order to protect them from a nonexistent threat – the threat of the selfish majority voter. While the voting public skews rich, educated, white, and male, this voting public tries to help everyone, not just rich, educated, white males.

To fix the Representativeness Argument, you need to say something like this: "Sure, voters are all trying to promote the common good. But even if the advantaged are trying to help the disadvantaged, the system would do a better job helping the disadvantaged if the disadvantaged voted more." Again, this seems like a reasonable speculation. But, again, speculation is not good enough. You have to go and check your premises.

2.4.4 *Do the Disadvantaged Know* How *to Help Themselves?*

Imagine your friend Bob wants to lose weight but has bizarre beliefs about how to do so. Bob believes that to lose weight, he must avoid exercise and eat 100 Oreos a day. Bob might intend to serve his self-interest, but his actions undermine rather than serve his self-interest.

What if voters are a bit like Bob?

The Representativeness Argument assumes, without argument or evidence, that nonvoters know *how* to vote in their self-interest. We shouldn't just assume this. The typical poor person knows she wants to be richer. She knows she wants more economic opportunity. But that does not mean she knows which set of policy platforms would in fact deliver those goods.

Suppose I want to support the candidate who will end violent crime in my neighborhood. One candidate proposes to ramp up the war on drugs, police raids, and mandatory sentencing. The other proposes to end the war on drugs, reduce occupational licensing, and reduce regulations and taxes within inner cities with the hope of fostering growth. If I just go on my gut feeling of which candidate is better, I might pick a counterproductive choice. To know which candidate, if any, I should support, I would need to have tremendous social scientific knowledge.

Most citizens lack this knowledge. Poor citizens especially tend to lack it, in part because we tend to give poor citizens crummy educations. As Thomas Christiano, himself an ardent supporter of democracy, says:

> It is hard to see how citizens can satisfy any even moderate standards for beliefs about how best to achieve their political aims. Knowledge of means requires an immense amount of social science and knowledge of particular facts. For citizens to have this kind of knowledge generally would require that we abandon the division of labor in society.[31]

Christiano thinks the typical citizen is competent to deliberate about and choose the appropriate aims of government. However, for citizens to know the best means for achieving those aims, they would have to become experts in sociology, economics, and political science. They don't have the time, let alone the will, to do so.

When citizens vote, they have at least two distinct sets of preferences:

1. *Policy preferences:* The set of policies and laws they want candidates to support. For instance: increase the estate tax, cut spending, increase tariffs, and escalate the war in Afghanistan.
2. *Outcome preferences:* The consequences they want candidates to produce. For instance: improve the economy, reduce the amount of criminal violence, increase economic equality, and reduce the danger of terrorism.

Generally, we form our policy preferences because we believe those policies would promote our outcome preferences. People support the war in Afghanistan because they believe it will reduce terrorism. People support the drug war because they believe it will reduce drug use. People support tariffs because they believe they will help produce economic prosperity. And so on. Bob eats Oreos because he wants to lose weight.

Here is the problem: sometimes – in fact, quite often – we make mistakes, just like Bob. We sometimes mistakenly believe a policy will promote our favored outcomes when that policy will in fact undermine those outcomes. So, for instance, Republicans sincerely believe cutting taxes and government spending will stimulate economic growth. Democrats sincerely believe increasing taxes and spending

[31] Christiano, "Democracy."

will stimulate economic growth. On this issue, at least half the country is *wrong*. They might all be wrong.

Politicians run on policy platforms, and they generally respond to voters' expressed policy preferences. Yet, if voters support the wrong policies, then giving them the policies they want prevents them from getting the outcomes they want. Voters need knowledge. As political scientists Michael Delli Carpini and Scott Keeter say in their famous study of voter ignorance and misinformation,

> Factual knowledge about politics is a critical component of citizenship, one that is essential if citizens are to discern their real interests and take effective advantage of the civic opportunities afforded them.... Knowledge is a keystone to other civic requisites. In the absence of adequate information neither passion nor reason is likely to lead to decisions that reflect the real interests of the public. And democratic principles must be understood to be accepted and acted on in any meaningful way.[32]

In fact, as I discuss at greater length in Chapter 4, the citizens who choose to abstain under voluntary voting tend to have significantly less political knowledge than the citizens who choose to vote. Most voters are ignorant, misinformed, irrational, and biased about political issues.[33] Yet the typical citizen who abstains from voting is even more ignorant, misinformed, irrational, and biased than the typical person who votes.[34] The poor are more likely to be ignorant or misinformed than the rich. Ethnic minorities are more likely to be ignorant or misinformed than majorities. Women are more likely to be ignorant

[32] Michael X. Delli Carpini and Scott Keeter, *What Americans Know about Politics and Why It Matters* (New Haven, CT: Yale University Press, 1996): 3.

[33] For example, see Brennan, *Ethics of Voting*: 179–84; Jamie Terrence Kelly, *Framing Democracy* (Princeton, NJ: Princeton University Press, 2012); Delli Carpini and Keeter, *What Americans Know*; Haidt, *The Righteous Mind*; Westen, *The Political Brain*; Bryan Caplan, Eric Campton, Wayne Grove, and Ilya Somin, "Systematically Biased Beliefs about Political Influence: Evidence from the Perception of Political Influence on Policy Outcomes Survey" (George Mason University, 2012), working paper.

[34] Delli Carpini and Keeter, *What Americans Know*: 135–77; Caplan, *Myth of the Rational Voter*: 255–6; Birch, *Full Participation*: 62; M. Mackerras and I. McAllister, "Compulsory Voting, Party Stability, and Electoral Advantage in Australia," *Electoral Studies* 18 (2) (1999): 217–34; Ian McAllister, "Compulsory Voting, Turnout, and Party Advantage in Australia," *Politics* 21 (1986): 89–93; Peter Selb and Romain Lachat, "The More the Better: Counterfactual Evidence on the Effect of Compulsory Voting on the Consistency of Party Choice," paper presented at the ECPR Joint Sessions of Workshops, Helsinki, May 11, 2007.

or misinformed than men. They are thus more likely than voters to choose candidates *inimical* to their outcome preferences. Forcing them to vote may hurt them rather than help them.

So the Representativeness Argument notes that certain demographic groups tend to vote less than others. Their voice in government is thus weaker. Yet those groups also tend to have little social scientific knowledge. This creates a dilemma: do we want government to represent their outcome preferences or their policy preferences? Should government give current nonvoters more of the policies they want at the expense of their preferred outcomes, or should it generate the outcomes they prefer at the expense of their preferred policies? If we want government to give them their preferred outcomes, then we often want it to ignore their policy preferences. Thus, if you care about the poor and disadvantaged, it does not follow that you want them to vote or get their way in government. It might instead mean that you hope they do not vote, or if they do, that politicians will ignore them.

I return to this point in Chapter 4. There I argue that forcing everyone to vote is like forcing the drunk to drive. I argue that the evidence supports the view that compulsory voting should slightly lower the overall quality of government.

Perhaps I am mistaken. Perhaps current nonvoters know more than I (or many other political scientists I cite) give them credit for. Or perhaps politicians will help the poor more if the poor vote more, even though the poor ask for the wrong things. However, note that because I do not have the burden of proof, I do not need to prove definitively that if we force nonvoters to vote, this will hurt them rather than help them. Rather, my point is that there are strong reasons to doubt that forcing the disadvantaged to vote will help them. Compulsory voting is presumed unjust until shown otherwise. Advocates of compulsory voting must decisively answer my objection.

One might try to argue that if we compel all citizens to vote, it will change their attitudes toward voting. Perhaps they will come to regard voting as an ethical obligation. Perhaps they will then become more interested in politics. Perhaps they will invest more in learning about politics. Perhaps they will increase their political knowledge and thus become better voters. So the advocate of compulsory voting responds, sure, right now nonvoters know too little to serve their own interests, but under compulsory voting, they would know much more. Compulsory voting advocate and former president of the American Political Science Association Arend Lijphart claims just that.[35] My former debating partner, Alfred Apps, does so as well.

At best, this is optimistic speculation. But it is worse than that. In fact, political scientists have studied whether compulsory voting tends to lead to a better-informed electorate. The evidence indicates it does not. Political scientist Annabelle Lever recently reviewed many empirical studies, and compulsory voting had "no noticeable effect on political knowledge or interest [or] electoral outcomes."[36] Antoine Bilodeau and André Blais tried to test whether Lijphart was correct that compulsory voting would increase voter knowledge.

> [They] could uncover no empirical studies to support Lijphart's claim. To fill the gap, they attempted to substantiate his claim in three ways. They first examined whether citizens in Western European countries with compulsory voting report that they discussed politics more than those in non-compulsory countries. Second, they examined the behavior of immigrants to New Zealand [which lacks compulsory voting] from compulsory-voting Australia. Third, they examined the behavior of immigrants to Australia.... In each case, they sought difference in reported levels of political discussion, interest in politics and attitudes toward voting, but were unable to find evidence of [increased political knowledge] due to compulsory voting.[37]

[35] Arend Lijphart, "Unequal Participation: Democracy's Unresolved Dilemma," *American Political Science Review* 91 (1997): 1–14, 10.

[36] Annabelle Lever, "Compulsory Voting: A Critical Perspective," *British Journal of Political Science* 40 (4) (2010): 897–915. See also Annabelle Lever, "'A Liberal Defense of Compulsory Voting': Some Reasons for Skepticism," *Politics* 28 (2008): 61–4; Peter John Loewen, Henry Milner, and Bruce M. Hicks, "Does Compulsory Voting Lead to More Informed and Engaged Citizens? An Experimental Test," *Canadian Journal of Political Science* 41 (2008): 655–67; Henry Milner, Peter John Loewen, and Bruce M. Hicks, "The Paradox of Compulsory Voting: Participation Does Not Equal Political Knowledge," *IRPP Policy Matters* 8 (2007): 1–48; Chris Ballinger, "Compulsory Voting: Palliative Care for Democracy in the UK?" paper presented at the European Consortium for Political Research Joint Sessions workshop "Compulsory Voting: Principles and Practice," Helsinki, May 7–12, 2007.

[37] Loewen, Milner, and Hicks "Does Compulsory Voting Lead": 656, summarizing Antoine Bilodeau and André Blais, "Le vote obligatoire exerce-t-il un effet de socialisation politique?" presented to Colloque int. vote obligatoire, Inst. d'tudes Polit. Lille, October 20–21, 2005. Birch also claims that according to the best available evidence, compulsory voting has no significant effect on voter knowledge (Birch, *Full Participation*: 49–51, 57–67, 140).

In short: Lijphart's and Apps's conjecture is probably wrong. Our evidence indicates that compulsory voting does not increase voter knowledge.

This should not be a surprise. Even though many citizens do not vote, the overwhelming majority of citizens *already* believe they have a moral duty to vote.[38] They already think voting is a civic duty, even though many of them fail to fulfill this purported duty. As we will discuss in Chapter 4, the reason most citizens do not invest in acquiring political information is that this investment does not pay, even if one has altruistic motives.

2.4.5 *If They Vote, Will Anyone Listen?*

The Representativeness Argument assumes that if we get disadvantaged voters to vote more, then political elites will respond more to their preferences. However, there are strong reasons to doubt this.

In the recently published *Affluence and Influence*, Martin Gilens measures how responsive different presidents have been to different groups of voters. In particular, Gilens wants to know when voters at the 90th and 10th percentiles of income disagree about policy, do presidents side with the rich or the poor? In fact, Gilens found, presidents are much more responsive to the policy preferences of the rich than the poor.[39] Note that, to his surprise, he found that George W. Bush was unusually responsive to the poor – Bush was much more likely to side with the poor than other presidents (including Kennedy and Johnson) had been.

Of course, the rich vote more than the poor, so thus far this does not appear to undermine the Representativeness Argument. However, Gilens also examines why presidents respond more to the rich than the poor. He concludes, "[T]he disproportionate responsiveness to the preferences of the affluent cannot be attributed to their higher turnout

[38] In the 1990 American Citizen Participation Study, when asked whether "doing my duty as a citizen" was a reason to vote, 78 percent said it was very important, and 18 percent said it was somewhat important (Sidney Verba, Kay Lehman Schlozman, Henry E. Brady, and Norman Nie, "American Citizen Participation Study," 1990 (Ann Arbor, MI: Inter-university Consortium for Political and Social Research [distributor], 1995); see data available at: http://dx.doi.org/10.3886/ICPSR06635.v1.

[39] Martin Gilens, *Affluence and Influence* (Princeton, NJ: Princeton University Press, 2012): 80.

rates or their greater involvement with political campaigns."[40] While the rich are slightly more likely to vote than the poor, presidents are about six times more responsive to the rich than the poor. If politicians were just trying to please their voting bases, they would be only slightly more responsive to the rich.

So the Representativeness Argument has yet another flaw. It speculated that getting the poor to vote more would make politicians side with their expressed opinions more. However, at least some empirical evidence indicates that politicians strongly tend to ignore the poor's political preferences and that this is not due to their lower turnout rates.[41] If so, then, because low turnout would not be the cause of the disease (if it is even a disease), there would be little reason to think increasing turnout would be the cure.

2.4.6 *Summary*

The Representativeness Argument seemed compelling at first glance, but it was full of false or questionable assumptions. It assumed, not only without evidence, but against overwhelming evidence to the contrary, that voters tend to vote selfishly. It assumed, without evidence and despite strong evidence to the contrary, that forcing nonvoters to vote would be in their best interest. It assumed that politicians would listen to the poor if the poor voted more. It also fails simply because – if we all want democracies to be more representative – voting lotteries are a superior alternative to compulsory voting.

I regard the Representativeness Argument as the strongest existing argument for compulsory voting. While I will continue to examine and undermine many more purported arguments for compulsory voting, things are already starting to look bad for compulsory voting.

2.5 Compulsory Voting, Trust, and Social Solidarity

Consider a different argument:

[40] *Ibid.*: 10, 234–52.

[41] For a contrary view, see Peter K. Enns and Christopher Wlezien (eds.), *Who Gets Represented?* (New York: Russell Sage Foundation, 2011).

The Trust and Solidarity Argument

1. It is good for citizens to trust their government and to feel solidarity with one another.
2. If there is high turnout, citizens will trust their government more and feel greater solidarity with one another.
3. If 1 and 2, then whatever increases trust and solidarity is justified.
4. Compulsory voting is necessary to ensure high turnout.
5. Therefore, compulsory voting is justified.

This argument faces several problems. First, premise 1 is not unconditionally true or false. Sometimes trust in government is good, but sometimes it is bad. Governments often act badly. For instance, my democratic government routinely murders innocent children in the third world in the name of a dubious war on terror. My government spies on its own people. My government started disastrous wars in Iraq and Afghanistan. Although the Iraqi war was a terrible idea, it enjoyed overwhelming popular support at the beginning of the war.[42] My democratic government has a long history of genocide and imperialism. My government asserts the rights to assassinate citizens without due process and to torture its enemies.

Accordingly, my government does not deserve citizens' trust. I prefer that my fellow citizens trust the government *less*, and I want them to act on this distrust.[43] It is good for citizens to trust their governments or their fellow citizens only if they *deserve* to be trusted. Thus, if someone claims that compulsory voting would lead Americans to trust their government more, I would oppose it for that very reason.

Sometimes societies need more distrust and less solidarity. After all, as Stanley Milgram illustrated in his famous experiments, in the attempt to conform to others' expectations, we can all be induced to

[42] Pew Research Center indicates that in March 2003, 72 percent of Americans supported the invasion. A year later, most people believed that the war was not going well. By 2006, most citizens thought the war was a bad decision. See Pew Research Center, "Public Attitudes toward the War in Iraq: 2003–2008" (March 19 2008); available at: http://pewresearch.org/pubs/770/iraq-war-five-year-anniversary.

[43] One might point out that the U.S. Congress has an approval rating hovering near 9 percent. However, presidents – the ones who perpetrate murderous policies – have much higher approval ratings. When I say I want citizens to act on this distrust, I do not mean I want them all to vote. Rather, I want those who do vote to vote better, to vote against hawks and civil rights abusers.

perform great evils. Dissent, disagreement, and partisanship are often good things.[44]

One might try to argue that if citizens voted en masse, then governments would, as a result, *become* more deserving of trust. For instance, one might try to argue that high turnout causes better government. Or one might argue that high turnout causes governments to be more representative of the people and the popular will. But this is really a distinct argument. I already considered and rebutted one version of this argument in Section 2.4, and I will turn to another version of it in Section 2.6.

The Trust and Solidarity Argument assumes (in premise 3) that government may force us to do things that improve social solidarity and mutual trust. However, as I explained in Chapter 1, even if coercing people would produce good results, this does not show coercion is permissible. The mere fact that something promotes social solidarity is not sufficient to justify compulsion, even if social solidarity is a good thing. Consider: we have strong evidence that bowling leagues, church membership, and fraternal societies encourage social solidarity and social capital.[45] Yet that would not entitle the government to penalize us for nonparticipation. If you think the Trust and Solidarity Argument justifies compulsory voting, then you should also favor compulsory membership in bowling leagues, churches, fraternal societies, and the like. If you do not in fact favor such compulsion, then it must be because you recognize premise 3 of the Trust and Solidarity Argument is false.

This argument also assumes (in premise 2) that great participation makes us trust each other more. Empirically, there does seem to be a positive correlation between trust and turnout. However, this does not show us that high turnout *causes* trust. Instead, it may be that trust causes high turnout. Or it may be that a third factor causes both trust and high turnout. The only way to know is to do empirical, social scientific work. In fact, there is empirical evidence showing that, all things being equal, when citizens trust politicians, each other, and the

44 See also Nancy Rosenblum, *On the Side of Angels: An Appreciation of Parties and Partisanship* (Princeton, NJ: Princeton University Press, 2010); Haidt, *The Righteous Mind*.

45 See Robert Putnam, *Bowling Alone* (New York: Simon and Schuster, 2001).

government, they are more likely to vote.[46] We have strong evidence that trust *causes* turnout, but there is no evidence (at least, as of yet) that turnout causes trust.

Given sad facts about political psychology, greater political engagement might even undermine rather than promote social solidarity. The political brain naturally tends toward polarization and conflict. We all know: if you want to ruin Thanksgiving dinner, just get people to talk about politics. Unfortunately, this may go for society at large as well. When confronted with contrary political beliefs, the overwhelming majority of people become angry and hateful. (There is a good chance that Section 2.4 made you angry with me.)

Psychologist Jonathan Haidt says, "Reasoning was not designed to pursue truth. Reasoning was designed by evolution to help us win arguments."[47] Here Haidt refers to a view known as the *argumentative theory of reasoning*.[48] The theory claims that we did not develop our reasoning capacities in order to become better scientific truth-seekers. Instead, we developed reasoning in order to communicate with, argue with, and manipulate one another. Hugo Mercier elaborates: "[R] easoning falls quite short of reliably delivering rational beliefs.... It may even be, in a variety of cases, detrimental to rationality. [People] ...

[46] Evans, *Voters and Voting*: 152, 118–45; Arend Lijphart, *Patterns of Democracy* (New Haven, CT: Yale University Press, 1999): 284–6; Michaelene Cox, "When Trust Matters: Explaining Differences in Voter Turnout," *Journal of Common Market Studies* 41 (2003): 757–70; Margaret Levi and Laura Stocker, "Political Trust and Trustworthiness," *Annual Review of Political Science* 3 (2000): 475–507. Timothy Besley suggests that poor democratic health is correlated with low turnout but also says it's hard to show what consequences that has for the welfare of citizens. The data he provides more strongly suggest that perceived low-quality governance causes decreased turnout rather than that increased turnout causes higher-quality governance (T. Besley, *Principled Agents? The Political Economy of Good Government* [New York: Oxford University Press, 2006]: 17–20). Mark Franklin attributes low voter turnout in the United States in part to the separation of powers and to the perceived strong influence of special interests on government policy (M. Franklin, *Voter Turnout and the Dynamics of Electoral Competition in Established Democracies since 1945* [New York: Cambridge University Press, 2004]: 91–118).

[47] Jonathan Haidt, "The New Science of Morality," *Edge* (September 17, 2010); available at: http://edge.org/conversation/a-new-science-of-morality-part-1.

[48] Hugo Mercier and Dan Sperber, "Why Do Humans Reason? Arguments for an Argumentative Theory," *Behavioral and Brian Sciences* 34 (2011): 57–111.

systematically strive for arguments that justify their beliefs or their actions."[49]

In politics (and elsewhere), we suffer from in-group/out-group bias or intergroup bias. *In-group/out-group* bias means we are tribalistic, in the most negative connotation of that term. We are biased to form groups and to identify ourselves strongly with our groups. We tend to develop animosity toward other groups, even when there is no basis for this animosity. We are biased to assume our group is good and just and that members of other groups are bad, stupid, and unjust. We are biased to forgive most transgressions from our own group and damn any minor error from other groups. We thus tend to treat political debates as rivalries between sports teams. Our commitment to our team can override our commitment to truth or morality.[50]

To illustrate: psychologist Henry Tajfel conducted experiments in which he randomly assigned subjects to groups. He would then lie to subjects by telling them that group members shared some frivolous trait. He then conducted experiments to see how people treated members of their own group and other groups. He repeatedly found that subjects would then show strong favoritism toward members of their own group and distrust toward members of other groups.[51]

Another illustration: psychologist Drew Westen wanted to study the phenomenon of motivated reasoning. *Motivated reasoning* occurs when the brain tries to converge on beliefs it finds appealing or pleasing. According to the theory of motivated reasoning, we do not always seek to believe what is true. Rather, we prefer to believe some things rather than others. Westen recruited committed Democrats and Republicans (as well as an uncommitted control group) to see

[49] Hugo Mercier, "The Argumentative Theory," *Edge* (September 18, 2010); available at: http://edge.org/conversation/the-argumentative-theory.

[50] Haidt, *The Righteous Mind*; Westen, *The Political Brain*; Drew Westen, Pavel S. Blagov, Keith Harenski, Clint Kilts, and Stephan Hamann, "The Neural Basis of Motivated Reasoning: An fMRI Study of Emotional Constraints on Political Judgment during the U.S. Presidential Election of 2004," *Journal of Cognitive Neuroscience* 18 (2007): 1947–58.

[51] Henry Tajfel, *Human Groups and Social Categories* (New York: Cambridge University Press, 1981); Henry Tajfel, "Social Psychology of Intergroup Relations," *Annual Review of Psychology* 33 (1982): 1–39; Henry Tajfel and J. C. Turner, "An Integrative Theory of Intergroup Conflict," in W. G. Austin and S. Worchel (eds.), *The Social Psychology of Intergroup Relations* (Monterey, CA: Brooks-Cole, 1979).

how they responded to evidence that various public figures had acted hypocritically. He found that the most politically engaged participants engaged most heavily in motivated reasoning. They dismissed evidence right in front of their faces. Worse, functional magnetic resonance imaging showed that as subjects acted irrationally, pleasure centers in their brains lit up. In politics, our brains reward us for epistemic vice.[52]

Many political theorists advocate deliberative democracy. In the theory of deliberative democracy, citizens are supposed to come together to reason and deliberate. They are supposed to air their opinions in an open and honest way. They are supposed to make decisions together based on reasons everyone can appreciate. They are supposed to seek consensus.

However, when political scientists study real-world political deliberation, they find that deliberative democracy falls far short of its goals. Deliberation tends to reduce in-group/out-group biases only when the opposing sides have equal numbers. Otherwise, deliberation exacerbates these biases. Deliberation and group discussion tend to increase rather than decrease polarization. Emotional appeals and manipulative language tend to rule the day. Sometimes groups behave nicely and reach consensus, but that is usually just because they choose to avoid the controversial topics.[53]

Getting people more involved in politics often causes greater conflict and increased polarization. It at least sometimes increases distrust. We can predict that, all things being equal, when people have happy feelings toward their government and each other, they participate more. But it does not follow that getting them to participate more would increase these happy feelings. On the contrary, more participation sometimes hurts. But, even if participation always did produce happy feelings, as we saw, that would not yet justify compulsory voting.

[52] Westen et al., "The Neural Basis of Motivated Reasoning"; Westen, *The Political Brain.*

[53] In support of all these claims, see Tali Mendelberg, "The Deliberative Citizen: Theory and Evidence," in Michael X. Delli Carpini, Leonie Huddy, and Robert Y. Shapiro (eds.), *Research in Micropolitics*, Vol. 6: *Political Decision Making, Deliberation, and Participation* (Amsterdam: Elsevier, 2002): 151–93. Mendelberg reviews nearly every empirical study done on deliberation.

2.6 Other Purported Consequences of Compulsion

Advocates often claim compulsory voting would produce certain good consequences. They make arguments with the following form:

The Generic Consequentialist Argument

1. Compulsory voting would produce good consequence *G*.
2. If compulsory voting would produce good consequence *G*, then compulsory voting is justified.
3. Therefore, compulsory voting is justified.

Different people will fill in the blank (*G*) in different ways.

Before looking at some of the purported good consequences of compulsory voting, let's reflect on what it takes to make a good argument here. The advocate of compulsory voting needs to do a few things.

First, he must show us that those purported consequences are in fact *good*. Suppose I said, "Compulsory voting will help Republicans win more elections." Few people, except for some Republicans, would regard that as a good argument for compulsory voting. It is too obviously a partisan value. Arguments that compulsory voting causes good outcomes need either to cite relatively uncontroversial, nonpartisan outcomes, or they must take a stance and show us why certain partisan outcomes are the right outcomes to impose through coercion.

Second, our advocate of compulsory voting must produce strong evidence that compulsory voting would in fact deliver the goods. All government coercion is presumed unjust until shown otherwise. Speculating that compulsory voting would produce good consequences is not good enough. The advocate must give us firm evidence.

Third, even if he has strong evidence that compulsory voting would in fact produce good results, our advocate must consider whether there are various deontological objections. After all, as we discussed in Chapter 1, even if forcing citizens to attend art events would produce an artistic renaissance, it is far from obvious that this would justify coercion. Citizens have their own lives to lead. Perhaps compulsory voting violates their rights. Or perhaps compulsory voting is objectionable on other grounds.

Fourth and final, our advocate must demonstrate that there are no other noncoercive (or less coercive) ways to produce the desired consequences. This was one of the (many) fatal problems with the Representativeness Argument. In general, we are not allowed to coerce people if we can get the purported benefits of coercion without coercion.

Arguments on behalf of compulsory voting generally begin with well-known statistics about low and unequal turnout. They then proceed by making a series of unsubstantiated empirical claims about what compulsory voting would do if we gave it a chance. These empirical claims often seem commonsensical, so the arguments seem strong. However, often political scientists have already studied, tested, and discredited these empirical claims.

In the social sciences, as in medicine, biology, and many of the natural sciences, one can often find one study claiming that *A* causes *B*, whereas another study claims that *A* does not cause *B* or that the authors were unable to show that *A* causes *B*. This is *normal* in all the sciences. For instance, even if most medical studies fail to find a link between some toxin and cancer, one can usually find at least one study somewhere that claims there is a link.

This does not mean we have to be agnostic, nor does it show we can just choose to believe whatever we want. (However, as I argued in Chapter 1, if you are agnostic or unsure about whether compulsory voting produces good consequences, then you are required to oppose it.) Rather, we must look at the balance of evidence. We try studying the same issue from many different angles, using many different data sets, using many different methods. If we consistently fail to show that *A* causes *B*, we conclude that it probably does not or at least that we are not justified in thinking it does. If we consistently show that *A* does cause *B*, then we should believe it does. If most studies show that *A* does not cause *B* but a few say it does, we usually must side with the majority. And so on. Rational belief formation in the natural and social sciences is all about balancing the available evidence.

Political scientist Sarah Birch's recent book, *Full Participation*, is a comprehensive review of nearly every empirical study on the effects of compulsory voting. In the social and natural sciences, a *review article* or book collects all the previous research that has been done on a topic, compares and weighs the research, and then makes conclusions based on the weight of the evidence.

Although (to my surprise) Birch herself seems to favor compulsory voting,[54] her book makes the consequentialist case for compulsory voting look exceptionally weak.[55] She says that compulsory voting has a clear positive effect on voter turnout and political participation. It gets citizens to the polls. It also improves citizens' feelings of satisfaction with democracy. By itself, this is not all that interesting a result and not enough to justify compulsion. A more interesting result is that many studies show compulsory voting is positively correlated with income equality (but only in Western Europe and parts of Latin America) and the reduction of corruption. We will take a closer look at this correlation later to determine whether this justifies compulsory voting.

Beyond that, Birch says, studies show that compulsory voting has a clear negative effect on citizens' feeling of political efficacy – that is, they feel *less*, not more, efficacious in compulsory-voting regimes. Otherwise, it has no significant effect on individual political knowledge, individual political conservation and persuasion, individual propensity to contact politicians, the propensity to work with others to address concerns, participation in campaign activities, the likelihood of being contacted by a party or politician, the quality of representation, electoral integrity, the proportion of female members of parliament, support for small or third parties, support for the left, or support for the far right.[56]

In short: compulsory voting gets people to the polls, but it does not do much else. Remember, this is not Birch offering the conclusions of her own individual studies but rather reviewing all the studies out there.

Many of my colleagues support compulsory voting because they believe it will help the Democrats (or the equivalent party or parties in other countries) win elections. But my colleagues are mistaken. Political scientists Raymond Wolfinger and Benjamin Highton say,

> [There is a] widespread belief that "if everybody in this country voted, the Democrats would be in for the next 100 years." … [T]his conclusion … is accepted by almost everyone except a few empirical political scientists. Their

[54] Sarah Birch, "The Case for Compulsory Voting," *Public Policy Research* 16 (2009): 21–7.

[55] See Birch, *Full Participation*, chaps. 4–6: 140.

[56] *Ibid.*: 140.

analyses of survey data show that no objectively achieved increase in turnout – including compulsory voting – would be a boon to progressive causes or Democratic candidates. Simply put, voters' preferences differ minimally from those of all citizens; outcomes would not change if everyone voted.[57]

Wolfinger and Highton agree that compulsory voting would bring at best modest changes in electoral outcomes. They conclude, "We found [even] less support for the conventional wisdom that higher turnout would be a boon for the Democrats."[58]

Now Birch says that income equality and compulsory voting are correlated. As far as I can tell, though, there is no clear evidence that compulsory voting *causes* income equality. Instead, whether a country chooses to adopt compulsory voting itself depends on the political opinions and dispositions of the electorate and their representatives. *Support* for compulsory voting is strongly correlated with income equality. Citizens from more ideologically egalitarian countries and countries with more income equality are more likely to support compulsory voting. Also, as Birch herself agrees, compulsory voting does not tend to help left-wing parties or have much partisan influence. It is not as though compulsory voting helps parties that favor higher levels of redistribution win elections. Thus it is unclear why compulsory voting would cause greater income equality. So, while there is indeed a positive correlation between compulsory voting and income inequality, we do not have strong grounds to believe that compulsory-voting laws lead to greater income equality. Instead, the kind of political culture that leads to greater income equality is itself more likely to lead to compulsory-voting laws. Compulsory-voting laws and income equality have a common cause.[59]

However, for the sake of argument, suppose compulsory voting really does reduce income inequality. Would that that be sufficient grounds to support it?

[57] Benjamin Highton and Raymond Wolfinger, "The Political Implications of Higher Turnout," *British Journal of Political Science* 31 (1) (2001): 179–223.

[58] Highton and Wolfinger, "Higher Turnout": 223. I add the qualifier *even* to signify the force of their quotation in context. Lijphart claimed that previous work with this conclusion also had a methodological flaw. Highton and Wolfinger say that even if one corrects for this supposed flaw, one gets the same result.

[59] Birch, *Full Participation*: 141–7.

Whether governments should try to equalize wealth is contentious, not just among conservatives and libertarians but also even among left-liberals and social democrats. *Material egalitarianism* is the doctrine that everyone ought to possess the same level of income or wealth. Few people really advocate material egalitarianism. If material egalitarianism were true, then it would be better for everyone to be equally poor than for everyone to be rich but unequal. However, it is better for everyone to be rich but unequal than for everyone to be equal and poor. John Rawls argued that the point of social justice is not to make people equal. Rather, the point is more to make sure that the worst off contributing members of society have enough to lead decent human lives.[60] Rawls asks us to imagine that the social product is a pie to be divided. We might think fairness or justice requires equal slices. However, suppose it is a magic pie. Suppose if we cut the pie into unequal slices, the pie gets bigger, such that everyone – even the person with the smallest slice – gets a bigger piece than she would if the pie were cut equally. In that case, Rawls says, only envy or malice would make us cut the pie equally. We should try to maximize the absolute size of the smallest slice, not try to make sure the slices are the same size. Rawls's point: society is just like that magic pie.

When Birch claims that compulsory voting and income equality are positively correlated, she measures income equality by a country's *Gini coefficient*, a statistical measure of income inequality. But had Birch taken her cue from Rawls, she would not care whether compulsory voting leads to income equality. Rather, she would ask whether compulsory voting helps the least advantaged workers get richer in absolute terms. She would instead try to determine whether compulsory voting improves the absolute lifetime income of blue-collar workers.

Note also that Birch and other researchers appear to be using pre–tax-and-transfer Gini coefficients rather than post–tax-and-transfer Gini coefficients. If so, this would bias the positive results of compulsory voting upward. Pre–tax-and-transfer inequality is higher than post–tax-and-transfer inequality. However, it seems like the relevant measure is post–tax-and-transfer inequality. After all, social democrats

[60] John Rawls, *A Theory of Justice* (Cambridge, MA: Harvard University Press, 1971).

themselves claim that pretax income is not much more than an accounting fiction.[61]

Birch also says there is positive correlation between compulsory voting and reduced political corruption. However, we must again ask whether this is because compulsory voting reduces corruption or, instead, whether less corrupt countries are more likely to instantiate compulsory voting in the first place. The less corrupt a country is, the greater is the support for compulsory voting. Thus, if compulsory voting and reduced political corruption are correlated, this may just mean that less corrupt countries are more likely to have compulsory voting, not that compulsory voting itself reduces corruption.

This is especially plausible when we think about how corruption takes place. One major form of political corruption is rent seeking. A firm, corporation, labor union, or special interest group engages in *rent seeking* when it tries to manipulate the legal environment for its own advantage at others' expense. Some firms induce legislators to pass favorable regulations, regulations that stifle competition. Others induce legislators to grant them subsidies, bailouts, or protective tariffs. And so on. Rent seeking is a major sign of corruption. However, rent seeking is generally a postelection phenomenon. Special interests groups win favors by lobbying, not by voting or by paying for campaigns.

Birch claims there is a positive correlation between reduced corruption and compulsory voting. However, as she would readily admit, we do not have an objective measure of government corruption. She uses Transparency International's Corruption Perceptions Index. This index surveys different analysts' *opinions* of how corrupt different governments are, which is not quite the same thing as surveying whether the government is actually corrupt.

More important, Transparency International itself warns not to make too much out of individual country rankings and scores. New Zealand is ranked number 1, Denmark number 2, the United States number 24, France number 25, Colombia number 80, and North Korea number 182 (dead last). We should take this as good evidence that New Zealand and Denmark are less corrupt than the United States

[61] Liam Murphy and Thomas Nagel, *The Myth of Ownership: Taxes and Justice* (Oxford, UK: Oxford University Press, 2002): 32–3, 36.

or France, but we do not really know that New Zealand is less corrupt than Denmark or that the United States is less corrupt than France. We should thus be cautious in trying to run statistical regressions, relying on fine-grade data, to determine whether compulsory voting correlates with reduced corruption.

Note also that Transparency International's thirteen least corrupt countries are New Zealand, Denmark, Finland, Sweden, Singapore, Norway, The Netherlands, Australia, Switzerland, Canada, Luxembourg, Hong Kong, and Iceland. One might notice that these are also *small* countries and, for the most part, *ethnically homogeneous* countries. Smaller, more homogeneous countries are generally less corrupt. Birch does not try to control for these other explanations.

However, even if we put all these concerns aside, a voting lottery remains superior to compulsory voting. Some people believe compulsory voting leads to more egalitarian outcomes. Suppose they are right. If we ask them why compulsory voting might do that, they will say that compulsory voting makes it so that a higher percentage of the voting public is poor and disadvantaged. Under voluntary voting, the electorate is demographically biased toward the rich and advantaged. The poor and disadvantaged are systematically less likely to vote.

As we saw when we discussed the Representativeness Argument, a voting lottery removes bias. A voting lottery makes the electorate statistically identical to the population of all eligible voters. But a voting lottery is cheaper and is noncoercive.

Thus there does not yet appear to be a good consequentialist argument in favor of compulsory voting. Compulsory voting gets people to vote, but that does not justify compulsion. Our best available evidence shows it does not have much of an effect beyond that. It does appear to be positively correlated with income equality and reduced corruption. However, correlation is not causation. And even if we grant that compulsory voting causes income equality, and even if we grant that the government should promote income equality, we can just use a voting lottery instead.

2.7 Conclusion

We have examined six major arguments on behalf of compulsory voting. These arguments claimed

1. Compulsory voting is necessary to ensure consent.
2. Compulsory voting is necessary to ensure legitimacy.
3. Compulsory voting is good because it makes democracy more democratic.
4. Compulsory voting is necessary to ensure representativeness.
5. Compulsory voting is good because it promotes trust and solidarity.
6. Compulsory voting causes a wide range of good consequences.

These arguments were all shown to be deeply flawed. In some cases they were self-contradictory or confused. In other cases they rested on disproven or unproven empirical assumptions. In many cases the arguments failed because a voting lottery would be a superior alternative to compulsory voting.

We are not done yet, though. In Chapter 3, I will consider (and rebut) a wide range of duty-based arguments for compulsory voting.

3

Do Your Share or Else

3.1 Introduction

In Chapter 2, I examined arguments that claimed compulsory voting is justified because it would produce good consequences. None of these arguments was sound. So far the case for compulsory voting isn't just weak – it's practically nonexistent.

In this chapter, I focus instead on deontological arguments for compulsory voting. Some of these arguments try to establish that, for one reason or another, citizens have a duty to vote. The arguments then try to show that this justifies government in making them vote. Others argue that compulsory voting would in some way make citizens more autonomous or more efficacious. I argue none of these arguments succeeds in justifying compulsory voting.

3.2 Not All Moral Duties Are Enforceable

For the sake of argument, suppose citizens have a moral duty to vote.[1] (Some people prefer to say we have a *civic* duty to vote, but that doesn't change anything. It just specifies what *kind* of moral duty the duty to vote is supposed to be.) Now spot the flaw in the following argument:

[1] This is in fact a controversial view. For two extended arguments that there is in fact no duty to vote, see Brennan, *Ethics of Voting*: 15–67; Loren Lomasky and Geoffrey Brennan, "Is There a Duty to Vote?," *Social Philosophy and Policy* 17 (2000): 62–86.

The Duty-to-Vote Argument

1. Citizens have a moral duty to vote.
2. If citizens have a moral duty to do something, then government may force them to do it.
3. Therefore, government may force citizens to vote (i.e., compulsory voting is justified).

Even if we grant premise 1, premise 2 appears to be false. Just because I have a moral duty to do something, it does not follow that government may force me to do it. On the contrary, it's usually wrong for government to force me to perform my moral duties. Most of my moral duties are unenforceable.

To illustrate, consider the following cases:

A. Mark promises Allison to drive her to the airport. When the time comes, he reneges, saying he'd rather play video games.
B. Mark promises to marry Allison. On the day of their ceremony, he reneges, saying he'd rather play video games. He offers to elope the next day instead, provided he beats the current level.
C. Mark forgets his first anniversary with Allison. He does not buy her a present or do anything special for the day.
D. Allison is a devout Catholic and so will not divorce Mark for any reason. Mark decides to sleep around, knowing Allison will not leave him, even though his infidelity hurts her.
E. When Mark and Allison have children, Mark does the minimum he can as a father, showing the children little affection or love. He provides them with the material goods they need, never abuses them, and does needed chores, such as driving them to soccer. He never says, "I love you," never cheers for them, and never smiles at them.
F. Mark wins millions of dollars in a lottery, more than he could ever use. He pays his taxes in full but never gives any money to charity. He does not help his sick mother with her medical bills. When he dies, he leaves no money to his children or grandchildren.
G. At work, Mark does the bare minimum not to get fired. He frequently promises his boss to get things done at certain times but doesn't do so.

H. Mark frequently promises coworkers that he will help them with projects, but he never does so.
I. Suppose God exists. Mark is aware that God exists, but never worships Him. In fact, he openly mocks God.
J. Mark is aware of his character flaws but actively chooses not to improve his character in any way.
K. Mark decides to smoke, overeat, and overdrink not because these things bring him joy but just to spite health fanatics.
L. Whenever Mark does something wrong, he refuses to say he is sorry or to make amends.
M. Mark never shows gratitude to anyone for anything.
N. Mark has a managerial job. He decides to promote workers who share his taste in music rather than promoting the best or most deserving workers.
O. Mark joins the Nazi Party and starts writing Nazi literature. He advocates that the state slaughter Jews and expel blacks.

Mark is a derelict boyfriend, husband, employee, father, and son. He's a jerk. He violates duties of beneficence, duties of special obligation, duties of gratitude, duties of justice, duties of self-improvement, and duties of fidelity.

In each case A–O, Mark violates a moral duty. Yet the state should not compel Mark to act better. It should not force him to pay even a small fine for his bad behavior. In each of these cases, intervention goes beyond the scope of the state's rightful authority over Mark. It's wrong for Mark to act badly, but it would also be wrong for the state to intervene.

Only in *special* cases may the state intervene to force us to perform our duties. Thus, for instance, the state may intervene to stop us from harming one another. It can intervene to force us to perform certain contracts (or, rather, to pay for damages when we fail to keep those contracts). It can force us to perform *some* of our special obligations, such as our duty to care for our kids. But *most* of our moral obligations are not enforceable.

So there is a huge gap between, "You have a duty to vote," and, "The state may force you to vote." Anyone who makes a duty-based argument for compulsory voting needs to close this gap. The defender of compulsory voting needs to show not only that there is a duty to vote but also that it is an enforceable duty.

With that in mind, consider the following argument, which I often see propounded in the popular press:

The Gratitude Argument

1. Citizens who fail to vote are ungrateful for their hard-won liberties. (Our troops died to protect those freedoms.)
2. People should be grateful.
3. Therefore, citizens should be compelled to vote.

Whatever one thinks of premise 1, this is not a compelling argument. Sure, people have a moral obligation to express and act on gratitude from time to time. But, in general, these obligations are *unenforceable*. We have a duty to express gratitude from time to time, but this duty is almost never enforceable. It's almost always wrong to coerce an adult into expressing gratitude.

3.3 Does Compulsory Voting Enhance Liberty?

Political theorist Justine Lacroix believes citizens have an enforceable duty to vote. She notes that some people might object that compulsory voting violates citizens' liberty. However, she says this objection to compulsory voting depends on a contentious view of liberty. On the contrary, she argues that compulsory voting actually enhances citizens' liberty.

In everyday English, we use the words *liberty* and *freedom* to refer to a wide range of different but related things.[2] Generally, philosophers claim that conceptions of liberty divide into two broad categories.

1. *Negative liberty.* Negative liberty connotes the absence of certain obstacles. For instance, Thomas Hobbes says that anything that gets in my way counts as an infringement of liberty. Other philosophers say that something infringes on my liberty only if it violates my rights.
2. *Positive liberty.* Positive liberty connotes the power or ability to achieve one's goals. So, for instance, one might say that a rich person has more positive liberty than a poor person because the rich person can use his money to do more.

[2] David Schmidtz and Jason Brennan, *A Brief History of Liberty* (Oxford, UK: Wiley-Blackwell, 2010): 1–29.

One popular conception of positive liberty equates liberty with *autonomy*. Lacroix says, "Liberty ... is rather akin to the concept of autonomy, that is to say that liberty does not mean the absence of law but rather the respect of the laws that men have made and accepted for themselves."[3] Lacroix does not elaborate much on what she means here. She seems to say that opponents of compulsory voting think that compulsion violates citizens' liberty by unjustly interfering with them. Opponents of compulsory voting rely on a negative conception of liberty.

In contrast, Lacroix thinks that compulsory voting might make citizens *more* free because it gets them to authorize the laws collectively.[4] Forcing citizens to vote is a petty violation of their negative liberty, but that violation is worthwhile because it enhances one form of positive liberty.

Thus let's consider the Autonomy Argument:

The Autonomy Argument

1. It is valuable for each person to be autonomous and self-directed and to live by rules of her own making.
2. In order for each person living in a shared political environment to be autonomous and self-directed and to live by rules of her own making, she needs to have and exercise her right to vote.
3. Compulsory voting ensures everyone exercises her right to vote.
4. Therefore, compulsory voting enhances autonomy.
5. If compulsory voting enhances autonomy, then compulsory voting is justified.
6. Therefore, compulsory voting is justified.

This argument is problematic for a number of reasons.

First – and one doesn't have to be a rabid libertarian or anarchist to say this – one might dispute whether government should *force us to be autonomous*. Some people are more autonomous than others. Some people have remarkable self-control. They lead lives of their own

[3] Justine Lacroix, "A Liberal Defense of Compulsory Voting," *Politics* 27 (2007): 190–5.

[4] Alternatively, Lacroix may just mean that compulsory voting does not violate citizens' autonomy and so is potentially permissible. However, Lacroix would then need to rely on another argument, such as the others I consider and rebut, to try to justify compulsory voting. In fact, her best argument just seems to be the Representativeness Argument, which was disposed of in Chapter 2.

making. They build up their own system of values through rational choice. They shape the world to fit them rather than being fit to the world. Other people are not so autonomous. They have an external locus of control. They are pushed around more by external forces. Their values and ideas are hand-me-downs from grandma or their peers. It is not obvious that the government should force us to be more like the former than the latter. Sure, autonomy is a form of freedom. But it might not be government's job to force us to be free in that way. (Instead, it is more plausible that government should help ensure that everyone has the chance to be autonomous.)

There are lots of ways of using compulsion to enhance citizens' liberty. We could force citizens to read Steven Covey's *The Seven Habits of Highly Effective People*, early nineteenth-century *Bildungsroman* novels, Romantic poetry, and John Stuart Mill's *On Liberty*, and this would probably enhance their autonomy. Or perhaps government could sponsor mandatory autonomy-improvement classes. It could fine citizens $20 if they fail to attend. Or the government could require every citizen to keep a journal in which he reflects on his daily decisions and asks himself how he could have done better. Citizens who failed to keep journals would be fined $100 per year.

Does any of this sound reasonable? If it is permissible to force citizens to improve their autonomy through voting, it should also be permissible to force them to improve their autonomy in other ways.

One might object that *political* autonomy is perhaps different from personal autonomy. Perhaps governments may permissibly use coercion against citizens to improve citizens' political autonomy but may not use coercion to improve their personal autonomy. Again, I'm not so sure. Suppose, for the sake of argument, it turned out that getting citizens to read books by Jean Jacques Rousseau, Philip Pettit, and Joshua Cohen significantly improved their political autonomy. That still would not seem to justify having government compel citizens to read those books. Similarly, suppose reading books by James Buchanan, Bryan Caplan, and Jason Brennan significantly impaired citizens' political autonomy. That would not justify the government in fining citizens $20 for reading those books.

Of course, voting takes less time than reading a book. So perhaps someone making the Autonomy Argument might say, "I'm in favor of political autonomy-improving government coercion, provided such coercion takes as little time as voting."

But that will not quite do. After all, it's hard to see why political participation makes me more autonomous unless I am also well informed. Autonomous people *know what they're doing*. Compulsory voting gets citizens to vote, but compulsory voting does not make them more informed (see Chapter 2). Perhaps the act of voting enhances our political autonomy, but only if we first become well informed about the social sciences and about current events. But that takes real time. One needs to do a ton of homework.

At any rate, so far I have been giving the Autonomy Argument too much credit. There's no reason to think that the act of voting gives citizens any real autonomy, any autonomy worth having.

If there is any connection between voting and autonomy, it must be that by voting, a person is in part the author of the laws, at least if her side wins. If she abstains, then she has no partial authorship over the laws, and thus the laws are in some way imposed on her.

There is a sure fire way to determine that you do not have autonomous control over a situation: no matter what you choose or what you decide, the same thing happens anyway. Your decisions make no difference. To illustrate: while writing this paragraph, I conducted an experiment. I decided that the Sun would set early. While editing this paragraph later at night, I decided that the Sun would rise early. Nothing happened. I repeated this experiment many times during subsequent editing. I conclude I lack autonomous control over the Sun.

So it goes with voting. In every election, I choose not to be governed by a populist, warmongering, civil rights–violating, immigrant-excluding, child-murdering plutocrat. Yet, in every election, a populist, warmongering, civil rights–violating, immigrant-excluding, child-murdering plutocrat comes to power nonetheless. And so it goes with your votes, too, even when you vote for popular candidates. Regardless of whether you choose to vote or not, and regardless of how you vote, the same result will occur. We might as well be willing the Sun to rise or set.

In contrast, today I also chose to eat tomato soup for lunch. After making the decision, I did in fact eat tomato soup. In later editing, I chose to eat different foods – and did in fact eat those different foods.

My experiments allow me to conclude that I have real autonomy over what I eat.

Now suppose that decision were taken from me and given over to democratic voting. Suppose we decided as a collective what I would eat. I would suffer a severe loss of autonomy. Or suppose we all decided as a collective what everyone would eat for lunch. We would each suffer a severe loss of autonomy. The collective would have power over each of us, and each of us would be effectively powerless.

Now there is some miniscule chance that my individual vote will change the outcome of the election. By voting, I have some small chance of making a difference; by abstaining, I have no chance. So one might claim that compulsory voting improves autonomy. But this is like saying that forcing a starving person to eat a breadcrumb improves his health. On the most optimistic estimates, a single voter can have as high as a 1 in 10 million chance of changing a presidential election, provided she is in a battleground state where other voters are split nearly 50–50.[5] However, on the more widely used method of estimating the probability of being decisive, our chances are vanishingly small, somewhere on the order of 1 in 10^{200} or less.[6] At any rate, even on the more optimistic estimates, the typical voter has almost zero chance of making a difference. To succeed, the Autonomy Argument would need citizens to have much more power than they in fact have.

For what it's worth, voters appear to agree. Political scientists have surveyed voters, asking them whether they agree, "No matter who people vote for, it won't make any difference to what happens." People who agree are said to have a low sense of political efficacy. Empirically, it turns out that compulsory voting lowers citizens' sense of efficacy, as it should.[7] The more people who vote, the lower is one's chance of making a difference.

Lacroix talks about freedom as autonomy, but there is a closely related conception of freedom called *freedom as nondomination*. A

[5] Aaron Edlin, Andrew Gelman, and Noah Kaplan, "Voting as a Rational Choice: Why and How People Vote to Improve the Well-Being of Others," *Rationality and Society* 19 (2007): 219–314.

[6] Brennan and Lomasky, *Democracy and Decision*: 56–7, 119; Lomasky and Brennan, "Duty to Vote?" 66.

[7] Birch, *Full Participation*: 140, 156.

person has *dominating power* over another just in case the first person has the capacity to interfere, arbitrarily, with another person's choices.[8] One might try to argue that by getting everyone to the polls, we prevent them from being dominated by other people.

Of course, on an individual level, my vote counts for too little for it to prevent me from being dominated. If tomorrow the rest of you decide to dominate me, my individual vote cannot stop you.

Compulsory voting could protect an individual from domination, provided it got enough other similar individuals to vote with the first individual such that they formed a big voting bloc that could protect itself. One could try to build an argument in favor of compulsory voting on this premise. However, this new argument would then just be a fancy variation on the Representativeness Argument, which we refuted in Chapter 2.

3.4 Fixing an Assurance Problem

Most people know that their individual votes make little difference. While people chant, "Every vote counts!" they also know that every vote counts for little. They certainly do not act as if their votes mattered much. After all, most people know very little about politics. If they believed their votes made a massive difference, they would take the time to know more.

However, one way to increase my political efficacy is to get like-minded people to vote with me. In that case, my individual vote still makes no difference. However, if I could be assured that everyone with my point of view would vote the same way, then I would at least feel like I was part of a movement making a difference. At least, I would if my movement were big enough to make a difference.

Sometimes like-minded people manage to organize themselves into groups that can make a difference. They form causes, political parties, public action committees, charities, and so on. They come together as a voting bloc and get their fellows to vote with them. As a collective, they produce real change.

[8] Philip Pettit, "Liberty as Anti-Power," *Ethics* 106 (1996): 576–604; Philip Pettit, *Republicanism: A Theory of Freedom and Government* (New York: Oxford University Press, 1997).

However, sometimes people lack the resources, time, and ability to self-organize. They would vote, if only they could be assured that others like them would also vote. They do not vote because they lack this assurance.

Lisa Hill argues that compulsory voting solves this assurance problem:

> Because compulsory voting ensures full turnout, it is able to overcome two of the most common causes of "rational abstention": informational uncertainty about other potential voters' intentions, on the one hand, and the transaction and opportunity costs of voting, on the other.... Rather than perceiving the compulsion as yet another unwelcome form of state coercion, compulsory voting may be better understood as a coordination necessity in mass societies of individuate strangers unable to communicate and coordinate their preferences.[9]

Hill argues that we should not find compulsion objectionable because it helps us coordinate our actions and gives us assurance that others will act. However, this line of reasoning at best removes an objection to compulsory voting. It does not give us grounds to endorse compulsory voting.

One problem with this line of reasoning is that it presupposes that citizens cannot overcome their assurance problem without involuntary compulsion. However, there is a large literature on the use of dominant assurance contracts as an alternative to coercion. In a *dominant assurance contract*, people pledge to provide some contribution or perform some action, conditional on a sufficiently high other number of people pledging to do the same (or conditional on the total monetary pledges meeting some bar). Perhaps community organizers could ensure turnout using assurance contracts for voting. "I pledge to vote provided [a sufficiently high number of other people] make this same pledge." I will not pursue this line of objection any further here, but I do want to make note of it.[10]

[9] Lisa Hill, "Low Voter Turnout in the United States: Is Compulsory Voting a Viable Solution?," *Journal of Theoretical Politics* 18 (2006): 207–32.

[10] See, e.g., Alex Tabarrok, "The Private Provision of Public Goods via Dominant Assurance Contracts," *Public Choice* 96 (1998): 345–62; Mark Bagnoli and Barton Lipman, "Provision of Public Goods: Fully Implementing the Core through Private Contributions," *Review of Economic Studies* 56 (1989): 583–601; David Schmidtz, *The Limits of Government: An Essay on the Public Goods Argument* (Boulder, CO: Westview, 1991).

Note that Hill is not arguing that the state should help people solve just any assurance problem they happen to have. She agrees it is not the state's job to help me get my Dungeons and Dragons club going or to help me ensure everyone in the neighborhood puts out luminarias on Christmas Eve.

Instead, Hill thinks compulsory voting is permissible because it solves the right kind of assurance problem. The state may compel citizens to vote because doing so would remove injustice. Hill says that the poor and disadvantaged vote at lower rates than the rich and advantaged. Candidates will thus pay more attention to the expressed interests of the rich and advantaged than of the poor and disadvantaged. Forcing everyone to vote would fix this problem.

If this sounds familiar, it is, because we have seen this argument before. Hill's point about curing an assurance problem is meant to remove an objection to compulsory voting, but it works in tandem with the assumption that compulsory voting will also produce certain good consequences. In fact, Hill is relying on versions of the Representativeness and Good Consequence Arguments we refuted in Chapter 2. Because the Representativeness and Good Consequence Arguments are unsound, Hill's assurance argument is immaterial.

There is one further problem with Hill's argument. Suppose she is right that citizens need compulsory voting to help them solve an assurance problem. If so, then we might expect citizens to be more amenable to compulsory voting than they in fact are. As Ben Saunders says in response, "If it really were the case that all want to vote, and people are only deterred by the problems of collective action, then one might expect universal support for compulsion. In fact, this is not the case."[11] Now perhaps citizens are misinformed about the value of compulsory voting – far be it for me to suggest that the average citizen can properly evaluate public policies! Still, on hearing Hill's proposal and argument, many citizens remain skeptical. Perhaps Hill is wrong about what citizens really want.

[11] Ben Saunders, "Increasing Turnout: A Compelling Case?," *Politics* 30 (2010): 70–7, 71.

3.5 Fixing Free Riding

William Galston offers the following argument for compulsory voting:

> The first [argument for compulsory voting] is straightforwardly civic. A democracy can't be strong if its citizenship is weak. And right now American citizenship is attenuated – strong on rights, weak on responsibilities. There is less and less that being a citizen requires of us, especially after the abolition of the draft. Requiring people to vote in national elections once every two years would reinforce the principle of reciprocity at the heart of citizenship.[12]

Because this excerpt is from a *New York Times* op-ed, Galston does not elaborate much on the "principle of reciprocity," but we can unpack this argument nonetheless. *Reciprocity* is the principle that when you receive a benefit from others, you should (under certain circumstances) return the favor. Galston thinks many Americans enjoy the good of government without doing anything, or without doing enough, to pay back the favor. He is thus advancing what I have elsewhere called the Public Goods Argument.[13]

The Public Goods Argument

1. Good governance is a public good.
2. No one should free ride on the provision of such goods. Those who benefit from such goods should reciprocate.
3. Citizens who abstain from voting free ride on the provision of good governance.
4. Therefore, all citizens should vote.[14]
5. If all citizens should vote, then government should compel them to vote.
6. Therefore, compulsory voting is justified.

This argument may seem plausible. But let's refute it.

[12] Galston, "Telling Americans to Vote": SR9.

[13] Peter Singer also advances a version of this argument in "Why Vote?" *Project Syndicate* (December 14, 2007); available at: http://www.project-syndicate.org/commentary/why-vote.

[14] Quoted from Brennan, *Ethics of Voting*: 38. In *The Ethics of Voting*, the Public-Goods Argument is just meant to establish a duty to vote. Here I add a further premise to link it to compulsory voting.

3.5.1 *Incompatibility with Other Arguments*

The Public-Goods Argument says that citizens have a moral duty to vote in order to avoid free riding on other citizens. Nonvoters take advantage of voters.

However, when Galston argues for compulsory voting, he does not just rely on the Public Goods Argument. He also advances a version of the Representativeness Argument. Maybe he thinks the more arguments, the merrier. On the contrary, a single person can't accept both the Public Goods Argument and the Representativeness Argument – they are in tension.

Remember, the Representativeness Argument claims that the rich and advantaged vote at higher rates than the poor and disadvantaged. It claims that this disparity in turnout causes the government to help the rich and advantaged more than the poor and disadvantaged. However, if so, the rich and advantaged could do the poor a favor by abstaining. If the rich and advantaged want to make government more representative, they *should* try to free ride on government. If Galston is right, it's *bad* for the poor and disadvantaged that he and I vote because he and I are rich, white, advantaged males. (Perhaps he and I are exceptions to the rule because we vote for freedom and social justice for all, not just for rich, white males. Or at least I do.)

In short: the Representativeness Argument treats citizens as competitors. One person's vote tends to come at other people's expense. The Public Goods Argument treats citizens as cooperators. One person's vote tends to benefit others, whereas abstention comes at their expense. The Public Goods Argument says that nonvoters take advantage of voters. The Representativeness Argument says that nonvoters advantage voters, whereas voters take advantage of nonvoters. At most, one of these arguments is sound.

These arguments would be especially in tension for those who believe that most voters vote selfishly. If voters were selfish, then they would do the rest of us a favor by abstaining. If you think that in the voting booth most people just try to exploit others for their own benefit, you should in general be happy when they abstain. (However, as we discussed in Chapter 2, voters do not in fact vote selfishly.)

3.5.2 *Is the Duty to Vote Enforceable?*

The Public Goods Argument first attempts to establish that there is a duty to vote and then concludes that compulsory voting is justified. However, as we discussed in Section 3.1, even if citizens have a civic or moral obligation to do something, it does not automatically follow that the government may force them to do it. On the contrary, most of our moral duties are not enforceable.

Premise 5 of the Public Goods Argument is thus controversial. Galston needs to defend premise 5 with another argument. Galston and others who advance this argument move too quickly from the claim that voting is a *responsibility* to the claim that government may force us to vote.[15]

Galston relies on something like what H. L. A Hart called the "principle of fairness":

> [W]hen a number of persons conduct any joint enterprise according to rules and thus restrict their liberty, those who have submitted to these restrictions when required have a right to a similar submission from those who have benefited by their submission.[16]

Hart calls this the principle of fairness, but it's really a principle of reciprocity. (What Hart means is that it's unfair for us not to reciprocate with one another.) Hart says that if you benefit from a good that a bunch of us burdened ourselves to produce, you should also incur a similar burden. You can see this idea spread over the first few premises of the Public-Goods Argument.

Robert Nozick has an influential critique of this kind of reasoning. Nozick asks you to imagine that your neighbors decide to create a public address system:

> They post a list of names, one for each day, yours among them. On his assigned day (one can easily switch days) a person is to run the public address system, play records over it, give news bulletins, tell amusing stories, ... and so on. After 138 days on which each person has done his part, your day arrives. Are you obligated to take your turn?[17]

[15] For a list of others making a similar argument, see Birch, *Full Participation*: 41–3.

[16] H. L. A. Hart, "Are There Any Natural Rights?," *The Philosophical Review* 64 (1955): 185.

[17] Nozick, *Anarchy*: 93.

Nozick thinks the answer is clearly no. You are not at your neighbors' mercy. They should not be able to just draft you against your will into their group projects, just because they provided you with a benefit. A moral code that allows for us to draft each other like that into our projects would be oppressive. If all my neighbors decide to decorate their houses with Christmas lights, and I *like* it, then I would suddenly have a duty to decorate my house. If my colleagues at the university start wearing makeup in the attempt to look sexier, and I *like* it, then I'd suddenly have a duty to improve my appearance. If my fellow citizens begin an artistic renaissance, and I *like* it, then I'd suddenly have a duty to produce or support art. And so on. That doesn't seem right. Sure, under *some* conditions, we should give back. But Hart's principle is far too strong. And Hart has not yet explained why we should be *forced* to give back.

One reason Hart's principle is too strong is that it implies our neighbors may engage in *speculative reciprocity*. As Schmidtz describes the problem, "*Speculating* in reciprocity involves doing favors without asking – not giving recipients the chance to decline – in order to obligate them."[18] My neighbors could conspire to do favors for me just because they want me to do them favors in return. I might wake up one morning to find the snow gone from my driveway. I turn to see my neighbor, shovel in hand, laughing, "Looks like someone owes me a nice dinner. Ha!" But that doesn't seem right.

Some citizens vote. Most citizens vote altruistically – they attempt to vote in ways that will benefit everyone. Perhaps we owe some of them – at least the well-informed voters – thanks.[19] Perhaps we owe them something back in return.

But does it follow that we can *force* citizens to vote as a way of expressing thanks or reciprocating? Probably not. As Schmidtz says:

> We receive benefits from diffuse and dispersed sources. Intuitively, we should feel grateful, and we should feel disposed to be part of the network of benevolence that makes people in general better off. Something goes wrong if we do not gladly join that network. Something equally goes wrong if other people force us to participate against our will.... [W]e do not jail people for failing to return favors.... We do not turn the other cheek, but neither do we resort to

[18] David Schmidtz, *The Elements of Justice* (New York: Cambridge University Press, 2006): 98.

[19] In Brennan, *Ethics of Voting*, I argue we owe most voters disapproval, not thanks.

official channels in search of retribution.... *Reciprocity in its canonical form is not enforceable.*[20]

Only in unusual circumstances may we *force* people to reciprocate. For instance, we can force people to reciprocate when they sign a contract. When a person signs a contract, she consents to being coerced to reciprocate. Other than that, are there any other cases where we may force people to reciprocate? I could not think of any uncontroversial examples.[21]

Schmidtz hypothesizes that debates like these – in which we are asking whether we can force people to reciprocate – are not really about reciprocity at all. Instead, some people worry that if we don't force (almost) everybody to provide some input, then we will fail to produce some vitally important output. The point here isn't to make sure people reciprocate with one another but to make sure we produce some crucial public good. With this in mind, Galston uses a few analogies to try to save his argument.

5.5.3 *The Jury-Duty Analogy*

Galston uses the analogy of jury duty. Juries play a vital role in the criminal justice system. No one – except foaming-at-the-mouth libertarians and anarchists – thinks it is unjust for government to compel citizens to serve on juries.

Galston also uses the analogy of the draft. If we are under a dire existential threat, we might have no choice but to compel young citizens to fight for our defense.

However, these analogies might undermine rather than support the case for compulsory voting. Consider jury duty again. Imagine someone said, "Jury duty plays a vital role in maintaining criminal justice. Therefore, we should compel all citizens to serve on the jury every time there is a criminal trial." That argument would seem absurd. We don't need or want *everyone* to be a juror on every trial. Rather, at most, we

[20] Schmidtz, *Elements of Justice*: 100 (italics mine).

[21] In private conversation, Bas van der Vossen suggests that some might respond here that it is permissible to force people to pay to use public transportation rather than literally free ride on it. However, notice that whether one has a duty to pay depends not just on whether one benefits from the bus but also on whether one chooses to use the bus. Also, it seems that the buses are government property, so if one rides them without paying, one is stealing.

want a small number of people to serve as jurors for each trial, say, twelve people per trial.

We don't compel every citizen to serve on every jury. We don't even compel every citizen to serve on at least one jury. Instead, we use a lottery system. To make sure we get the jury members we need, we randomly select a small subset of qualified citizens to serve as jurors. Most Americans never serve on a jury their entire lives.

Similarly, when using a draft, we would not force every American to fight unless we needed every American to fight. Rather, we would use a lottery. If we need 50,000 troops, we randomly select 50,000 citizens from a pool. Maybe we instead select 70,000 to ensure we meet our needs. But we don't force everyone to take up arms.

With jury duty and the draft, the point is not to make *every* citizen serve. Rather, the point is to ensure that *enough* people serve. So it should go with voting, too. We shouldn't force *everyone* to vote. At most, we should try to make sure that the right number of people vote or that people vote in right proportions.

Like many other defenders of compulsory voting, Galston thus needs to explain why the voting lottery is not preferable to universal compulsory voting. In a presidential election, instead of forcing all citizens to vote, why not randomly select 20,000 citizens, imbue them (and only them) with the power to vote, and then pay them $1,000 to vote? This would solve the free-rider problem.

We use a lottery to select jurors. We don't complain that citizens who have not served on a jury free ride on citizens who have served. They would have served if they had been selected. Thus we should not complain that, in a voting lottery, citizens who are not selected to vote free ride on citizens who do vote. They would have voted if they had been selected. Galston's Public Goods Argument does not justify compulsory voting. At most, it justifies using a voting lottery instead. So the Public Goods Argument is unsound.

Because Galston thinks jury duty, the draft, and voting are in some way analogous, it's also worth pointing out that we don't just allow anyone to serve in the military or on a jury. We select people at random. However, if they then turn out to be incompetent, or if we know they will not act in good faith, we don't make them serve. I will return to this point in Chapter 4, when I argue that a large percentage of both voters and nonvoters are incompetent at politics.

5.5.4 *Are Nonvoters Free Riders?*

Premise 5 of the Public Goods Argument is false, so the Public Goods Argument is unsound. However, let's go after premise 3 as well. The Public Goods Argument presupposes that nonvoters free ride on voters. Anyone who benefits from good government incurs a debt and should be forced to pay that debt. To pay that debt, one must vote.

There are at least two views on how a person can avoid free riding:

1. If you receive a good of type *P*, then you must provide goods of type *P* back in return.
2. If you receive a good of type *P*, then you must provide sufficiently valuable goods of *any* type back in return.

The first view says that if you enjoy good governance, you must, in turn, contribute to good governance. Otherwise, you are a free rider. The second view says that if you enjoy good governance, you must provide some mix of goods and services back, in turn, to avoid free riding, but you do not necessarily have to contribute directly to good governance. Most people seem attracted to the first view. However, I will now argue they should endorse the second view instead.

Consider what's at stake if you endorse the first view. At any given moment, you benefit from all sorts of positive externalities. You receive benefits from diffuse and dispersed sources. Your neighbors, your neighbors' neighbors, and people across the globe contribute to different charities and community organizations, which improve your life in all sorts of ways, many of which you hardly notice. You enjoy art and music you never directly pay for. Thanks to others' organizing efforts, you benefit from reduced crime and reduced disease. You have instant access to most of the knowledge humanity has produced. The very language you use to speak and think is a social product, produced by other people. What have you done in return?

If we're allowed to say that nonvoters free ride on voters, we should also say that nonscientists free ride on scientists, noncommunity volunteers free ride on community volunteers, nonartists free ride on artists, and so on. If the first view is correct, you are constantly free riding on hundreds or thousands of different collective activities, many of which you don't even know about. You'll never do your share. You'll always have thousands of small debts you'll never pay.

If we take Galston's Public Goods Argument seriously, we should not just conclude that nonvoters free ride on voters. We should conclude that all of us are constantly free riding on everybody else, and there's hardly anything we can do about it. Even if you tried to avoid free riding by giving back in kind everything you've taken, you'd fail.

Note one other problem with the first view. Galston thinks nonvoters free ride on voters because nonvoters enjoy the good of government without doing their share. But Galston's argument doesn't prove you need to vote. At best, it shows you should do *something* to contribute to good government. Besides voting, you can pay taxes, support good candidates, write books about justice and injustice, write letters to the editor, campaign, and so on. Galston doesn't give us any reason to think you must specifically *vote*. So Galston doesn't have an argument for compulsory voting. At most, he has an argument for compulsory political participation *of some sort*.

The first view of how to avoid free riding is deeply problematic. This brings us to the second view. It faces no such problems.

In a modern liberal society, we have a division of labor. Citizens of liberal societies receive a bundle of different kinds of goods, including economic, cultural, social, and political goods. Most citizens – except the extremely lazy or unlucky – in turn contribute to the bundle other citizens receive. But they do it in different ways.

Some citizens provide political goods. They vote, fight in just wars, write senators, serve in office, and so on. Others volunteer at soup kitchens or for Habitat for Humanity. However, others also work productive jobs producing goods and services others want. Others contribute to good culture by producing art, music, crafts, food, and so on. Steve Jobs, James Hetfield, Maya Angelou, and Thomas Edison did a lot more for society by creating iPhones, thrash metal, poetry, and light bulbs than they ever could have done by voting.

People often talk as if we have a "debt to society" for all the goods we receive. I'm skeptical that we have any such free-floating debt. However, if we have such a debt, we should be able to pay it with multiple different currencies. As members of a modern liberal society, we enjoy a bundle of different kinds of goods. If we incur a debt, we should be able to pay for that bundle by providing enough of any mix of goods (or perhaps just one kind of good) back in turn. Some citizens pay by providing good governance, others by providing good culture, and others by providing economic opportunity. Most citizens will provide a mix of different kinds of goods, but some will specialize in producing one good to the exclusion of all other goods. Citizens who provide nonpolitical goods are not free riding on the provision of good governance. If, over the course of our lifetimes, society is better off with each of us than without us, then we've paid whatever debt to society we've incurred.

Imagine Superman were real. Now imagine Superman never votes or participates in politics. Imagine Galston said to Superman, "You're a jerk. You free ride off of voters' efforts. You benefit from good government but don't do your part." Superman could respond, "Remember all the times I saved the world? That's how I did my part."

Let's take a less extreme case. Suppose there is a medical genius, Phyllis the Physician. Phyllis is such a genius that she produces new medical breakthroughs hourly. If Phyllis cares about serving the common good, she has little reason to vote. An hour at the voting booth is worth less than an hour at the lab. Now imagine Galston said to Phyllis, "You're a jerk. You free ride off of voters' efforts." Phyllis could respond, "No, I've paid voters back by producing my research. I don't owe them anything more."

Superman and Phyllis are extreme cases that prove the general point. There's no reason to hold that nonvoters specifically owe a debt to voters. Rather, if we have a debt, it's a debt that each of us has to millions of other people because we benefit from all sorts of positive externalities. However, we can pay that debt any number of ways. For any given citizen, given what other citizens are doing and are good at doing, there will be an optimal mix of political and nonpolitical ways for him to pay his debt. For some citizens, this will mean heavy political engagement at the expense of other pursuits. For other citizens, it will mean complete disengagement so as to free the citizen to pursue nonpolitical activities. For most citizens, the optimal mix will be some combination of political and nonpolitical engagement. Although each citizen might contribute in different ways, they can all pay their debts.

Also, by contributing one kind of good, I thereby also help indirectly to produce other kinds of goods. In a modern liberal society, people specialize in different tasks. When I specialize in producing one sort of good or service, I don't just become better myself at producing that good, I also help to create and maintain the conditions under which other people can specialize in producing other sorts of goods. If Peter specializes in growing apples, he thereby frees up Quentin to specialize in catching fish. Peter's specializing in apple growing *enables* Quentin to specialize in fish catching, and vice versa. Peter produces apples directly, but he indirectly contributes to the production of fish. Quentin produces fish directly, but he indirectly contributes to the production of apples.

This extends to politics as well. Some people specialize in producing good governance. Others specialize in producing other kinds of goods. The former depend on the latter just as much as the latter depend on the former.

This doesn't mean that literally everyone pays his or her debt to society. Over the course of a lifetime, some people are a net loss to society. As a collective, we would have been better off without them than with them. For a small number of those people, it's their fault that they are a net loss. But these people are rare.

I often hear people claim that citizens who fail to vote aren't "doing their part." In my view, when people say that, they disrespect their fellow citizens. They dismiss the contributions their fellow citizens do make. They fail to recognize that most of their fellow citizens are doing their part and are paying their "debt to society." In my view, when Galston calls nonvoters free riders, he insults his fellow citizens. He owes them an apology.

3.6 Conclusion

In this chapter, we searched for viable arguments for compulsory voting, arguments that did not rely on the claim that compulsory voting would make the world a better place or produce better consequences. Our search came up short. The arguments we considered here depended on flawed empirical or normative premises. And even if we granted these flawed premises, a voting lottery was once again a superior alternative.

4

Should We Force the Drunk to Drive?

4.1 The State of the Debate

The main argument *against* compulsory voting is the sheer weakness of the arguments *for* it. Over the past three chapters, we examined many attempts to justify compulsory voting. Some of these arguments were incoherent or self-contradictory. Others relied on questionable or discredited empirical speculations. Others relied on false or implausible normative premises. Even if we ignored these serious flaws, none of these arguments could then explain why a voting lottery would not be superior to compulsory voting. All the arguments were defective. The best of the arguments gave us little reason to support compulsory voting. Most of the arguments gave us no reason to support it at all.

At this point, we must conclude compulsory voting is unjust. Governments may not impose compulsory voting on their citizens, even if the overwhelming majority of citizens enthusiastically support compulsory voting. Australia, Belgium, and other countries must repeal their compulsory-voting laws immediately.

In this chapter, I stop refuting arguments for compulsory voting and instead produce an independent argument against it. In a sense, previous chapters argued that compulsory voting is bad because it is not good. This chapter argues compulsory voting is bad because it is bad. Remember, however, that the other side bears the burden of proof. Strictly speaking, to undermine compulsory voting, I do not need my argument in this chapter to succeed. The arguments of the other three chapters suffice.

4.2 The Magic Wand

Imagine you had a magic wand. Waving the wand would instantly make the median American voter more misinformed, more ignorant, and more irrational about politics. The quality of candidates who make it on the ballot and who win elections would then be worse. We would then get worse government, policies, and laws.

Compulsory voting may be just such a magic wand. As we saw in Chapters 2 and 3, many people mistakenly believe that compulsory voting is a magic wand that produces better government. On the contrary, I argue here that it should produce slightly worse government, all things being equal.

The *all things being equal* qualifier is important. Many factors influence and affect the quality of government. So, for instance, Australia has compulsory voting; the United States does not. Australia has waved the magic wand; the United States has not. But this does not mean Australia has worse government than the United States. On the contrary, as I have argued elsewhere, Australia enjoys better government than the United States.[1] Compulsory voting probably lowers the overall quality of Australian governance, but other factors compensate for that.

In a similar vein, economics textbooks say that, all things being equal, protectionism hurts economic growth. This does not mean that all countries with trade quotas are worse off than all countries without them. After all, again, many factors – such as formal legal institutions, technological innovations, and culture – influence economic growth. Instead, economists mean that, in general, any given country would do better without tariffs than with them. Similarly, I think Australia would be better off without compulsory voting than with it, even though Australia with compulsory voting has better government than the United States.

In this chapter, I advance the following argument against compulsory voting:

[1] See Brennan, *Libertarianism*: 31, 59, 122, 136–7, 177–8.

The Worse-Government Argument

1. The typical and median citizen who abstains (under voluntary voting) is *more* ignorant, misinformed, and irrational about politics than the typical and median citizen who votes.
2. If so, then if we force everyone to vote, the electorate as a whole will then become more ignorant, misinformed, and irrational about politics. Both the median and modal voter will be more ignorant, misinformed, and irrational about politics.
3. If so, then compulsory voting will lead to at least slightly more incompetent and lower-quality government,
4. It is unjust to impose more incompetent and lower-quality government.
5. Therefore, compulsory voting is unjust.

I'll examine and defend each of these premises at some length.

4.3 Imposing Less Competent and Lower-Quality Government Is Unjust

Let's begin by looking at premise 4 of the Worse-Government Argument.

From a moral point of view, how we vote matters. Voting is not some private form of self-expression. How other people vote is *my* business. They make it my business because they impose their decisions on me, against my will, using the coercive power of government.

Politics is high stakes. If we make bad choices at the polls, we suffer from sexist, homophobic, or racist legislation. We leave the poor behind, or we intervene in ways that make their lives worse. We ghettoize and destroy inner cities. We start unnecessary wars. We create bubbles that ruin the economy. We throw the wrong people in jail or put them in jail for too long. And so on. Voting does not just decide morally arbitrary issues, such as flag colors or national anthems

Sometimes voters choose the law directly, such as when Californian voters banned same-sex marriage. Other times, voters choose leaders who, in turn, choose the laws (and appoint other leaders). Representative democracy removes us one or two levels from final decision making, but it does not relieve us of responsibility. Candidates run on policy platforms. Many candidates have voting records. Candidates have ideological slants. All things equal, electing a candidate who supports certain policies tends to increase the likelihood we will endure those policies. Picking a hawkish presidential candidate makes it more likely we will go to war. Selecting a "tough-on-crime" district attorney tends to mean more people will go to jail. Picking an anti-immigration sheriff tends to mean more Mexicans will be deported. And so on.

Some democratic theorists, in their romantic exuberance for democracy, claim that there is no independent or external moral standard by which anyone can judge whether a government is low or high quality. Good government is whatever the people say it is, or so these theorists say.[2]

But I doubt anyone really believes this, and even if they did, it's not a plausible view.[3] Consider that in 1932, a majority of German voters voted for either the Nationalist or National Socialist parties. They thus imposed horrific government on their fellow citizens, and the entire world had to suffer the consequences. When people make bad choices at the polls, they harm innocent people. If you really do believe that there is no external standard for judging democratic decisions as better or worse, then you should be fine with the Nazi-Nationalist coalition ruling the Reichstag. You should be also fine with Jim Crow laws. You should be fine with California's Proposition 8.

Some people think that voting is morally neutral because, in democracy, the people choose for themselves. But this is a mistake. Democracy is never everyone choosing for themselves but always some people choosing for everyone.

Voting is not like choosing what to eat from a restaurant menu. At a restaurant, I choose for myself. Except in bizarre circumstances, no one else bears the consequences of my decisions. If I choose to eat cake at every meal, I get fat, but no one else gets fat. In the language of economics, we say that the costs of my decisions are *internalized*. So we have good reasons to treat my meal choices as subjective or indifferent from a moral point of view.

With voting, the costs of our decisions are never internalized. They are always *externalized*. If a majority coalition gets its way, it imposes its preferences on innocent people, both foreign and domestic, who

[2] For example, see Michael Walzer, "Philosophy and Democracy," *Political Theory* 9 (1981): 379–99.

[3] See Estlund, *Democratic Authority*, for a lengthy refutation of this idea.

do not consent to the outcome. Voting is all externalities all the time. That's the whole point of politics. Politics is about imposing one rule (or ruler) on all. The place where everyone gets her own way and her own niche isn't the political forum but the market.

It is unjust to impose bad or worse government on innocent people. To see why, consider an analogy to a capital murder trial. A defendant has been charged with first-degree murder. Imagine the jury is about to decide the case. The jury's decision will be imposed involuntarily, through violence or threats of violence, on a potentially innocent person. That person does not consent to the outcome of the decision. The decision is high stakes. How should the jury act?

Jurors have been entrusted with important decisions. They have a presumptive monopoly on decision-making power in the cases they hear. Juries hold serious power over defendants. A jury's decision can significantly alter a defendant's life prospects and deprive him of property, liberty, and life.

With that in mind, consider these three hypothetical juries:

1. *The ignorant jury.* The jurors pay no attention during the trial. When asked to deliberate, they are ignorant of the details of the case but find the defendant guilty anyway. After the trial, they admit they decided the case this way.
2. *The irrational jury.* The jurors pay some attention to the details of the case. Yet they find the defendant guilty not on the basis of the evidence but on the basis of wishful thinking and various bizarre conspiracy theories they happen to believe. After the trial, they admit they decided the case this way.
3. *The morally unreasonable jury.* The jurors find the defendant guilty because he is Muslim and they are Christians who think Muslims mock the Word of God. After the trial, they admit that they decided the case this way.

In each of these cases, the jurors have acted in deeply unjust ways.

The jury has a clear duty to try the case competently. They should not decide the case selfishly, capriciously, irrationally, or from ignorance. They should take proper care, weigh the evidence carefully, overcome their biases, and decide the case from a concern for justice. Jurors owe the defendant and the rest of us competence and good faith.

Most people will accept this view about juries. However, if we think jurors have a fiduciary duty to act competently and in good faith, we should also hold that government as a whole must act competently and in good faith. After all, the following seem to be the features that explain why the jury owes us good faith and competence:

1. The jury is charged with making a morally momentous decision because they must decide how to apply principles of justice. They are the vehicle by which justice is to be delivered.
2. The jury's decision can greatly affect the defendant's and others' life prospects, and they can deprive the defendant of life, liberty, and/or property.
3. The jury is part of a system that claims sole jurisdiction to decide the case. That is, the system claims a monopoly on decision-making power, and it expects the defendant and others to accept and abide by the decision.
4. The jury's decision will be imposed, involuntarily, by force or threats of force.

Notice that the government as a whole shares these features:

1. Governments are charged with making morally momentous decisions because they must decide how to apply principles of justice and how to shape many of the basic institutions of society. They are one of the main vehicles through which justice is to be established.
2. Political decisions are high stakes. They can significantly alter the life prospects of citizens and deprive them of life, liberty, and property.
3. The government claims sole jurisdiction for making certain kinds of decisions over certain people within a geographic area. Governments expect people to accept and abide by their decisions.
4. The outcomes of decisions are imposed involuntarily on innocent people through violence and threats of violence.

It is an injustice to try a defendant with an incompetent jury or a jury that acts in bad faith. If so, then it is also an injustice to expose innocent citizens to an incompetent government or government that acts in bad faith.

When elections are decided out of ignorance, capriciousness, misinformation, irrationality, or malice, this exposes the governed to undue risk of serious harm. Because the governed are *forced* to comply with political decisions, negligent decision making is intolerable.

Not only is incompetent political decision making unjust, but it is also presumptively unjust to go make an already incompetent decision procedure worse. Imagine, for example, that the President is already incompetent. However, right before he makes a decision about whether to start a new war, you wave the magic wand and make him slightly more incompetent. Or right before an incompetent judge sentences a defendant, you wave the wand and make the judge even more incompetent. Or right before an already incompetent parliament votes on welfare reform, you wave the wand and make them even more incompetent. In each case, you have done something unjust. So, if I am right that compulsory voting is like a magic wand that makes the electorate and our elected leaders more incompetent, then compulsory voting is, on its face, unjust.

4.4 Political Ignorance

Having established the main normative premise of the Worse-Government Argument, let's look at the empirical premises.

In the 1950s, researchers at Columbia University, the University of Michigan, and elsewhere began cataloging what typical citizens (including both voters and nonvoters) know and don't know about politics. They found that most citizens have extremely low levels of political knowledge. About 35 percent of voters are "know-nothings."[4] As Ilya Somin summarizes, "The sheer depth of most individual voters' ignorance is shocking to many observers not familiar with the research."[5] Jeffrey Friedman adds, "[T]he public is far more ignorant than academic and journalistic observers of the public realize."[6]

[4] Ilya Somin, *The Problem of Political Ignorance* (Palo Alto, CA: Stanford University Press, 2013): chap. 2.

[5] Somin, *Political Ignorance.*

[6] Jeffrey Friedman, "Democratic Competence in Normative and Positive Theory: Neglected Implications of 'The Nature of Belief Systems in Mass Publics,'" *Critical Review* 18 (2006): i–xliii.

Most voters cannot identify their representatives or senators, even on a multiple-choice test. In an election year, most cannot identify any of the candidates running against the incumbents. Most cannot identify the incumbents either. Most cannot recall any major laws or bills passed in the previous few years. For instance, immediately before the 2004 election, 70 percent of Americans were unaware that Congress had passed Medicare Part D, the biggest increase in entitlement spending and largest welfare program since Johnson's Great Society.[7] Few citizens know much about the candidates' voting records. And so on. Most of these results are well known, so I won't belabor the point here.

While tests of voters' or citizens' political knowledge indicate that most know little about politics, these tests also tend to *overstate* how much voters and citizens know.

One reason they overstate voter knowledge is that these surveys often take the form of a multiple-choice test. When many citizens do not know the answer to a question, they guess. Some of them get lucky, but our surveys mark them as knowledgeable.

Another reason these surveys overstate knowledge is that they often focus on easily verifiable questions. They ask citizens to pick the current president from a list or identify which party controls the House of Representatives. These are the kinds of questions one might find on a middle-school civics exam. While most voting Americans cannot answer such questions, these questions do not concern specialized social scientific knowledge. You could Google the answer to all these questions in a few minutes.

Yet to be well informed, it is not enough to know the candidates' names. A citizen would also need to know the candidates' policy platforms, how they are likely to vote, and how much influence the candidates are likely to have if they win.

Yet even this is not enough. Now, if you just know who the candidates are and what policies they are likely to implement if elected, you thereby know more than almost all other citizens. But even then you don't yet know enough to choose among the candidates. A truly well-informed voter needs to be able to assess whether the candidates'

[7] Somin, *Political Ignorance*.

preferred policies would tend to promote or impede the voter's favored outcomes. Thus, a well-informed voter needs a strong background in the social sciences.

Suppose you want to make your country more prosperous. Suppose you know that candidate Adam would implement free trade, whereas candidate Philipp would impose protectionism. Suppose Adam and Philipp are identical in all other respects. To choose between Adam and Philipp, it is not enough to know what they stand for. You also need to know the likely consequences of their different trade policies. You would need some background in economics. (If you had that background, you'd choose Adam.)[8]

So it's one thing to be able to identify which candidates are running for Congress in your district. It is yet another thing to be able to identify what policies the candidates support. It is yet another thing to be able to identify whether the candidates have any real chance of implementing those policies. And it is yet another thing to be to be able to judge what consequences those policies are likely to produce. Being well informed about politics requires specialized knowledge, knowledge most citizens lack and could not quickly acquire.

Political scientists and economists debate just *why* citizens are so ignorant. Without entering that debate myself, I will just recite one standard explanation. For most people, acquiring political information would be worthwhile only if they could use this information to change political policies. However, even if you are an altruistic person, the cost to you of acquiring this information exceeds the benefits of using it when you vote. Economists say that voters are "rationally ignorant." That is, for most people, the benefits of acquiring political information are not worth the costs.

In contrast, some people *enjoy* acquiring political knowledge. They find political knowledge intrinsically interesting and value it for its own sake. Others – such as college professors in certain disciplines – are expected to be knowledgeable about politics. They might not find the information interesting, but they acquire it to avoid embarrassment. However, these two kinds of people are in the minority.

[8] In Brennan, *Ethics of Voting*, I argue that even this is not enough. Voters also need to have *moral* knowledge and must vote in good faith.

However, the fact that many citizens are badly informed does not by itself tell us whether compulsory voting is good or bad. I need to show

1. That political ignorance or misinformation is not uniform. Some people know more than others.
2. That compulsory voting *lowers* the typical and median voters' level of knowledge.
3. That this knowledge matters – it tends to change policy outcomes.

After all, if everyone were equally ignorant, then compulsory voting would make no difference. If compulsory voting did not lower the median or typical level of knowledge among voters, my argument here would fail. (For instance, suppose it turned out empirically that current nonvoters were better informed than voters. In that case, compulsory voting would tend to improve the quality of government.) Or, if leaders did not respond at all to voters' preferences, my argument would fail.

4.5 Differential Ignorance and Misinformation

Now let's turn to premise 1 of the Worse-Government Argument.

Most people are ignorant about politics. However, ignorance is not uniform. Some people know a great deal. Others know nothing. Others know less than nothing – they are systematically misinformed or in error.

The American National Election Studies survey voter opinion and knowledge. (They survey both potential voters before the election and actual voters after the election.) As Philip Converse says, "[T]he two simplest truths I know about the distribution of political information in modern electorates are that the mean is low and the variance is high."[9]

To this, Scott Althaus adds:

> Just how high [the variance is] is made clear when we add up the number of correct answers to these questions and divide respondents into knowledge

[9] Philip Converse, "Popular Representation and the Distribution of Information," in John A. Ferejohn and James H. Kuklinski (eds.), *Information and Democratic Processes* (Urbana: University of Illinois Press, 1990): 372.

quartiles. While people in the highest knowledge quartile averaged 15.6 correct answers out of 18 possible, people in the lowest averaged only 2.5 correct answers.[10]

On this simple, objective test of political knowledge, the top 25 percent are well informed, the next 25 percent are badly informed, the next 25 percent are know-nothings, and in fact, the bottom 25 percent are systematically misinformed.

It can be shocking to discover just how badly informed some people are. Suppose you had very low standards for what count as "informed" voting. You do not ask voters to know anything about economics or political science. You do not ask them to be able to identify the consequences of the policies they support. You do not ask them to be able to explain their ideology – if they even have one – or defend it from objections. You just say to voters, "If you're on the left, vote for the left-wing party. If you're on the right, vote for the right-wing party. That's all I ask."

You asked too much. The bottom 25 percent of voters cannot even follow this advice. For example, in the 1992 American National Election Study, voters were asked to identify which party, the Democrats or the Republicans, was more conservative on average. Only 12 percent of people in the lowest knowledge quartile could do so. They were also asked to identify the relative ideological position of the two major party candidates (sitting president) George Bush or Bill Clinton. Only 17.9 percent of people in the lowest knowledge quartile could do so. Only 17.1 percent of them could identify which candidate, Clinton or Bush, was more pro-choice. Only 9.7 percent of them could identify which candidate, Clinton or Bush, wanted to expand government services or the welfare state more.[11] (Similar results hold for other election years.)

The bottom 25 percent are not just ignorant. They know *less than* nothing. (If they became ignorant, this would actually be an improvement.) The American National Election Survey gives them a multiple-choice test, and they do much worse than chance. They make systematic mistakes on these basic questions. A random-answer generator would

[10] Scott Althaus, *Collective Preferences in Democratic Politics* (New York: Cambridge University Press, 2003): 11–12.
[11] *Ibid.*: 11.

do better than the bottom quartile of voters. Monkeys pressing buttons would do better.

Suppose you have a different set of low standards for "informed" voting. You say to voters, "You don't need to be informed. All I ask is that you select well-informed leaders." Again, you have asked too much. Through a long series of well-replicated experiments, psychologists David Dunning and Justin Kruger have shown that (1) the politically incompetent do not know how little they know, and (2) they are bad at identifying who knows more than they do. As Dunning says, "To the extent that you are incompetent, you are a worse judge of incompetence in other people."[12] If asked to identify experts, most incompetent people fail. They select those who are slightly more competent than they are, but they do not select highly competent people.[13]

Political knowledge and economic literacy are not evenly spread among all demographic groups. For instance, political knowledge of the sort tested by the American National Election Studies is strongly positively correlated with having a college degree but negatively correlated with having a high school diploma or less. It is positively correlated with being in the top half of income earners but negatively correlated with being in the bottom half. It is strongly positively correlated with being in the top quarter of income earners and strongly negatively correlated with being in the bottom quarter. It is positively correlated with living in the Western United States and negatively correlated with living in the South. It is positively correlated with

[12] Natalie Wolchover, "People Aren't Smart Enough for Democracy to Flourish, Scientists Say," *Life's Little Mysteries* (February 28, 2012); available at: http://news.yahoo.com/people-arent-smart-enough-democracy-flourish-scientists-185601411.html.

[13] See, e.g., Mato Nagel, "A Mathematical Model of Democratic Elections," *Current Research Journal of the Social Sciences* 2 (2010): 255–61; Joyce Ehrlinger, Kerri Johnson, Matthew Banner, David Dunning, and Justin Kruger, "Why the Unskilled are Unaware: Further Explorations of (Absent) Self-Insight Among the Incompetent," *Organizational Behavior and Human Decision Processes* 105 (2008): 98–121; David Dunning, Kerri Johnson, Joyce Ehrlinger, and Justin Kruger, "Why People Fail to Recognize Their Own Incompetence," *Current Directions in Psychological Science*, 12 (2003): 83–6; Justin Kruger and David Dunning, "Unskilled and Unaware – But Why? A Reply to Krueger and Mueller," *Journal of Personality and Social Psychology*, 82 (2002): 189–92; Justin Kruger and David Dunning, "Unskilled and Unaware of It: How Difficulties in Recognizing One's Own Incompetence Lead to Inflated Self-Assessments," *Journal of Personality and Social Psychology* 77 (1999): 1121–34.

being or leaning Republican but negatively correlated with being or leaning independent or Democrat. It is positively correlated with being between the ages of thirty-five and fifty-four but negatively correlated with other ages. It is negatively correlated with being black and strongly negatively correlated with being female.[14] These factors compound: high-income older men do about 2.5 to 3 times better on basic knowledge surveys than low-income black women.[15]

We discussed the Representativeness Argument in Chapter 2. The Representativeness Argument claimed (correctly) that blacks, minorities, the uneducated, women, the young, and the poor were less likely to vote than whites, ethnic majorities, the educated, men, the old, and the rich. But blacks, ethnic minorities, the uneducated, women, the young, and the poor also have a lower level of basic political knowledge. Under voluntary voting, the people who vote generally know more than the people who abstain.

The Pew Research Center finds similar results. Pew finds that Republicans, the well-educated, and older people are generally more knowledgeable than Democrats, the less-educated, and younger people. It also finds that, on average, nonvoters – citizens who are not registered to vote – know less about politics than likely voters. As Pew Research Center summarizes, "On average, people who are not registered to vote answer 4.9 out of 12 questions correctly compared with 7.2 among voters. Just 22 percent of non-voters know that Republicans control the House of Representatives."[16] Less than a third of nonvoters

[14] Althaus, *Collective Preferences*: 16; Delli Carpini and Keeter, *What Americans Know*: 135–77. For example, less than 40% of all blacks can identify which political party was more conservative, but the majority of whites can (Delli Carpini and Keeter, *What Americans Know*: 166). On the 1988 survey, high-income older men get average scores that are nearly three times as high as the average score of low-income black women (Delli Carpini and Keeter, *What Americans Know*: 162). See also Michael X. Delli Carpini and Scott Keeter, "Stability and Change in the U.S. Public's Knowledge of Politics," *Public Opinion Quarterly* 55 (1991): 583–612; W. Russell Neuman, *The Paradox of Mass Politics* (Cambridge, MA: Harvard University Press, 1986); Thomas Palfrey and Keith Poole, "The Relationship between Information, Ideology, and Voting Behavior," *American Journal of Political Science* 31 (1987): 510–30; Scott Althaus, "Information Effects in Collective Preferences," *American Political Science Review* 92 (1998): 545–58.

[15] Delli Carpini, *What Americans Know*: 162.

[16] Pew Research Center, "What Voters Know about Campaign 2012" (August 10, 2012); available at: http://www.people-press.org/2012/08/10/what-voters-know-about-campaign-2012/#knowledge-differences-between-voters-and-non-voters.

know that Romney is pro-life. Only 41 percent know that Romney opposes gay marriage. On each of the Pew Research Center's political "News IQ" quiz questions, voters score between 10 and 25 percentage points higher than nonvoters.

Let's also consider differences between voters and nonvoters in knowledge of basic economics. Adam Smith's 1776 *The Wealth of Nations* was, among other things, a refutation of an erroneous economic ideology he labeled "mercantilism." Economists today, regardless of whether they lean left or right, universally reject mercantilism. Yet mercantilism remains the dominant economic worldview of most Americans. For instance, while the overwhelming majority of economists believe that government should not use price controls to curb inflation, most voters believe the government should use such controls. Most voters favor economic protectionism, whereas economists favor free trade.[17]

Most Americans are innumerate about economics, but Americans are not equally innumerate. Some voting citizens think like economists, whereas others subscribe to a wide range of economic fallacies. The rich, whites and Asians, the well-educated, people with high IQs, and men tend to be more literate about economics than others.[18] Many of the demographic factors that positively correlate with abstention also positively correlate with being misinformed about economics. The median and typical voter understands economics better than the median and typical nonvoter.

One might object: of course, rich white men are more likely to think like economists. After all, rich white men are more likely to be economists, and economists are more likely to be rich white men than poor, black, or female. However, we can test (and have tested!) whether demographic differences explain economists' and citizens' differing beliefs about the economy. They do not.[19] So this objection, while sensible, has been discredited empirically.

[17] Caplan, *Myth of the Rational Voter*: 51.

[18] Bryan Caplan, "What Makes People Think Like Economists? Evidence on Economic Cognition from the 'Survey of Americans and Economists on the Economy,'" *Journal of Law and Economics* 44 (2001): 395–426.

[19] To test this, one just needs to collect citizens' and economists' demographic information at the same time that one surveys their opinions about economic issues. With those data in hand, one can see *how* demographic factors influence people's economic

To summarize: white, male, affluent, and older people are more likely to vote than nonwhite, female, poor, and young people. However, it also turns out that, in general, being white, male, affluent, and older is correlated with political and economic knowledge, whereas being nonwhite, female, poor, and young is correlated with political and economic ignorance and misinformation.[20] The people who vote tend to be more knowledgeable than those who abstain. The people who vote tend to better understand relevant social science than those who abstain.

Now one might try to argue that nonvoters are politically disconnected. If we force them to vote, they'll become better informed. However, as we discussed in Chapter 2, political scientists have already discredited this thesis. Compulsory voting does not improve voter knowledge. It turns nonvoters into voters, but it doesn't turn them into good voters.

4.6 Ignorance Matters

Now let's turn to an objection to premises 2 and 3 of the Worse-Government Argument.

Many political theorists and philosophers believe in the "miracle of aggregation." The miracle-of-aggregation thesis holds that large democracies with only a tiny percentage of informed voters perform just as well as democracies made up entirely of informed voters.

The assumption behind this is that ignorant voters will vote randomly. Imagine our society has 100 million voters. Two percent are well informed. Suppose each of the well-informed voters prefers candidate *A* to candidate *B*. The other voters are completely ignorant. Because they are completely ignorant, they have no basis whatsoever for preferring *A* to *B* or *B* to *A*. Thus, many political theorists allege, ignorant people will vote randomly. For them, casting a vote is like flipping a coin. If you flip a coin 100 million times, you're going to get very close to 50 percent heads and 50 percent tails. Thus, among the ignorant voters, 50 percent will vote for *A* and 50 percent will vote for

beliefs. One can statistically simulate what Americans would believe if we kept their demographic factors the same but gave everyone the knowledge needed to get a Ph.D. in economics. See Caplan, *Myth of the Rational Voter*.

[20] For example, see Althaus, "Information Effects": 545–58 and note 12 above.

B. The uninformed voters cancel each other out, leaving the informed voters to decide the election. The informed voters all vote for candidate *A*. Thus *A* will end up with 51 percent of the total vote, and *B* will get 49 percent. *A* will win the election.

I sometimes wonder whether the people who advance this argument sincerely believe it. If you believe errors cancel out, that ignorance doesn't hurt, or that democracies with only a tiny percentage of informed voters do just as well as democracies in which everyone is informed, then at first glance it seems that civics education is a waste of time and money. Public schools routinely try to create a public well educated in politics. Apparently they fail. But even if they had succeeded, as the miracle-of-aggregation argument seems to imply, we would still have wasted our time and money. We only need a tiny percentage of Americans to be well informed about politics – we don't need to educate everyone. Yet most theorists who make the miracle-of-aggregation argument support widespread civic education through public schooling. Perhaps these theorists support civic education for other reasons.

The miracle of aggregation is intuitively appealing, but it isn't real. First, it's mistaken for empirical reasons – as a matter of fact, badly informed people do not vote randomly. Second, the miracle-of-aggregation argument is mistaken even in principle because it is based on fallacious or mistaken mathematical reasoning. I will discuss each of these problems in turn.

First, notice that the miracle-of-aggregation defense of democracy is an a priori argument. It assumes without empirical evidence that uninformed voters vote randomly. The argument is that if someone is truly uninformed, he has no basis whatsoever for his opinions and so will choose candidates at random. However, we know from empirical research that real-life voters are not like that. The real-life voters whom we call *ignorant* do not have random preferences. Rather, they make systematic mistakes.

As we discussed in the preceding section, the least well-informed voters do *worse than chance* when evaluating the relative ideological positions of the two major parties or the two major candidates. Also, as we discussed, because of the Dunning-Kruger effect, politically incompetent citizens are systematically bad at identifying who is more competent than they are. They cannot identify the most competent political candidates, nor can they identify which pundits are the best to turn to for advice.

Well-informed and badly informed citizens also have systematically different policy preferences.[21] As people (regardless of their race, income, gender, or other demographic factors) become more informed, they favor less government intervention and control of the economy. They are more in favor of free trade and less in favor of protectionism. They are more pro-choice. They favor using tax increases to offset the deficit and debt. They favor less punitive and harsh measures on crime. They are less hawkish on military policy, although they favor other forms of intervention. They are more accepting of affirmative action. They are less supportive of prayer in public schools. They are more supportive of market solutions to healthcare problems. They are less moralistic in law; they don't want government to impose morality on the population. And so on. In contrast, as people become less informed, they become more in favor of protectionism, abortion restrictions, harsh penalties on crime, doing nothing to fix the debt, more hawkish intervention, and so on. (Note that these effects are not due to differing demographics between low- and high-information voters.) The problem is that *ignorant* voters do not vote randomly.

Misinformed voting is dangerous. The economy is a major concern in most elections. Economist Bryan Caplan asks, "What happens if voters are not only uninformed but misinformed about how the economy works?"[22] In any given election, foreign policy is a major issue. What happens if the median voter has mistaken views about international relations? In any given election, candidates will spout statistics to defend their views. What happens if the median voter failed "Introduction to Statistics"? In any given election, candidates will

[21] Althaus, *Collective Preferences*: 129; Caplan, *Myth of the Rational Voter*. Both Althaus and Caplan are correct for the influence of demographic factors.

[22] Bryan Caplan says, "If the wisdom of crowds functions as advertised, we would expect laymen and experts to have the same *average* beliefs. They do not; systematic disagreement between economists and the public is the rule, not the exception. The SAEE's raw belief gaps are statistically significant for thirty-three out of thirty-seven questions. They are also very large in magnitude. Caplan (*Myth of the Rational Voter*: 406) calculates that in the SAEE, the disagreement between laymen and experts is more than 70 percent larger than the disagreement between America's extreme left and extreme right. See Bryan Caplan, "The Myth of the Rational Voter and Political Theory," in Hélène Landemore and John Elster (eds.), *Collective Wisdom: Principles and Mechanisms* (Cambridge, UK: Cambridge University Press, 2012): 322.

complain about social issues. What happens if the median voter has silly views about sociology?

Two things happen:

1. The electorate is more likely to make a bad choice among the candidates on the ballot.
2. The candidates who make it on the ballot will be lower quality to begin with.

When a misinformed electorate votes, it is more likely to choose the worse rather than the better candidate. However, that is not even the worst of it. The quality of candidates who make it on the ballot depends on the quality of the electorate. If voters are systematically mistaken about political issues, then good candidates do not stand a chance.[23]

Uninformed voters make systematic mistakes. However, there is an entirely different set of reasons why the miracle of aggregation does not occur. Empirically, it also turns out that voters also have various quirks and biases in how they answer surveys and polls. These biases prevent even completely ignorant voters from voting randomly.

For instance, voters tend to prefer names that sound familiar and tend to avoid names that connote the wrong ethnicity. Imagine an election between Tom Smith and Aaqib Rahim. Suppose there are 10 million voters. Imagine most voters know nothing about the candidates or even about the office – they just see the two candidates' names on the ballot. The miracle of aggregation predicts that each candidate will get 5 million votes. Not so. Citizens are ethnocentric and religiocentric. They will tend to pick Smith over Rahim. (One may recall that before the 2008 U.S. presidential election, Republicans repeatedly emphasized that Barack Obama's middle name is *Hussein*.)

Ignorant voters are not completely ignorant. Even though most voters cannot identify the incumbent, as a whole, low-information

[23] See also Rebecca Morton, Marco Piovesan, and Jean-Robert Tyran, "The Dark Side of the Vote: Biased Voters, Social Information, and Information Aggregation Through Majority Voting," working paper (Cambridge, MA: Harvard University, 2012).

voters are biased to select the incumbent over the challenger. As Somin summarizes the research:

> A recent attempt to test the [miracle of aggregation] on samples drawn from six recent presidential elections (1972–1992) found that, controlling for various background characteristics of voters, poor information produces an average aggregate bias of 5 percent in favor of the incumbent.[24]

Five percent is, of course, more than enough to prevent the miracle of aggregation from occurring.

Voters also tend to suffer from a *position bias* or *order bias*. That is, when given a list of alternatives, all things equal, people are most likely to pick the top-listed alternatives, second most likely to pick the bottom-listed alternatives, and least likely to pick the middle alternatives. Imagine I give 100 million Americans a one-question multiple-choice test, written in a language they cannot understand. The test has four answers, also written in the unknown language, marked *A*, *B*, *C*, and *D*. Subjects must circle the letter corresponding to the correct answer. Suppose I offer to pay the subjects $10 if they get the right answer. Because, by hypothesis, no one can read the test, one might expect the test taker to guess randomly. One might expect each answer (*A–D*) would get 25 percent.

Not so – in fact, answer *A* will probably get the most, *D* the second most, and *B* and *C* the least. Thus even completely ignorant voters do not vote randomly – they are more likely to pick the first candidate than the fourth on a list. One might think that we can solve this problem just by randomly assigning candidates different positions on different voters' ballots, but this turns out not to work.[25] (The explanation for why it doesn't work is technical, so I won't review it here.) Position bias on its own is sufficient to stop the miracle of aggregation from occurring.

[24] Ilya Somin, "Voter Ignorance and the Democratic Ideal," *Critical Review* 12 (1998): 413–58. For empirical confirmation of these claims, see Larry Bartels, "Uninformed Votes: Information Effects in Presidential Elections," *American Political Science Review* 40 (1997): 194–230; Michael Alvarez, *Information and Elections* (Ann Arbor: University of Michigan Press, 1997).

[25] Niels J. Bunch, "Position Bias in Multiple-Choice Questions," *Journal of Marketing Research* 21 (1984): 216–20.

Yet another problem is that voters are followers. Suppose early in the political process some relatively uninformed voters randomly settle on supporting a particular candidate. When other uninformed voters see this, they, in turn, are more likely to support that candidate. Ignorance compounds rather than cancels out.[26]

Yet another problem is that voters try to use informational shortcuts to make decisions. But these shortcuts tend to cause them to make systematic mistakes. As Ilya Somin summarizes, "As a result, ill-informed voters often draw non-random, misleading inferences about economics conditions and other issues."[27]

Thus empirical work overwhelmingly shows that low-information voters do not in fact vote randomly. They have systematic errors, beliefs, and biases. At the very least, the miracle-of-aggregation argument does not apply to the real world. People do not in fact behave the way the model predicts.

Moreover, the problem is not just that the miracle of aggregation rests on an a priori model, a model that has impeccable mathematics but that fails to correspond to the real world. Rather, the miracle-of-aggregation argument appears to be mistaken, even in principle. The argument rests on an equivocation. As Scott Althaus explains:

> [I]n order for random errors to sum to zero, they must be scaled in standardized form with a mean of zero. *While the expected value of standardized random error is zero, the expected value of unstandardized random error is equal to the midpoint of the range of possible responses....* Random errors do not, strictly speaking, cancel out.... [T]hese random errors ... continue to influence the location of means and modes as well as the shape of marginal percentages.[28]

To simplify (when applying this to political issues): random voting will tend to fall along what statisticians call a *normal distribution*. Smart voting will also tend to fall along a normal distribution. But these distributions will have different peaks. What the mean and median random voters want will often be different from what the mean and median smart voters want. Even on a simple left-and-right scale,

[26] Keith Jakee and Guang-Zhen Sun, "Is Compulsory Voting More Democratic?" *Public Choice* 129 (2006): 61–75.

[27] Somin, "Voter Ignorance": 431.

[28] Althaus, *Collective Preferences*: 40.

random voting will tend to shift the balance of public opinion one way or another. The more random voting there is, the worse is the effect.[29]

Keith Jakee and Guang-Zhen Sun produce a similar criticism. The miracle of aggregation claims that informed voters will always decide the election as long as a tiny percentage of voters are informed, and the ignorant majority votes randomly. If the miracle-of-aggregation argument holds, then democracy should get the right answer 100 percent of the time. Democracy should be perfectly reliable. Jakee and Sun try to model this argument mathematically and conclude that, on the contrary, the more citizens who vote randomly, the more random will be the outcome of the election. If there are 98 million ignorant voters voting randomly and 2 million smart voters with a distinct preference, the decision of the electorate as a whole will be no more reliable than a coin flip.[30]

The miracle-of-aggregation argument assumes that low-information voters will vote randomly, and thus these low-information voters will have no effect on the outcome of the election. Empirically, this assumption turns out to be flat out wrong. What's more, the argument may be mistaken even in principle because the mathematical model is itself controversial. Ignorance matters, alas.

4.7 The Ideological Elephant in the Room

Let's be really frank here. There is an unstated reason why many political theorists, political scientists, and philosophers are sympathetic to compulsory voting. Most of my American colleagues are Democrats. Many of them sensibly believe compulsory voting would help the Democratic Party. (Similar remarks apply to my colleagues outside the United States with respect to their favored left-leaning parties.) As we saw in Chapter 2, they are mistaken – the best available evidence indicates that compulsory voting has few partisan effects and does little to help left-leaning parties or causes. However, suppose compulsory voting would in fact increase the power of the Democratic Party. If so, should that give my Democratic colleagues at least some reason to favor compulsion?

[29] *Ibid.*: 29–58.
[30] Jakee and Sun, "Is Compulsory Voting More Democratic?"

Perhaps not. Democrats are not united in their moral and political outlooks. High-information Democrats have systematically different policy preferences from low-information Democrats. Rich and poor Democrats have systematically different policy preferences. Compulsory voting gets more poor Democrats to the polls. But poor Democrats tend to be low-information voters, whereas affluent Democrats tend to be high-information voters. The poor approved more strongly of invading Iraq in 2003. They more strongly favor the Patriot Act, invasions of civil liberty and torture, protectionism, and restricting abortion rights and access to birth control. They are less tolerant of homosexuals and more opposed to gay rights.[31] In general, compared with the rich, the poor – including poor Democrats – are intolerant, economically innumerate, hawkish bigots. If compulsory voting were to help Democrats at all, it would probably help the *bad* Democrats. The Democrats would end up running and electing more intolerant, innumerate, hawkish candidates.

4.8 Mitigating Factors

Compulsory voting changes the quality of the electorate. Under voluntary voting, the median and typical voter is better informed, less biased, and less bigoted than the median and typical nonvoter. Compulsory voting thus makes the median voter and the typical voter more ignorant, misinformed, biased, and bigoted. It is like a magic wand that makes the electorate dumber about politics. Government tends to give the people what they want. Thus compulsory voting should produce somewhat lower-quality and more incompetent government. However, while I expect compulsory voting would produce lower-quality and less competent government, I do not expect it would be a disaster.[32]

When 60 percent or more of the population is voting, most voters are already ignorant, biased, economically innumerate, and misinformed. Sure, the median voter is better informed than the median

[31] Gilens, *Affluence and Influence*: 106–11.

[32] I once wrote a *New York Times* op-ed titled, "Mandatory Voting Would Be a Disaster," but an editor chose the title, not me (J. Brennan, "Mandatory Voting Would Be a Disaster," *New York Times* [November 7, 2011]; available at: http://www.nytimes.com/roomfordebate/2011/11/07/should-voting-in-the-us-be-mandatory-14/mandatory-voting-would-be-a-disaster.)

nonvoter, but not by much. But even under voluntary voting, only a tiny minority of voters is well informed about current events, candidates, and relevant background social science. Only a tiny minority processes political information in an unbiased and rational way. With 60 percent or more of citizens voting – the majority biased and irrational about politics – most of the damage has already been done.

Another mitigating factor is that politicians may not be equally responsive to all voting groups. As I discussed in Chapter 2, political scientist Martin Gilens has produced significant evidence that presidents do not respond equally to the preferences of the rich and poor. When citizens at the 90th and 10th percentiles of income disagree about policies, presidents tend to side with the 90th percentile rather than the 10th percentile. (Recall that Gilens shows that this is not because citizens at the 90th percentile vote more. The 90th percentile is slightly more likely to vote than the 10th percentile, but the 90th percentile has something like six times the influence of the 10th percentile.[33]) Voters at the 90th percentile of income are generally much better informed than voters at the 10th percentile. They tend to have higher IQs, are better educated, and are more likely to think like economists.[34] Thus, whereas compulsory voting floods the electorate with bad voters, politicians tend to be more responsive to the better voters. So flooding democracy with more bad voters may tend to produce worse results, but the effect might be nonlinear. Now, Gilens' results are not without controversy, but they are least some evidence that compulsory voting would not be too bad.

Gilens suspects that the reason politicians are more responsive to rich voters is that rich voters donate more money to political campaigns. If he's right, this has an interesting implication: many political theorists want to eliminate privately funded elections and instead have mandatory publicly funded elections. But if Gilens is right, this means that politicians would then become more responsive to dumb voters and less responsive to smart voters.

[33] Gilens, *Affluence and Influence*: 10, 234–52.

[34] For example, see Bryan Caplan and Stephen Miller, "Intelligence Makes People Think Like Economists: Evidence from the General Social Survey," *Intelligence* 38 (2010): 636–47.

4.9 The Burden of Proof Revisited

In this chapter, I presented evidence that compulsory voting lowers the intellectual quality of the electorate and that this would probably lower the quality of government to some degree. Forcing everyone to vote is like forcing the drunk to drive. It subjects all of us to government leaders and political policies that appeal to uninformed, biased, and misinformed voters.

Remember that proponents of compulsory voting bear the burden of proof. They want government to use coercion to make people vote. They want to restrict citizens' liberty. As I argued in Chapter 1, they are like prosecutors in a criminal trial. They must defend their position using a high standard of evidence.

In contrast, I play the role of the defense. I can undermine their position by giving strong reasons to be skeptical of it, even if I do not definitively nail down my counterarguments. We could spend more than one book debating the effects of voter ignorance and misinformation, but we have spent just one chapter on it here.

A proponent of compulsory voting might try to argue that while compulsory voting makes the median and typical voter dumber about politics, compulsory voting produces other good consequences or realizes some other values that in some way outweigh the harmful effects of dumb voting.

However, we just spent three chapters looking in vain for decent arguments on behalf of compulsory voting. Most of the arguments relied on confused normative premises or speculative or mistaken empirical premises. None of these arguments could show why a voting lottery would not be superior to compulsory voting.

If you want to produce a successful defense of compulsory voting, you must show that compulsory voting is either necessary or at least the best way to realize some important value. You must show that there are no superior, noncoercive ways of realizing that value. You must show that compulsory voting really does produce that value – you cannot rely on speculation or unproven empirical assertions. You must also show that it is morally permissible to use government coercion to realize that kind of value.

Participation rates are low in some countries. So what? Instead of asking how we can make them higher, we should instead ask how we could induce people to vote smarter. It is important that enough people vote and, when they do vote, that they vote well. That does not imply that we need *everyone* to vote, especially if many of them do not know enough to vote well.

Many democracies seem diseased. Compulsory voting is not some easy cure. It is not penicillin for democratic pathologies. Compulsory voting is like medieval medicine. At best, it is useless, like wearing amulets and carrying posies. At worse, it's harmful, like bloodletting.

PART II

COMPULSORY VOTING DEFENDED

Lisa Hill

5

Compulsory Voting: Background, Effects, Feasibility, and Basic Premises

5.1 Introduction

Simply put, compulsory voting exists where the state imposes a legal requirement to vote. The idea of being compelled to vote is anathema to many who live in Western democracies because it seems to run counter to both democratic and liberal values. But even though I agree that, in principle, voluntary political participation is preferable to obligatory participation, I argue in the following chapters that requiring people to vote can be reconciled with both liberal and democratic values.

In defending compulsory voting, I write as a normative political theorist, but I also approach the issue as a political scientist who is wary of normative arguments about elections and voting that do not engage with the empirical world. These kinds of arguments tend, either consciously or unconsciously, to embody assumptions about that world that, in turn, justify real-world laws and practice. Therefore, my argument is informed, where possible, by the empirical data and actual trends in electoral and political behavior. But, in the end, it is a normative argument written from a political-theory perspective.

Much has been written and said about compulsory voting, but quite a lot of it is controvertible. For this reason, the following set of arguments tends to be structured in response to criticism of compulsory voting and the high and socially even turnout it is able to deliver.

5.2 Basic Premises

In terms of basic premises, I do not deny that democracy can deliver suboptimal and sometimes perverse policy outcomes[1] or that an epistocracy might sometimes deliver better policy decisions than a participatory electoral democracy.[2] Nevertheless, because participatory electoral democracies are what we do have – and are likely to have for the foreseeable future – we should try to get them to work as well as we can and with as much procedural fairness as possible.

I also stand for substantive political equality as well as equality of political opportunity[3] (meaning I don't just want people to have the right to vote but to *exercise* that vote) and, as far as the boundary problem of the *demos* is concerned (i.e., the question of who should be included in the electorate), I follow Robert Dahl in the view that "[t]he Principle of Affected Interests is very likely the best general principle of inclusion" available. This principle holds that "everyone who is affected by the decisions of a government should have the right to participate in that government."[4] But I go further than Dahl in suggesting that all affected interests not only should be entitled to participate but also should *exercise* that right through voting.

Because conceptions of democracy vary widely,[5] I am going to keep it simple and go with an idea of democracy familiar to everyone. This idea was summed up in the words of Abraham Lincoln, who described a true *democracy* as being "[g]overnment of the people, by the people, for the people." Thus, when assessing the effects of compulsory voting against those of voluntary voting, I will be attempting to judge how well it conforms to this ideal. The other standards I use are Robert Dahl's five criteria for judging the legitimacy of elections. These are political equality, "effective participation," "enlightened understanding," "final control of the agenda by the *demos*," and inclusiveness.[6]

[1] For example, see Caplan, *Myth of the Rational Voter.*

[2] Estlund, *Democratic Authority.*

[3] Others, for example, are happy with equality of political opportunity alone; see, e.g., Brennan, *Ethics of Voting*: 6; and Saunders, "Increasing Turnout."

[4] See Robert Dahl, *After the Revolution: Authority in a Good Society* (New Haven, CT: Yale University Press, 1971): 64.

[5] There is, for example, pluralist democracy, radical democracy, deliberative democracy, polyarchy, elitist democracy, and equilibrium democracy (Weale, *Democracy*: 19).

[6] Dahl, *After the Revolution*: 101–8.

I assume that there is nothing inherently undemocratic about compelling people to do things that they might otherwise choose not to do: after all, paying our taxes and educating our children are both compulsions and yet are good ideas to which most of us readily assent. After all, democracy is just another way of arriving at decisions that are binding on all citizens. The real question is whether the compulsion to vote is justified to the extent that being required to pay taxes and send our children to school is justified. I aim to show that it is.

5.3 Approach and Plan

I offer both utilitarian and rights-based justifications for compulsory voting.[7] While this approach may lack elegance, I have adopted it for several reasons; first, compulsory voting needs to be justified in terms of two separate (often related, sometimes conflicting) sets of values: the liberal and the democratic. These values emphasize, in varying degrees, both processes and outcomes. In Chapters 6 and 8, I focus more on the democratic, whereas Chapter 7 deals more with the relationship of compulsory voting to liberal values. But, as I aim to show, these two sets of values are not as easily separated as is often thought. Second, I accept Joseph Raz's insight that any theory that attempts to reduce all morality to a single type of basic concern will be impoverished.[8] After all, when formulating policies, liberal democratic governments are constantly seeking to balance utility with rights and, where possible, to serve both through compromise. Third, I agree with Russell Hardin that, in general, rights are ultimately justified by their good effects and are best thought of as "institutional devices for achieving good outcomes."[9] It turns out that there are many reasons why compulsory voting is a good idea, and I do not wish to omit any of them for the sake of neatness. As I hope to show, furthermore, all these reasons are intimately related.

The plan of my argument is as follows: in the remainder of this chapter, I provide some background to the topic, lay out some important

[7] Although the greater burden of my argument tends to rest on an account of the consequences of near-universal voting participation.

[8] Joseph Raz, *The Morality of Freedom* (New York: Oxford University Press, 1986): 193–216.

[9] Russell Hardin, "The Utilitarian Logic of Liberalism," *Ethics*, 97 (1986): 47–74.

qualifications to my argument, establish the turnout-enhancing capacity of compulsory voting, and explore the efficacy of other, less coercive mechanisms for raising voter turnout. I also provide some information about compulsory voting practice in Australia as an example of a best-practice regime. In Chapter 6, I deal with the problem to which compulsory voting is a purported solution: low voter turnout. I argue that, contrary to the claims of some observers, high turnout offers superior democratic outcomes to low turnout. In Chapter 7, I consider whether compulsory voting represents an unwarranted burden on individual liberty, including whether it is a violation of an alleged right not to vote. I also argue that the tension between democratic and liberal values is not as great as is normally assumed in the compulsory-voting debate because, in enhancing democracy via compulsory voting, liberty is also enhanced. In Chapter 8, I explore the impact of compulsory voting on the derogation and/or realization of democratic values that have not been dealt with in earlier chapters, such as whether compulsory voting leads to "overinclusiveness," higher levels of "bad" voting and therefore worse government. In Chapter 9, I summarize my overall argument and make some additional observations about the potential role of compulsory voting in preserving at-risk electoral democracies.

5.4 An Important Qualification

Before continuing, an important qualification should be made: the arguments offered in the following chapters apply only to voting within properly functioning and authentic democracies. I do not defend all types of compulsory regimes, only those that meet certain quite-high standards and where compulsory voting is – or has a good chance of being – administered properly. For a compulsory-voting regime to be both effective, in terms of ensuring high turnout and enjoying high levels of public acceptance, and appropriate, insofar as it is not being used as a mechanism to forge consent or legitimize one-party contests, a number of conditions need to be met. Chief among them is a well-established system of democratic institutions[10] with adequate civil and political rights protection (including universal suffrage), the apparatus

[10] It is also preferable if there is some degree of genuine choice reflected in the candidates on offer and the voting system in use. For example, some degree of proportionality is optimal (as opposed to a simple plurality system) so that voters can achieve at least some degree of meaningful representation.

of constitutionalism, limits on political power, and free, competitive, and fair elections. From an administrative point of view, the following is also desirable: a developed national infrastructure,[11] reasonable levels of cooperation between regional and central governments (particularly within federal structures), and professional, well-funded, independent, and accountable electoral commissions. In order to ensure that the obligation is not burdensome, voting should be relatively easy with few opportunity and transaction costs to voters. Further, sanctions should be applied consistently but without zealotry.[12] Where any of these conditions fail to be satisfied, the effectiveness and/or legitimacy of the compulsion may be in question.

A good compulsory-voting system is not easy to achieve; apart from the obvious cultural resistance, which could mean that the laws enabling it might never be passed, there are also the practical problems associated with making such a system work well and in a fashion that is acceptable to the voting public as well as the courts. Nevertheless, the establishment of such a system is not impossible, as the Belgian, Dutch (before 1970), and Australian examples amply demonstrate. I will be referring to practice in these highly successful best-practice cases – particularly the Australian case – throughout my argument.

But before moving on to the normative part of the discussion, I will address briefly some of the practical aspects of compulsory voting, outlining what it tends to entail and what it is capable of achieving so as to be clear about what it is that I am about to defend.

5.5 Background and Practical Matters

The term *compulsory voting* is somewhat misleading in that it does not generally involve the requirement to actually mark the ballot but

[11] Timothy J. Power and J. Timmons Roberts, "Compulsory Voting, Invalid Ballots and Abstention in Brazil," *Political Research Quarterly* 48 (1995): 795–826.

[12] See Graeme Orr, *Australian Electoral Systems: How Well Do They Serve Political Equality?* (Canberra: Democratic Audit of Australia, 2004). For example, the penalties in Australia for failure to attend a polling booth are fairly mild, and noncompliance is handled in a reasonable fashion. Initially, the Electoral Commission sends the absentee a "please explain" letter with the option of paying a $20 fine to settle the matter. If a satisfactory reason for abstention is provided, the matter is dropped. Nevertheless, in the past, there have been rare cases where electors who have repeatedly refused to pay fines have served short jail sentences. Fortunately, this no longer seems to happen.

rather to attend a polling place on election day. Because of the secret ballot in places such as Belgium and Australia (and The Netherlands before 1970, when the laws were repealed), it is technically only *attendance* at a polling place that is – or can be – legally required. In fact, when voting was required in The Netherlands, the Dutch employed the term *opkomstplicht* to denote "obligatory attendance" at the polls. This distinction is quite important because I do not endorse requiring electors to mark ballots formally if they would rather not,[13] even though I think it is more productive from a democratic perspective for them to do so. Rather, I tend toward endorsing compulsory attendance at a polling place.[14] Nevertheless, what generally happens is that where people are required to attend a polling place, they do end up voting, and so the best way to get more people to vote – even where it is possible to lodge a blank ballot – is to make attendance obligatory.

Contrary to the common perception that compulsory voting is a curiosity, compulsory voting has been used successfully in many settings and over long periods of time. Around thirty democracies worldwide claim to have compulsory voting, but a much smaller number use it (or have used it) with reasonable levels of support and enforcement.[15] Some voluntary-voting established democracies have shown interest in the idea, such as Great Britain,[16] where a private member's bill was (unsuccessfully) put before parliament for its

[13] I do not endorse compelling people to mark the ballot because this is too coercive. While this may sound odd and perhaps arbitrary coming from someone who advocates compulsory attendance, I believe voters should retain the right to mark the ballot as they see fit. After all, the point of elections is to find out what voters really think, and if they really think that none of the candidates is worth voting for, parties and candidates ought to get that message. Further, it isn't arbitrary because (1) requiring attendance usually gets the job done anyway (i.e., people *do* end up voting), and (2) for the practical reason that asking for more than attendance from voters would bring the institution of compulsory voting into disrepute.

[14] Or, at least, the lodgement of a ballot, whether in person or by post and whether marked validly or otherwise.

[15] These regimes are Argentina, Australia, Austria (two länder only), Belgium, Brazil, Cyprus, Fiji, Greece, Italy (until 1993), Liechtenstein, Luxembourg, Nauru, Peru, Singapore, Switzerland (one canton only), Uruguay, and Venezuela (until 1993). Of these, the older democracies of Australia, Belgium, Cyprus, Greece, Luxembourg, and until 1970, The Netherlands, have evinced the most serious commitment to the regular institutionalization and support of compulsory-voting laws.

[16] The U.K. Electoral Commission and the Electoral Reform Society have both undertaken research into the topic to gauge its suitability for the British context.

adoption.[17] Likewise, there have been calls for its introduction in the United States,[18] Canada,[19] New Zealand, India, and Jordan. Although a "significant minority of citizens in voluntary voting states are open to the idea of making voting compulsory," most continue to find the idea of being compelled to vote objectionable.[20] Public resistance is therefore a major obstacle to the introduction of compulsory voting in settings where it could significantly boost turnout.

5.6 Compulsory Voting and Voter Turnout: Are There Other, Less Coercive Ways of Raising Turnout?

In authentic democracies, compulsory voting is usually introduced to address the problem of low and declining turnout, something that has become a universal feature of voluntary-voting systems in advanced democracies worldwide. There are, of course, less coercive means by which to raise turnout. Yet recent experiments using such methods have met with mixed to poor success.[21] Because complicated registration procedures have long been thought to depress voting participation,[22] making voter registration easier is often the measure of first resort. The

[17] See T. Watson and M. Tami, *Votes for All: Compulsory Participation in Elections* (London: The Fabian Society, 2000). The bill was introduced by Gareth Thomas, MP, on November 27, 2001 (C. Sear and P. Strickland, "Compulsory Voting," Standard Note SN/PC/954 for members of the House of Commons [Canberra, Australia: Parliament and Constitution Centre, 2001]).

[18] See, e.g., Sean Matsler, "Compulsory Voting in America," *Southern California Law Review* 76 (2002–3): 953–78; J. P. W. Halperin, "Note: A Winner at the Polls: A Proposal for Mandatory Voter Registration," *Journal of Legislation and Public Policy* 69 (1999–2000): 69–117.

[19] Canada's most senior election officer, Jean-Pierre Kingsley, speaking of compulsory voting, once observed that "[s]ometimes, in order to save democracy ... you have to do things that might seem to run a little bit against it" (J. D. Solomon, "Even Those Who Don't Vote Should Have to Go to Polls," *USA Today* [October 24, 2002]; available at: http://www.usatoday.com/news/opinion/2002–10–24-oped-solomon_x.htm.)

[20] Birch, *Full Participation*: 144.

[21] See Lisa Hill, "Low Voter Turnout in the United States: Is Compulsory Voting a Viable Solution?" *Journal of Theoretical Politics*, 18 (2006): 207–232. This is not to suggest that any of the other turnout-raising strategies would be redundant were compulsory voting adopted. In fact, they are all features of a well-functioning compulsory-voting regime like Australia's.

[22] See, e.g., G. E. Mitchell and W. Wlezein, "The Impact of Legal Constraints on Voter Registration, Turnout and the Composition of the American Electorate," *Political Behaviour* 17 (2) (1995): 179–202.

National Voter Registration Reform Act of 1993 (effective January 1995)[23] was one notable attempt in recent history to increase turnout rates and close the particularly wide socioeconomic status (SES) gap that exists in the United States. But it failed to achieve the dramatic results for which many hoped.[24] Making registration less onerous and "costly" is not the only option. There are a number of other institutional means by which turnout can be enhanced, such as to move election day to a Saturday or declare it a national holiday.[25] Countries that conduct elections on a weekend or holiday have 6 percent higher turnout than would otherwise be expected.[26] Lowering the voting age has also been mooted as a possible solution; however, doing so is unlikely to have much positive effect – quite the contrary. According to Mark Franklin's study, by inflating the electoral rolls with citizens with a low likelihood of voting in the first place (the young), the average decline in registered voter turnout tends to be around 2.5 percent.[27]

Other ergonomic solutions involve providing for absentee voting, siting polling places in shopping malls to reduce the opportunity costs of voting, or extending voting over two or more days. Alternatively, it has sometimes been suggested that voters should be offered incentives

[23] "The 103rd Congress passed – and President Clinton signed – the National Voter Registration Act (NVRA), a federal mandate which required states to offer voter registration opportunities at driver's license and motor vehicle bureaus, welfare offices, and military recruiting stations." It was thought that "[i]f new residents, young people, and the poor could be reached at the time that they were applying for, or renewing, a driver's license or public assistance benefits, the disenfranchisement of those populations might be partially overcome and turnouts might continue to climb." Neither turnout nor the SES gap was significantly affected by the measure. In fact, they were officially exacerbated (Michael D. Martinez and David Hill, "Did Motor Voter Work?" *American Politics Quarterly*, 27 [3] [1999]: 296–315).

[24] For a detailed account of the history and effects of the "Motor Voter" Act, see R. E. Wolfinger and J. Hoffman, "Registering and Voting with Motor Voter," *PS: Political Science and Politics*, 34 (1), (2001): 85–92.

[25] Or, as Wattenberg suggests, combining it with Veterans Day (Wattenberg, "Where Have All the Voters Gone?" 6–7).

[26] Mark Franklin, "Electoral Participation," in L. LeDuc, R. G. Niemi, and P. Norris (eds.), *Comparing Democracies: Elections and Voting in Comparative Perspective* (Thousand Oaks, CA: Sage, 1996).

[27] Mark Franklin, *Voter Turnout and the Dynamics of Electoral Competition in Established Democracies since 1945* (Cambridge, UK: Cambridge University Press, 2004): 78–9.

to vote. However, the "carrot" approach, while more acceptable to voting libertarians, is rarely as effective as the "stick."[28]

Proportional representation is often touted as the best voluntary remedy of low turnout, but its capacity to raise turnout is modest compared with that of compulsory voting. While it is true that countries with proportional representation have higher turnout than those that are majoritarian, the gain in switching from a majoritarian to a proportional representation system has been estimated at variously 3, 7, and 12 percent.[29] By contrast, compulsory voting increases turnout from a minimum of 12 percent to a maximum of 30+ percent.[30] When it is administered effectively, with appropriate sanctions[31] and high levels of electoral integrity, compulsory voting is the most efficient and effective means for raising and maintaining high and socially even turnout.[32] In fact, it is the *only* institutional mechanism that can achieve turnout rates of 90 percent and above on its own.[33] This tends to be the case not just in prosperous, well-resourced settings but also in compulsory systems generally.[34] Further, its effect on turnout is *immediate*.

Now, it is true that there are some voluntary-voting regimes that continue to enjoy very high turnout rates, and critics of compulsory voting often point to levels in such places as Austria, Luxembourg, Iceland, New Zealand, Denmark, and Malta as evidence that compulsory voting is not required to achieve high turnout. But anecdotal evidence such as this can be misleading because such settings tend to be characterized by an unusually large coincidence of variables known to

[28] Hasen, "Voting without Law": 2136, 2169.

[29] Jonathon Louth and Lisa Hill, "Compulsory Voting in Australia: Turnout with and without It," *Australian Review of Public Affairs* 6 (2005): 25–37.

[30] Birch, *Full Participation*: 96; Louth and Hill, "Compulsory Voting in Australia."

[31] Louth and Hill, "Compulsory Voting in Australia"; Costas Panagopoulos, "The Calculus of Voting in Compulsory Voting Systems," *Political Behaviour* 30 (4) (2008): 455–67; S. Singh, "How Compelling Is Compulsory Voting? A Multilevel Analysis of Turnout," *Political Behavior* 33 (1) (2011): 95–111.

[32] Louth and Hill, "Compulsory Voting in Australia"; W. Hirczy, "Explaining Near-Universal Turnout: The Case of Malta," *European Journal of Political Research* 27 (1995): 255–72.

[33] Arend Lijphart, "Compulsory Voting Is the Best Way to Keep Democracy Strong," in R. E. DiClerico and A. S. Hammock (eds.), *Points of View*, 8th ed. (New York: McGraw-Hill, 2001): 74.

[34] Birch, *Full Participation*; Louth and Hill, "Compulsory Voting in Australia."

enhance turnout. The case of Malta, for example, is particularly problematic because it is far from representative: whereas Malta regularly achieves very high turnout rates (92 percent registered voters at the last national election), this is due to the coexistence of an unusually large number of features congenial to high turnout: a small, urbanized, and geographically concentrated population; unitary, concentrated government[35]; high levels of partisanship; proportional representation; highly competitive elections resulting in one-party governments (despite proportional representation); extremely intense election campaigns; and a polarized electorate of partisan, committed voters.[36] New Zealand is another setting that happens to enjoy reasonably high turnout levels. Yet, eccentrically,[37] although New Zealand is a voluntary-voting system, *enrollment* is effectively compulsory in New Zealand. Further, New Zealand elections are especially salient to the electorate because of the unitary and unicameral structure of government there and the intimacy of the political culture.[38] Finally, any optimism about comparable turnouts with New Zealand should be dampened by the fact that its own turnout rate is currently in decline. At the last national election in 2011, turnout had slid to 74.2 percent (registered voters). This is much lower than the turnout figure of 93 percent (registered voters) achieved in 2010 by its near neighbor, Australia. Therefore, despite anecdotal evidence from settings where conditions would be virtually impossible to replicate elsewhere, in general, compulsory voting is the most decisive means by which to raise voting levels. It is the only measure that really works consistently and over long periods.

According to Mark Franklin, compulsory voting does not address the "real" cause of low turnout: low electoral salience. This is where he believes reformers should be directing their energies.[39] The salience

35 A. Siaroff and J. Merer, "Parliamentary Election Turnout in Europe since 1990," *Political Studies* 50 (5) (2002): 916–27.

36 Hirczy, "Explaining Near-Universal Turnout": 255.

37 Denmark and New Zealand are rarities among industrialized nations in upholding this practice in isolation from the compulsion to vote (Richard Rose, "Evaluating Election Turnout," in *Voter Turnout from 1945 to 1997: A Global Report on Political Participation* [Stockholm: International IDEA, 1997]: 45–6).

38 S. Jackman, "Non-Compulsory Voting in Australia? What Surveys Can (and Can't) Tell Us," *Electoral Studies* 18 (1) (1999): 29–48.

39 Mark N. Franklin, "Electoral Engineering and Cross-National Turnout Differences: What Role for Compulsory Voting?" *British Journal of Political Science* 29 (1999): 205–24.

of elections is diluted by factors such as how competitive, visible, and consequential an election is, and it can be undermined by federalism, divided government, the separation of powers, and the choice-restricting effect of a simple plurality system, all of which are thought to weaken the perceived strength of the relationship between voting and policy consequences.

But even if it could be definitively shown that electoral salience is the main reason for low turnout, this knowledge is of limited value because it would be extremely difficult, if not impossible, to comprehensively reform the systemic sources of low salience in any democracy. One of the beauties of compulsory voting is that, unlike most other remedies for low turnout, it does not rely on a contested hypothesis about the underlying cause of voting abstention. We do not have to have a definitive answer to the question of why so many people fail to vote in order for compulsory voting to work at changing voting behavior and even attitudes (e.g., people in compulsory-voting systems are more likely to regard voting as a duty than those in voluntary systems). Similarly, it is much harder to address the deeper sociological "causes" of socially uneven turnout (i.e., economic and social inequality; see Chapter 6) than it is to apply the legal solution. Of course, it would be ideal if we could attack the turnout problem by reducing disparities in advantage, but this is unrealistic.

Therefore, because compulsory voting is the most – indeed, *only* – really decisive and reliable means by which to keep turnout high, it should be the first – rather than last – resort in attempts to address the turnout problem. Yet, for obvious, usually cultural, reasons, it isn't. It is also possible that resistance to the idea is fueled by the perception that establishing a good mandatory voting regime is just too difficult. But, although doing so takes effort, it is not impossible. The Australian system provides a good example of an effective and well-accepted regime.

5.7 A Real-World Example

In Australia – where turnout is routinely in the 90+ percent (registered voters) range – voting is easy and the system remarkably free from interference and corruption; for example, between 1998 and 2007, not a single Australian was prosecuted for multiple voting.[40] This is noteworthy considering proof of identity is not required to vote. Electoral offices are organized, reasonably integrated and cooperative (despite federalism), professional, well-funded, independent, accountable, and apolitical.[41] As a result, there is a very high level of trust around the election process and its outcomes.

It is worth noting that the comparatively high standard of service delivered by Australian electoral offices has been substantially driven by the fact that voting is compulsory: high turnout levels coupled with the expectation that no Australian, however disadvantaged or isolated, should be excluded from the electoral process has led to a comprehensive and rigorous regime of electoral management. As Orr and colleagues have noted, the compulsion to vote in Australia "colours electoral authority activity in a positive way" by encouraging "electoral commissions to treat every vote as sacred and to expend considerable efforts in ensuring adequate access to the ballot."[42]

Voting in Australia is a comparatively painless affair for voters because the Australian state meets almost all the opportunity and

[40] Joint Standing Committee on Electoral Matters (JSCEM), "Fact Sheet: Report on the 2007 Election," *Issues* (June 23, 2009), Parliament House, Canberra. Independent inquiries and audits carried out on the integrity of the federal electoral roll have found that the roll is reliable, accurate, and of "high integrity" (Colin Hughes and Brian Costar, *Limiting Democracy: The Erosion of Electoral Rights in Australia* [Sydney: UNSW Press, 2006]: 38–43). The Australian National Audit Office review (2002) has also rated the federal electoral roll as "over 96% accurate, 95% complete and 99% valid" (Graeme Orr, Bryan Mercurio, and George Williams, "The Australian Electoral Tradition," in G. Orr et al. [eds.], *Realising Democracy: Electoral Law in Australia* [Leichhardt: Federation Press, 2003]: 16).

[41] Australian Electoral Commissions, which "are staffed with expert public servants" who "[a]s a rule ... have traditionally been exceptionally apolitical" (Graeme Orr, Bryan Mercurio, and George Williams, "Australian Electoral Law: A Stocktake," *Election Law Journal* 2 [2002]: 383–402). Within its typology of electoral authorities ("independent," "government," and "mixed"), IDEA has classified the Australian system as independent, that is, institutionally independent from the executive (see Alan Wall et al., *Electoral Management Design: The International IDEA Handbook* [Stockholm: International IDEA, 2006]). Nevertheless, because executive governments have the power to appoint the heads of electoral commissions, "bi-partisanship over appointments" can occasionally "deteriorat[e]" (G. Orr, B. Mercurio, and G. Williams, "The Australian Electoral Tradition," in G. Orr, B. Mercurio, and G. Williams [eds.], *Realising Democracy: Electoral Law in Australia* [Leichhardt: Federation Press, 2003]: 400).

[42] Orr et al., "The Australian Electoral Tradition": 390.

transaction costs involved. The Australian state (via its state and commonwealth electoral commissions) assumes a high degree of responsibility for making feasible what it requires of voters. Electoral commissions go to considerable lengths to accommodate aging and immobile people, the homeless, those living in remote regions, prisoners, and people who have a disability or are ill or infirm, housebound, living abroad, approaching maternity, hospitalized, have literacy and numeracy problems, or are from a non-English-speaking background. There are also special provisions for "silent enrollment" (for those who believe that having their name on a public roll endangers either themselves or their families) and itinerant enrollment ("for homeless people, or people who travel constantly and have no permanent fixed address").[43] In any given federal election, up to 500 mobile teams will visit 2,000 special hospital locations; mobile teams will visit 300 or so remote outback locations and over 40 prisons; and there will be hundreds of prepoll voting centers and around 100 overseas polling places to which approximately three tons of election-related and staff training materials will be air-freighted immediately prior to polling. Finally, Australians living in the Antarctic and based on Antarctic supply ships are supplied with voting materials and facilities.[44]

It would be hard to find an electoral authority in a voluntary setting anywhere that goes to nearly this much trouble to ensure full voting inclusion. No one, no matter how marginalized, isolated, or immobile, is expected to meet the potentially high transaction and opportunity costs of voting, costs that the state would be unlikely to offset were voting voluntary. Because Australian electoral commissions actively seek and assist with registration; provide electoral education; offer absent voting, mobile polling, and postal voting; and ensure that elections are held on a Saturday and that polling booths are generally close at hand, voters don't have to sacrifice much in terms of cost and opportunities for work or leisure to vote. This high standard of service and integrity has, in turn, undoubtedly reinforced the view that being required to vote is an acceptable infringement on liberty: the public approval

[43] This enables them to vote. Their details are later checked to determine why their names did not appear on the roll.

[44] Voting is not compulsory for Australians living in the Antarctic due to the impossibility of ensuring the secrecy of the ballot.

rating for compulsory voting in Australia has hovered between 70 and 77 percent for decades.

It might be thought that the costs of such a system are prohibitive: in fact, the average cost to the taxpayer of voting in Australia is around AU$5 per vote. The costs of Australian elections are further contained by the fact that there is so little postelection contestation and litigation.

But all this talk about the benefits and feasibility of compulsory voting assumes that there is something wrong with low turnout, whereas many argue that it is not necessary – or even desirable – for everyone to vote and that low turnout presents no problems for democracy. I turn to this issue in Chapter 6.

6

Turnout, Abstention, and Democratic Legitimacy

6.1 Introduction

Before embarking on a specific defense of the requirement to vote, it is important to discuss the problem to which compulsory voting is a purported solution: low voter turnout. As Ben Saunders has pointed out, "If high turnout is not necessarily democratically better than low levels of turnout, then compulsory voting cannot be justified on the grounds that it is necessary to realize democracy."[1]

Despite the assumed importance of elections and voting, some commentators have argued that it is not necessary – or even desirable – for everyone to vote and that low turnout therefore presents no problems for democracy or democratic legitimacy. Is there actually anything wrong with low turnout? Can democracy really do without voters? And can we, as individuals, do without voting?

Before starting, it may be worth clarifying what this chapter is *not* about: it is not about whether aggregative democracy is superior or inferior to other forms of democracy (such as deliberative democracy) as a means for preference gathering and self-government; further, it is not about which voting system best serves democratic values.[2]

[1] Ben Saunders, "The Democratic Turnout 'Problem,'" *Political Studies* 60 (2012): 306–20.

[2] Nevertheless, a proportional system is preferable to a simple plurality system, especially in a mandatory system, because it tends to offer more opportunity for some representation and more choice to offset the compulsion.

Neither does it challenge the idea that voting is self-defeating because of the ambiguities and instabilities that can plague voting methods (as per William Riker and Kenneth Arrow). Rather, it takes the following as facts of political life that must be taken into account rather than wished away: namely, that voting – with all its distortions and problems – remains the primary mechanism for establishing legitimate governments in advanced representative democracies and, further, that things are likely to stay this way for the foreseeable future. Given this reality, does low turnout matter?

6.2 The Turnout Problem

Voter turnout is in steady decline throughout the industrialized voting world.[3] Because much of this turnout decline is driven by the civic demobilization of young people, it signals a future crisis in electoral democracy.[4] Many people observe this trend with alarm and are keen to arrest it. But whether declining turnout is a problem in need of remedy is disputed by others who claim that voting abstention is either democratically neutral or actually serves – and is an expression of – democratic values. Some argue that high turnout makes no difference to political outcomes and that low turnout is a sign of contentment with the political status quo; others characterize voting abstention as a positive choice and apathy as a "political virtue"; and there are those who deny that low-turnout elections are less legitimate than high-turnout ones. This chapter explores whether such claims have merit by assessing them in light of both empirical trends and normative concerns about democratic legitimacy. It will be argued that low-turnout elections produce different and less democratically desirable outputs than high-turnout elections and that they do not, therefore, have the same level of democratic legitimacy as high-turnout elections. It is further argued that, even if low-turnout elections did not produce

[3] Andre Blais, E. Gidengil, N. Nevitte, and R. Nadeau, "Where Does Turnout Decline Come From?" *European Journal of Political Research* 43 (2004): 221–36; Andre Blais, "Political Participation," in L. LeDuc, R. G. Niemi, and P. Norris (eds.), *Comparing Democracies 3: Elections and Voting in the 21st Century* (London: Sage, 2010): 165–83.

[4] A. Blais and D. Rubenson, "The Source of Turnout Decline," *Comparative Political Studies* 46 (1) (2013): 95–117.

divergent outputs, they would still be less procedurally democratic than high-turnout elections. The meaning and significance of persistent voting abstention are also explored here. Overall, I aim to show that when turnout is high and socially even, not only are elections more procedurally legitimate, but the governments they deliver are also more able to be "of the people, by the people, for the people."

I begin by laying out Robert Dahl's conception of a legitimate procedural democracy.

6.2.1 Legitimacy in a Procedural Democracy

A political system cannot be legitimized unless the process that establishes it is itself legitimate. Obviously, within a representative (i.e., procedural) democracy, this requires that elections are properly managed and are free from corruption so that the result can be deemed legal. But it means more than this: in procedural democracies, such as those under consideration in this book, voting in elections – the primary mechanism for making binding decisions on members of a *demos* – is central to legitimizing the authority of the governing regime. On this view, it is vitally important that electoral procedures are duly complied with for the result to be deemed legitimate. According to Robert Dahl, certain conditions must be met in evaluating the proposed procedures, and he identifies five criteria: "political equality," "effective participation," "enlightened understanding," "final control of the agenda by the *demos*," and "inclusiveness." Political equality demands that the mechanism for "determining outcomes" takes "equally into account, the expressed preferences of each member of the *demos*"; further, because the claims of each member of the *demos* are equally valid, each individual is entitled to equal voting "shares" or an "equal vote." "Effective participation" requires that citizens have not only "an adequate opportunity" but also "an *equal* opportunity, for expressing [their] ... preferences as to the final outcome." On this criterion, procedures are judged according to "the adequacy of the opportunities they provide for, and the relative costs they impose on, expression and participation by the *demos* in making binding decisions." "Enlightened understanding" requires that "in order to express his or her preferences accurately, each citizen ought to have adequate and equal opportunities for discovering and validating ... what his or her preferences are on the matter to be decided." On this criterion, it is unacceptable to "cut off" or suppress information that could affect decisions made or to afford some citizens easier access to information of crucial importance. By "final control of the agenda," Dahl means that "the people must have the final say, or must be sovereign," and it demands that "the terms on which the *demos* delegates authority" are determined by the people. By "delegation," Dahl means "a revocable grant of authority, subject to recovery by the *demos*."[5] Finally, "inclusiveness" requires that the *demos* include "all adult members of the association except transients." This universal inclusion criterion is intended to prevent any distribution of benefits that violates the principle that the "good interest of each human being is entitled to equal consideration."[6] If a system can satisfy these five criteria, it can be regarded as "a full procedural democracy."[7]

These procedural criteria focus mainly on inputs to the voting process (a process Dahl calls the "decisive stage") so as to confer legitimacy on it. But they (and the legitimacy that they are intended to confer) also exist to produce outputs that optimize the interests of *demos* members; in other words, the democratic inputs are assumed to affect democratic outputs. As I will show, biases in electoral inputs affect democratic outputs in ways that are problematic for democratic legitimacy *in general* and for procedural legitimacy *in particular*. But, as I will also show, biases in inputs alone are enough to compromise the legitimacy of procedural democracies.

6.3 Does Higher Turnout Confer Greater Democratic Legitimacy on Election Outcomes?

Establishing the legitimacy of government has been defined as a key function of elections.[8] Many people assume that the higher the turnout,

[5] Dahl, *After the Revolution*: 98–108.

[6] *Ibid.*: 124–5.

[7] Not everyone regards procedural fairness as necessary. For example, despite doing so in earlier work, in his later work, David Estlund "gives little or no role to procedural fairness." Rather, his position is reduced to the values of epistemic proceduralism, which he posits as providing fairer outcomes: "Democratic legitimacy requires that the procedure can be held, in terms acceptable to all qualified points of view, to be epistemically the best (or close to it) among those that are better than random" (Estlund, *Democratic Authority*: 66, 98).

[8] R. S. Katz, *Democracy and Elections* (New York: Oxford University Press, 1997): chap. 7, *passim*; R. H. Salisbury, "Research on Political Participation," *American*

the greater is the legitimacy of the government that has won office. Others disagree: Annabelle Lever argues that high turnout is "a poor proxy for legitimacy" because even when people "fail to vote, they may rightly deem their government legitimate." Voting, says Lever, "is, at best, only one form of democratic participation and, from some perspectives, not an especially important or attractive one."[9] Similarly, Ben Saunders denies that "a country with universal suffrage and high levels of turnout" better realizes "the ideal of democracy ... than one with similarly universal suffrage but lower levels of turnout."[10]

It is conceded that elections can be rather blunt instruments for aggregating preferences and communicating mandates; therefore, turnout is not a perfect proxy for legitimacy. But are there any equally reliable and consequential alternatives? After all, it is still elections that determine who rules and in what way. The suggestion that voting is not "more important than other forms of collective choice and action"[11] is questionable given the centrality of representative parliaments in determining the breadth and legality of democratic activity. The idea that we can participate in self-governing activities in spheres other than (or instead of) legislative politics is flawed because it is the legislature that usually determines the democratic framework, that is, whether these other spheres "of collective choice and action" will be allowed to exist. It can, for example, limit free speech and the right of protest, it can outlaw certain interest groups, and it can make strikes illegal.[12] In order to enjoy the voluntary aspects of democracy, there must be democratic spheres left within which to participate voluntarily; participating in the selection of those who make decisions about those spheres is therefore an important self-governing activity. And even if I do participate in other kinds of self-governing activities, it needs to be shown that such activities actually provide me with *better* and *more effective* kinds of representation than legislative ones, particularly if I am disadvantaged. Voting for our democratic representatives

Journal of Political Science 19 (1975): 326–7; C. B. Gans, "The Empty Ballot Box: Reflections on Non-voters in America," *Public Opinion* 1 (1978): 54–7.

[9] Lever, "Compulsory Voting": 909.

[10] Saunders, "Democratic Turnout": 310.

[11] Lever, "Compulsory Voting": 911.

[12] In some settings, such as the United States, the courts are also extremely influential in determining such issues.

is a *special* activity, not just one of many ways in which we can participate politically.

Further, can it really be the case that the legitimacy conferred by elections with 60 percent turnout is as high as that conferred by turnout of 95 percent? Now, perhaps it can: after all, these are only numbers, and if there is nothing qualitatively different about the information communicated by 60 percent – as opposed to, say, 95 percent – of the population, it may not matter. Leaving aside the question of whether the information gathered in low-turnout elections is the same (I will address this issue presently), should we attach any significance to the raw turnout figures? How low is too low? Twenty percent? Ten percent? At what point do we start to worry about this problem, if at all? Does it matter that democracy is becoming the exclusive business of elites?[13] Is there any point at which we might admit that "the people" are no longer sovereign, even when they retain the formal right to vote? Some might argue that the people's choice to abstain is an expression of their sovereignty, but do we still say the people are sovereign if *no one* is voting anymore? Do we still say that the people are sovereign simply because they are entitled to vote?

For Dahl, democratic legitimacy is like a reservoir: provided the water remains at a given level, political stability is assured. When it falls below a certain level, legitimacy is compromised. What exactly is this level? Dahl is unable to help here because his criteria "do not specify any particular procedure"; rather, they are standards against which to evaluate procedures. However, he does stipulate that the number should be "significant."[14] It has been observed that political scientists have yet to determine an agreed "optimal level of political participation" (the implication being that this may be too difficult a task).[15] I would suggest that identifying this ordained level is not beyond us and that we might begin looking for it at the tipping point where turnout

[13] Some might interpret Dahl to say that elite rule is acceptable. After all, he does stipulate that the only plausible rival to democracy is rule by a "meritorious minority, an elite possessing superior knowledge and virtue" (Dahl, *After the Revolution*: 131–2). However, as Dahl is well aware, although voters are generally better educated than nonvoters, there is no evidence that they are more virtuous. The fact that they tend to vote in their own class interests and therefore against those of less advantaged nonvoters strongly suggests that they are neither more nor less virtuous.

[14] Dahl, *After the Revolution*: 100.

[15] Gans, "The Empty Ballot Box": 55.

becomes socially uneven enough to affect the behavior of governments in favor of voters (in other words, when the "inclusiveness" criterion becomes compromised). This seems to happen when turnout dips to below around 90 percent (registered voters), but this is something that could be worked out more precisely by empirical researchers.

It has also been suggested that "universal turnout is not necessary for decisions to be representative since we may instead consult a random-sample of the population."[16] If by this is meant substituting elections for the random sample, then it sounds like a sensible idea in principle, if only because it would allow us to canvass the preferences of a representative sample of the population (this is also one advantage of Brennan's idea of a voting lottery; see Chapter 2). But, although we *may* do this, we don't and almost certainly *won't* start doing this. What we *do* have, though, is elections with low and socially uneven turnouts that are becoming worse over time. So, given the reality of the situation – namely, that voting is the agreed procedure – we need to decide whether low turnout really is acceptable in an advanced procedural democracy.

6.4 *Opportunity* to Vote Not *Actual* Voting Is What Counts

It has been argued that it is only necessary that everyone has the "opportunity to influence political decision-making, not that all must exercise this."[17] Because on this view, it "is only the opportunity that matters"; a democracy can still be legitimate and "well-functioning" even where large numbers of potential voters do not take up the opportunity to participate.[18] There are several responses to this idea. An important reason why *actual* voting is preferable to the *opportunity* to vote lies in the value of complete information. High to universal participation provides a much higher level of information about citizens' preferences than low participation does. Such information cannot be supplied authoritatively by random samples, polls, or postelection surveys (discussed later). The more completely the preferences of the majority are registered, the more democratic (i.e., representative) will be the system.

[16] Saunders, "Increasing Turnout": 12–13; Birch, *Full Participation*: 26.
[17] Saunders, "Increasing Turnout": 75; Saunders, "Democratic Turnout": 311.
[18] Saunders, "Democratic Turnout": 311–13, 317.

This might seem like an obvious – even banal – point, but for some it is controversial because it is disputed that higher turnout delivers more authoritative information about voters' preferences. Does obtaining *more* information yield any qualitatively *new* or different information? This is a legitimate objection that needs to be addressed.

One reason why the mere opportunity to vote is not enough to make a system fully procedurally democratic is that, in practice, low turnout invariably means low and *socially uneven* turnout. Low-turnout elections therefore aggregate the preferences of an unrepresentative sample of the voting population. Many defenders of low turnout gloss rather easily over the fact that turnout in most industrialized democracies is not only low and uneven but also declining and becoming ever more uneven as time passes.[19] In other words, because declining turnout is steepest among the disadvantaged and the young, it is an escalating problem signifying not only the gradual death of electoral democracy but also the decline of democratic *equality*. In industrial democracies worldwide, failure to vote is generally concentrated among groups already experiencing one or more forms of exclusion or deprivation, namely, the young,[20] the poor, the unemployed, the less well educated, the homeless, indigenous peoples, remote citizens, new citizens, prisoners, and people with low literacy, numeracy, and majority-language competence.[21] To make matters worse, political demobilization among the poor escalates during periods of widespread economic crises; the worse off people become, the less likely they are to vote at the point at

[19] For example, the participation gap between manual and nonmanual workers more than doubled in the two British elections between 1997 and 2005, rising from 5 percent in 1997 to 11 percent in 2005 (E. Keany and B. Rogers, *A Citizen's Duty: Voter Inequality and the Case for Compulsory Turnout* [London: Institute for Public Policy Research, 2006]).

[20] Youth can be generally treated as a surrogate for other forms of social and economic exclusion.

[21] H. E. Brady, S. Verba, and K. Schlozman, "Beyond SES: A Resource Model of Political Participation," *American Political Science Review* 89 (2) (1995): 271–94; Lijphart, "Unequal Participation"; M. Hooghe and K. Pelleriaux, "Compulsory Voting in Belgium: An Application of the Lijphart Thesis," *Electoral Studies* 17 (1998): 419–24; P. Beramendi and C. J. Anderson, "Income Inequality and Democratic Representation," in P. Beramendi and C. J. Anderson (eds.), *Democracy, Inequality and Representation* (New York: Russell Sage Foundation, 2008): 3–25; A. Fowler, "Electoral and Policy Consequences of Voter Turnout: Evidence from Compulsory Voting in Australia," *Quarterly Journal of Political Science* 8 (2013):159–82.

which those crises are worst. People grappling with economic hardship deploy their scarce resources in the task of getting by.[22] What appears to be a "rational choice" (i.e., the preservation of scarce resources in times of crises) works out, in the long term, to be a counterproductive sacrifice of economic well-being. Democratic responsiveness and the idea that there should be "a revocable grant of authority, subject to recovery by the *demos*,"[23] is what is at stake here because those most inclined to punish the government are the least likely to do so. During periods of economic crises, incumbent governments have the best chance of escaping electoral retribution from those most affected by any mismanagement on their part.

Low and socially uneven voting levels operate as the functional equivalent of weighted votes for the well-off,[24] thereby impugning two fundamental criteria of procedural democracy: equality of voting power[25] and inclusiveness. This, in turn, affects the legitimacy of the democracy in question, assuming that inclusiveness and political equality are considered important for such legitimacy.

Formal equality (the mere opportunity to vote) is not enough to make a system as democratic as it could be, just as formal equality of economic opportunity is not enough to eradicate poverty in developed economies. An opportunity to vote is not the same as *actually* voting, as the empirical studies on the effects of voting canvassed below demonstrate. For the moment, though, I would stress

[22] See Hill, "Compelling Citizens to Vote," for a review of the literature here.

[23] Dahl, *After the Revolution*: 98–108.

[24] Lijphart, "Unequal Participation": 7.

[25] Hans Kelsen defines *democratic elections* as "those which are based on universal, equal, free and secret suffrage," whereas Robert Dahl lists "equal votes" or "political equality" first in his list of five criteria for judging the democratic legitimacy of procedural democracies (see H. Kelsen, "Foundations of Democracy," *Ethics* 66 [2006]: 1–101, 3; and R. Dahl, "Procedural Democracy," in P. Laslett and J. Fishkin [eds.], *Philosophy, Politics and Society*, 5th Series [New Haven, CT: Yale University Press, 1979]: 101–31). Democratic equality means not only that "everyone should be treated equally; it also means that everyone should have a place in the exercise of political authority." The basis for this belief is (1) "that each citizen is as well qualified as any other to contribute to political decision-making" (see H. Sidgwick, *The Elements of Politics* [London: Macmillan, 1891]: 587) and (2) the nonpaternalist principle that each person is the best judge of her own interests (see D. F. Thompson, *The Democratic Citizen* [Cambridge, UK: Cambridge University Press, 1970]: 13–19; A. Weale, *Democracy* [New York: St. Martin's Press, 1999]: 54–5).

that while the formal opportunity to vote is certainly a *necessary* condition of democracy, whether it is a *sufficient* one (for satisfying procedural criteria) is debatable. Further, it is not even clear that everyone *does* have an equal opportunity to vote, as will also be argued presently.

6.5 Is Failure to Vote Neutral?

Does it make any difference if people fail to vote? According to Loren Lomasky and Geoffrey Brennan, failure to vote is neutral: there are no "morally unsatisfying properties" of nonvoting – and therefore low turnout – because the dynamic is self-equilibrating. On their reasoning, "[w]hen an eligible voter abstains, thereby lowering *E*, the total size of the electorate, the probability *P* of one's own vote proving decisive increases. That is, each remaining voter is rendered better off by the lower level of electoral competition.... Therefore, ... the process ... [is] self-stabilizing."[26]

This argument is seriously challenged by the character and effects of actual voting behavior. It is based on the faulty assumption that potential voters can be understood as generic interest-bearers and that the only democratic issue at stake is maintaining the raw quantity of electoral power. But the empirical trends referred to earlier reveal a less benign picture; when a young, poor, isolated, homeless, or new citizen abstains, her voting power does not revert to another young, isolated, poor voter but generally to a well-off, middle- to upper-class, educated, home-owning, established citizen. The dynamic is not a neutral, self-equilibrating one but a zero-sum game: a straightforward transference of power from weak to already strong interests. Therefore, failure to vote does give rise to a number of "morally unsatisfying properties" – at least for procedural, egalitarian, and participatory democrats – among them, exacerbation of elite power, political exclusion, socioeconomic bias, unfairness, violation of the one-vote, one-value principle, and unrepresentativeness, all of which undermine the participatory democratic ideal.

[26] L. Lomasky and G. Brennan, "Is There a Duty to Vote?" *Social Philosophy and Policy* 17 (1) (2000): 62–86.

6.6 Is It True That It Would Make No Difference to Government Policy (Outputs) if Everyone Voted?

One common genre of argument that underplays the importance of turnout is that democratic outputs are unaffected by the uneven inputs of low turnout.

One variant of this argument is that low turnout is fine because voters' issue priorities and policy preferences differ minimally from those of the voting population in general; therefore, it would make no difference to the way governments behave if "more people voted."[27] Another argument in this genre is that it makes no difference if everyone votes because election results invariably reflect nonvoters' partisan (as opposed to policy) preferences. Anthony Ciccone notes that polling organizations, using a sample as small as 1,600 people, have been able to predict with "at least 95 percent accuracy, the expected outcome of pending presidential elections"; it is therefore unnecessary, he argues, for everyone to vote "in order to accurately reflect the majority interest."[28] The same type of argument has been made using survey data (as opposed to polls).[29] (Note that this claim is

[27] R. E. Wolfinger and S. J. Rosenstone, *Who Votes?* (New Haven, CT: Yale University Press, 1980). See also D. T. Studlar and S. Welch, "The Policy Opinions of British Non-Voters: A Research Note," *European Journal of Political Research* 14 (1986): 139–48; R. A. Texeira, *The Disappearing American Voter* (Washington, DC: Brookings Institution, 1992); D. Rubenson, A. Blais, E. Gidengil, N. Nevit, and P. Fournier, "Does Turnout Matter?" *Electoral Studies* 26 (2007): 589–97. One significant difference that Highton and Wolfinger underplay is that voters and nonvoters differ markedly on attitudes to welfare (Highton and Wolfinger, "Higher Turnout": 185). Further, their data do not sit well with what we know about the differences between the young (whose turnout is generally low) and the old (whose turnout is generally high) on policy opinions. According to Martin Wattenberg, "Survey research consistently indicates that young people are ... much more supportive of government spending for public schools and jobs programs. They are also more in favor of spending to protect the environment, an equal role for women in society, and abortion rights. In terms of ideology, young people are virtually as likely to say they are liberals as conservatives, whereas among senior citizens, conservatives outnumber liberals by 20 percent. In sum, if young people had turnout rates equal to older people, voting behavior and public policy would probably be shifted leftwards" (M. P. Wattenberg, "Why Don't More Americans Vote?" *Boston Globe* [September 21, 2003]).

[28] A. Ciccone, "The Constitutional Right to Vote Is Not a Duty," *Hamline Journal of Public Law and Policy* 23 (2001–2): 325–57.

[29] J. Nagel and J. E. McNulty, "Partisan Effects of Voter Turnout in Senatorial and Gubernatorial Elections," *American Political Science Review* 90 (1996): 780–93; J. Petrocik, "Voter Turnout and Electoral Preferences: The Anomalous Reagan

contested, with many people suggesting that high turnout benefits left-of-center parties.[30])

If one accepts the claim that turnout levels are unimportant if the policy or partisan preferences of nonvoters are reflected in the outcome, then one should also accept the stronger claim that it is acceptable for David Cameron to skip the next election and just appoint himself Prime Minister as long as his policies reflect the surveyed preferences of the majority of the electorate and provided the required number of nonvoters agree they would have voted for him anyway. In other words, no one need vote at all. I say this not to be glib or provocative, but to draw attention to the fact that these sorts of arguments are missing something important about the role of properly observed *procedures* in securing the legitimacy of representative (i.e., procedural) democracies. Even if it were true that polls unfailingly predict election outcomes (they don't), that surveys accurately register the preferences of voters (this is controvertible), and that we could be certain that political outcomes would be exactly the same if everyone voted (we can't), it does not give grounds for the conclusion that low and unequal turnout is of no consequence. The reason is simple: polls and surveys are not elections, and they are certainly nothing like elections with high and socially even turnout. It is not opinion polls, representative samples, or postelection surveys – no matter how authoritatively and carefully conducted – that confer democratic legitimacy but *elections* – real elections with real electors casting votes on real ballot papers. It is elections that are the *acknowledged* and decisive procedure. And the more complete and socially representative is the information about

Elections," in K. Schlozman (ed.), *Elections in America* (New York: Allen and Unwin, 1987); P. A. Pettersen, "Comparing Non-Voters in the USA and Norway," *European Journal of Political Research* 17 (1999): 351–9; Rubenson et al., "Does Turnout Matter?"

30 A. Pacek and B. Radcliff, "Turnout and the Vote for Left-of-Centre Parties: A Cross-National Analysis," *British Journal of Political Science* 25 (1995): 137–43; J. Citrin, E. Schickler, and J. Sides, "What if Everyone Voted? Simulating the Impact of Increased Turnout in Senate Elections," *American Journal of Political Science* 47 (2013): 75–90; T. G. Hansford and B. T. Gomez, "Estimating the Electoral Effects of Voter Turnout," *American Political Science Review* 104 (2010): 268–88;T. L. Brunell and J. D. Nardo, "A Propensity Score Reweighting Approach to Estimating the Partisan Effects of Full Turnout in American Presidential Elections," *Political Analysis* 12 (2004): 28–45; J. Sides, E. Schickler, and J. Citrin, "If Everyone Had Voted, Would Bubba and Dubya Have Won?" *Presidential Studies Quarterly* 38 (2008): 521–39; M. P. Wattenberg, *Is Voting for Young People?* (New York: Pearson, 2008): 150–1.

electors' preferences, the more legitimate is the result, assuming we accept Dahl's procedural legitimacy criteria of "equal votes," "effective participation," and "inclusiveness." In a way, the outcome of elections is beside the point here; rather, the legitimacy of elections derives from the fact that it is *the peoples'* expressed choice – that they have, in fact, communicated their preferences/consent/dissent and that the government that wins is actually "by" and "of" the people.

6.6.1 Voting Does Affect Outputs

There is another – and perhaps more serious – problem with the argument that turnout does not affect democratic outputs: it ignores the way political elites respond to political participation in formulating policies and allocating resources.[31] Political science has long known that "if you don't vote, you don't count."[32] Generally speaking, governments are more attentive to the demands of habitual voting groups such as senior citizens and the middle classes at the expense of those who abstain. It seems that voters' preferences count more. A significant number of studies have found a strong relationship between electoral participation rates and the design and implementation of public policies that affect spending in important areas such as health services, education, and public amenities.[33]

Because voting is concentrated among the more prosperous members of society, it tends to help "those who are already better off."[34] This effect has been demonstrated in a large range of single-setting and cross-national studies. Paul Martin has found a close relationship between geographic voting patterns and "the allocation of federal

[31] P. S. Martin, "Voting's Rewards: Voter Turnout, Attentive Publics and Congressional Allocation of Federal Money," *American Journal of Political Science* 47 (2003): 110–27.

[32] W. D. Burnham, "The Turnout Problem," in J. Richly (ed.), *Elections American Style* (Washington, DC: Brookings Institution, 1987): 99.

[33] S. Verba, S. L. Schlozman, H. Brady, and N. H. Nie, "Citizen Activity: Who Participates? What Do They Say?" *American Political Science Review* 77 (1993): 303–18; S. Verba, "Would the Dream of Political Equality Turn Out to Be a Nightmare?" *Perspectives on Politics* 1 (2003): 663–79; A. Gallego, "Understanding Unequal Turnout: Education and Voting in Comparative Perspective," *Electoral Studies* 29 (2010): 239–48.

[34] S. Verba and N. Nie, *Participation in America: Political Democracy and Social Equality* (New York: Harper and Row, 1972): 338.

discretionary spending to those locations"; in other words, U.S. counties with high turnout rates "are rewarded with higher per capita federal expenditures."[35] Griffin and Newman's study of the aggregate roll-call behavior of U.S. senators provides empirical support for the hypothesis that government is more likely to represent voters than nonvoters. Although "senators may not know with certainty who votes and what their preferences are, their patterns of roll-call voting respond to voters' opinions but not to non-voters opinions."[36] Other and earlier U.S. research came to the same conclusion. For example, two important studies have shown that the provision to African-American citizens of public services (such as fire stations and recreational facilities, garbage collection, and street paving) improved when they fully entered the electorate after the enactment of the Voting Rights Act of 1965.[37] In fact, there is no shortage of studies that confirm that voters' preferences count more.[38]

Chong and Olivera's cross-country analysis of ninety-one countries over the period 1960–2000 shows that properly enforced compulsory voting improves income distribution.[39] In Europe and Latin America, high turnout induced by compulsory-voting laws is associated with a reduction in wealth inequality.[40] O'Toole and Strobl's cross-national study of the effect of compulsory-voting rules on government spending concludes that compulsory voting "decreases the proportional amount of government expenditure on defence and economic services" while increasing that spent on "health, ... housing

35 P. S. Martin, "Voting's Rewards: Voter Turnout, Attentive Publics and Congressional Allocation of Federal Money," *American Journal of Political Science* 47 (1) (2003): 110–27.

36 J. D. Griffin and B. Newman, "Are Voters Better Represented?" *The Journal of Politics* 67 (2005): 1206–27.

37 W. Keech, *The Impact of Negro Voting: The Role of the Vote in the Quest for Equality* (Chicago: Rand McNally, 1968); J. W. Button, *Blacks and Social Change: Impact of the Civil Rights Movement in Southern Communities* (Princeton, NJ: Princeton University Press, 1998).

38 See, for example, C. S. Bullock III, "Congressional Voting and the Mobilization of a Black Electorate in the South," *Journal of Politics* 43 (1981): 662–82; K. Q. Hill and J. E. Leighley, "The Policy Consequences of Class Bias in State Electorates," *American Journal of Political Science* 36 (1992): 351–65.

39 A. Chong, A. and M. Olivera, "On Compulsory Voting and Income Inequality in a Cross-Section of Countries," Inter-American Development Bank Research Department Working Paper 533, New York, May 2005.

40 Birch, *Full Participation*: 131

and transfers increases."[41] Vincent Mahler's study of thirteen developed democracies (including European and North American countries as well as Britain and Australia) found that "the rate of electoral turnout is positively related to the extent of government redistribution." This relationship was "especially true of redistribution that is accomplished by way of transfers" affecting "the lower part of the income spectrum."[42] Other studies have shown that in constituencies where the electoral participation of the disadvantaged is greater, welfare policies are more generous, and the state tends to be more redistributionist.[43] According to Kenworthy and Pontusson, voter turnout should be "treated ... as a proxy for the electoral mobilization of low income workers, condition[ing] the responsiveness of government policy to market income inequality trends."[44] In Australia, for example, the introduction of compulsory voting – which brought with it near-universal voting participation – coincided with a "dramatic increase in pension spending."[45]

Martin Gilens has found that U.S. presidents are six times more responsive to the rich than the poor. But as he also points out, this disproportionate level of "responsiveness to the preferences of the affluent cannot be attributed to their higher turnout rates or their greater involvement with political campaigns."[46] Gilens is correct, but this does not mean that turnout is of no consequence. In fact, there are two reasons why presidents are more responsive to those in the top

[41] They define economic services as "expenditure on regulation, regional development and trade promotion as a percentage of government expenditure" (F. O'Toole and E. Strobl, "Compulsory Voting and Government Spending," *Economics and Politics*, 7 [3] [1995]: 271–80).

[42] V. A. Mahler, "Electoral Turnout and Income Redistribution by the State: A Cross-National Analysis of the Developed Democracies," *European Journal of Political Research* 47 (2008): 161–83.

[43] S. E. Bennett and D. Resnick, "The Implications of Nonvoting for Democracy in the United States," *American Journal of Political Science* 34 (1990): 771–802; A. M. Hicks and D. H. Swank, "Politics, Institutions, and Welfare Spending in Industrialized Countries, 1960–82," *American Political Science Review* 86 (1992): 658–74; K. Q. Hill, J. E. Leighley, and A. Hinton-Anderson, "Lower-Class Mobilization and Policy Linkage in the U.S. States," *American Journal of Political Science* 39 (1995): 75–86; D. C. Mueller and T. Stratmann, "The Economic Effects of Democratic Participation," *Journal of Public Economics* 87 (2003): 2129–55.

[44] L. Kenworthy and J. Pontusson, "Rising Inequality and the Politics of Redistribution in Affluent Countries," *Perspectives on Politics* 3 (3) (2005): 449–71.

[45] Fowler, "Electoral and Policy Consequences of Voter Turnout."

[46] Gilens, "Affluence and Influence": 234–52.

10th percentile of wealth, and both relate to the fact that the wealthy are more politically engaged and better politically resourced than the poor. First, they are, as we know, more likely to vote. But second, and this hardly needs pointing out, they are more likely to contribute *money* to campaigns; further, only the rich are able to contribute *large* sums, thereby effectively amplifying their political power and their ability to attract government attention. So, clearly, campaign finance is the key to understanding how governments respond to the electorate, but this does *not* mean that turnout is of no consequence. In fact, it is still vitally important because high turnout ameliorates the disproportionate power of the rich at election time simply by diluting that power with the votes of the poor and less well-off.

In any case, politicians regard concentrations of consistent voters as "attentive publics."[47] Attentive publics, in turn, enjoy the close attentions of politicians,[48] hence the oldest cliché of politics: pork-barreling. After all, as Martin Wattenberg puts it so neatly, "Politicians are not fools; they know who their customers are."[49] Therefore, the claim that high turnout makes no difference to the way governments behave is controvertible. High turnout seems to give us not only *more* but qualitatively *different* kinds of information about the policy preferences of citizens. It also seems to give us different outcomes that serve the objective interests of typical nonvoters. So, in low-turnout elections, greater inequalities in procedural input lead to greater inequalities in democratic output, with the result that the legitimacy criteria of "equality," "inclusiveness," and "final control of the agenda" by the *demos* are undermined.

However, I should reiterate that my argument does not rely solely on the claim that the information garnered in high-turnout elections is qualitatively different insofar as it yields distinct outputs. As foreshadowed previously, it also relies on a procedural point: even if the *content* of the additional information were exactly the same under high

[47] *Attentive publics* are "those citizens who are aware that a specific issue is on the congressional agenda, know what alternatives are under consideration, and have relatively firm preferences about what Congress should do" (D. R. Arnold, *The Logic of Congressional Action* [New Haven, CT: Yale University Press, 1990]: 64–5).

[48] Martin, "Voting's Rewards": 112.

[49] M. P. Wattenberg, "Where Have All the Voters Gone," paper presented in the Political Science Seminar Series, RSSS, ANU, May 13, 1998: 6.

turnout (so that high-turnout elections produced the same outputs as low-turnout elections), the information would still be different simply by virtue of the fact that it is more complete and socially representative. Regardless of their expressed preferences, the fact that all affected interests have submitted their preferences makes the outcome different from one in which they haven't. The procedural democratic criteria of "equality," "effective participation," and "inclusiveness" aren't valued and upheld only when they yield particular outcomes; they are valued and upheld *regardless* of the outcome. This is not to say that they don't exist for the sake of the output (so I'm not claiming that they are ends in themselves because I've already argued for the good consequences of universal voting), only that they don't exist for the sake of a *particular* output. We don't stop valuing them when we don't get the output we expect; rather, it is the proper performance of *procedures* that is of central importance[50] so that the government really ends up being "of" the people.

6.7 Just Turning Up?

This last point might give the impression that I am advocating turning up to vote just so it can be said that people have gone through the democratic motions. After all, compulsory voting can only really guarantee *attendance* at the polls (although, it does, in fact, tend to ensure that most people vote). Compelling reluctant citizens to vote seems like a waste of theirs and everyone else's time if it means they will either only spoil their ballots (I address the problem of spoiled ballots in Chapter 8) or record positive abstention (i.e., a "none of the above" option). I suggest that when this latter option is available,[51] it offers the disaffected an opportunity for democratic expression that is superior to staying at home. This idea is not as outlandish as it

[50] The procedures aren't just valued as ends in themselves but because they are believed to be the best means for making binding democratic decisions. However, should the procedures routinely produce outcomes that we wouldn't expect or desire – for example, if high-turnout elections started to exacerbate rather than ameliorate bias – the procedures would need to be reevaluated.

[51] I believe it *should* be available in order to offset the compulsion. It is certainly better to vote this way than to lodge a blank or spoiled ballot because it communicates something meaningful, namely, that the voting public would like more and different candidate choice.

sounds: Russian presidential elections have, in the past, offered voters the option "Against all." In the March 26, 2000, election, 1.88 percent of the electorate chose this category.[52] The British Electoral Commission of 2001, when it explored the idea of compulsory voting for Britain, also contemplated the possibility of providing an entry on ballot papers for "positive abstention," whereby voters could vote for "None of the above."[53]

Even if people only turn up to vote for "None of the above," this is still meaningful activity and delivers more democratic information than failure to turn up at all. Positive abstention conveys vitally important information to politicians, potential politicians, and other voters; it communicates that there is a constituency of citizens whose votes are up for grabs and that an, as yet, unavailable electoral alternative needs to be framed. For those who fail to vote because they find none of the existing candidates acceptable, this option could eliminate at least one source of alienation from politics. In any case, as I've already mentioned, once we've found a way to get people to turn up, they tend to use the opportunity to vote, usually in their own interests.

6.8 Apathy Is a Virtue: Low Turnout Is a Function of Democratic Choice and an Expression of Self-Government

Those who see low and declining electoral turnout as unproblematic rarely conceive it as a problem about deprivation but are more likely to frame it in positive, agentic terms as an expression of "democratic choice" and freedom and even as the expression of a desire for "self-government."[54] For Jason Brennan, "so long as I have an equal right to

[52] RFE/RL Newsline, "None of the Above Finishes Sixth," Radio Free Europe/Radio Liberty (April 6, 2000); available at: http://www.rferl.org/content/article/1142131.html.

[53] C. Trueman, "The Electoral Commission of 2001," *History Learning Site*: http://www.historylearningsite.co.uk/electoral_commission_of_2001.htm (last accessed April 2, 2013).

[54] Saunders, "The Democratic Turnout 'Problem'"; Lever, "Compulsory Voting"; K. M. Swenson, "Sticks, Carrots, Donkey Votes and True Choice: A Rationale for Abolishing Compulsory Voting in Australia," *Minnesota Journal of International Law* 16 (2007): 525–52.

vote, choosing not to vote can be an autonomous act."[55] But the reality is more complicated than this, as will be shown presently.

Some have gone so far as to describe apathy as a "political virtue" that benefits "the tone of political life" by providing an "effective counter-force to the fanatics who constitute the real danger to liberal democracy."[56] Political apathy has also been characterized as "a sign of social and political stability,"[57] reflecting "contentment with the available political choices or, at least, confidence that the winner, whoever it is, will be worthy of support."[58] Some see low turnout as "a blessing" because those more strongly inclined to vote are posited as more competent to perform the mandate and accountability functions of elections than those who aren't so inclined.[59] Others regard abstention as a choice that needs to be respected; abstainers need not be alienated or neglected, they say, but are making a principled decision to leave the decision to others who are (allegedly) more "affected" by the outcome of elections.[60] It has also been argued that the silence of abstention is a form of political communication (or even speech) signifying alienation or protest.[61]

[55] Jason Brennan, "Polluting the Polls: When Citizens Should Not Vote," *Australasian Journal of Philosophy* 87 (2009): 535–49.

[56] W. H. M. Jones, "In Defence of Apathy: Some Doubts on the Duty to Vote," *Political Studies* 2 (1954): 25–37.

[57] Mayo's reasoning here seems incoherent: "A large public which is not constantly excited and interested in political questions is probably healthy in any democracy" because "[i]nterest (and voting) go with partisanship, and it is virtually impossible to increase one without the other. The heavier the vote, therefore, the less likely are the voters to be the rational citizens of classical theory, calmly contemplating the 'public good'" (H. B. Mayo, "A Note on the Alleged Duty to Vote," *Journal of Politics* 21 [1959]: 319–23). On this logic, surely those who do turn out to vote are more partisan and therefore not the "calm contemplators of the public good" Mayo values. Better, then, that the less-partisan participate.

[58] Lever, "Compulsory Voting: A Critical Perspective": 18.

[59] For example, J. H. Abraham, *Compulsory Voting* (Washington, DC: Public Affairs Press, 1955); M. Rosema, "Low Turnout: Threat to Democracy or Blessing in Disguise? Consequences of Citizens' Varying Tendencies to Vote," *Electoral Studies* 26 (2007): 612–23.

[60] For example, Saunders, "Increasing Turnout."

[61] See Blomberg, "Protecting the Right Not to Vote"; Lerman, "Voting Rites"; and *Hoffman* v. *Maryland* (928 F.2d 646, 648–9, 4th Cir. 1991), where the plaintiffs argued (unsuccessfully) that the right not to vote is fundamental because it is a form of political expression. See also Lardy, "Right Not to Vote," where she discusses, but does not defend, the idea of voting as expression.

There are a number of responses to these kinds of arguments: first, the idea that we should be complacent about the silence of abstainers is problematic because silence is extremely ambiguous. If it is a form of political communication in this context (it can be in other contexts), it is certainly a rather incoherent form of political expression compared with voting, which, at the very least, communicates a message about partisan preferences. Notably, the courts are very skeptical about this type of argument,[62] but even if I accepted that silence is a form of political communication, it is questionable whether it expresses contentment and assent, as has been alleged (I explore this issue empirically below). It could, in fact, mean many things, such as, "I'm homeless and find it difficult to register"; "I'm experiencing an economic crisis and am too demoralized to vote"; "I'm ill"; "I'm isolated"; "I'm a new migrant"; "I have literacy and numeracy problems"; "I have mobility problems"; "I'm a young voter alienated from the political system"; or "I have low feelings of either internal or external political efficacy"[63] (or both) (these are all well-established triggers/correlates of abstention). It could also mean, of course, that "I'm perfectly satisfied with things as they are and don't care about the election outcome one way or another." But it is difficult, if not impossible, to perceive which of these things is explaining the abstention of any particular person. On the other hand, not only does the *formal* vote reveal more information about what is going on in the mind of the electorate, so too does the *informal* vote. Blank ballots, spoiled ballots, protest votes, ballots marked with slogans and political rhetoric ("No dams"[64]; "I am

[62] It would be hard to successfully make the case that voting abstention is a form of political speech because the U.S. Supreme Court has already denied that voting can be regarded as such. In the 1992 case *Burdic* v. *Takushi*, the Court upheld Hawaii's ban on write-in votes, ruling against a voter's claim that the ban deprived him of the right to cast a protest vote for Donald Duck. According to the Court, elections are about choosing representatives not about self-expression (R. L. Hasen, "Voting without Law," *Pennsylvania Law Review* 144 [1996]: 2135–79). See also *Hoffman* v. *Maryland* (928 F.2d 646, 648–49, 4th Cir. 1991).

[63] Lijphart, "Compulsory Voting"; Lijphart, "Unequal Participation"; Lisa Hill, "Compulsory Voting, Political Shyness and Welfare Outcomes," *Journal of Sociology* 36 (1) (2000): 30–49.

[64] In 1979, the Tasmanian Hydro Electric Commission proposed to construct a dam on the lower Gordon River. The building of the dam would have significantly damaged a wilderness area that had just received a World Heritage listing. Under pressure from a fierce campaign waged by environmentalists, the incumbent Labor government proposed a "compromise" that involved damming a different part of the Gordon. This

an anarchist"; "Voting is the opiate of the masses") convey a wealth of information. All are legitimate forms of political expression that should be appreciated as such.[65]

Second, there is little empirical evidence to support the view that low turnout keeps political extremism at bay or that high turnout favors extremist parties.[66] In any case, extremism is not the real problem here but, rather, elite dominance. Where there is a large proportion of nonvoters, governors are disproportionately influenced by elites and intense issue activists.[67]

Third, even if it were true that habitual abstainers have lower levels of political competence than habitual voters, this should not surprise us given that disadvantage is a primary characteristic of the abstainer. But, because disadvantage seems to be substantially responsible for the relative political incompetence of the abstainer (who tends, for example, to be less well educated; see Chapter 8), and because failure to vote seems to exacerbate disadvantage, endorsing abstention hardly seems constructive in the long term. Significantly, Dahl does not recommend that when "enlightened understanding" is lacking in some *demos* members, we should exclude them from political decisions; rather, his implication is that we should ensure that everyone has the capacity for making informed political choices in the first place.[68] He also says that exclusions cannot be justified unless it can be compellingly shown that the *demos* will give equal consideration to the interests of the excluded. However, as he regretfully notes, "[e]xperience

plan was rejected by both the environmentalists and the Legislative Council (the Tasmanian Upper House), which supported the original proposal. As a result, the two proposals were put to the Tasmanian people in a referendum that took place in December 1981. The environmentalists encouraged voters to reject this "choice" by writing "No dams" on their ballot papers. This would render the ballots informal; nevertheless, more than 38 percent of voters did so. This protest had a powerful effect, and the case was eventually won by environmentalists in the High Court.

[65] In fact, the Australian Electoral Commission carefully tracks, records, and analyzes blank and deliberately spoiled ballots for the purposes of interpretation.

[66] It should be noted, however, that in compulsory-voting systems that systematically sanction noncompliance, it seems to provide some benefit to far-right parties (Birch, *Full Participation*: 125).

[67] Bennett and Resnick, "Implications of Nonvoting"; see also Verba and Nie, *Participation in America*.

[68] Obviously, it is preferable if the functions of elections are performed well rather than poorly. I simply dispute that excluding the less well-informed and competent is either a desirable or effective long-term solution.

has shown that any group of adults excluded from the *demos* will be lethally weakened in its own defense; and an exclusive *demos* will fail to protect the interests of those who are excluded."[69] Therefore, Dahl deems almost all exclusions unjustified.

Finally, I am skeptical of the assumption that people who fail to vote are, by and large, *choosing* not to because they perceive it as a means to "self-government" or else feel contented, are not affected, are "principled," or do not feel neglected. Such assumptions rely on a naive model of political quiescence. Although it is doubtless true that there are some people who abstain from voting for these kinds of reasons, it is also true that, generally speaking, the more socially and economically marginalized a person is, the less likely she is to vote. We should therefore be skeptical of any explanation for low turnout that relies on the assumption that disadvantage is correlated with satisfaction. Silence does not necessarily connote consent: survey data consistently tell us that abstainers are less satisfied with the state of democracy than are voters. We know, for example, that young American nonvoters tend to be considerably less satisfied than voters about the state of their democracy, whereas alienated all-age Americans are "less likely to vote, even after controlling for all of the other demographic factors that affect voter turnout."[70] In their study of Senate voters and nonvoters, Lyn Ragsdale and Jerrold Rusk found that the most common characteristic of Senate nonvoters was "dissatisfaction."[71] British youth, whose voting participation is notoriously low, report continued interest in politics but "very negative perceptions of the world of politics."[72] Canadian nonvoters partially

[69] Dahl, *After the Revolution*: 127.

[70] P. L. Southwell, "The Effect of Political Alienation on Voter Turnout, 1964–2000," *Journal of Political and Military Sociology* 36 (2008): 131–45; for a contrary view, see S. E. Bennett and D. Resnick, "Implications of Nonvoting." See also R. Brody and B. Page, "Indifference, Alienation and Rational Decisions," *Public Choice* 15 (1973): 1–17; Pettersen, "Comparing Non-Voters in the USA and Norway"; A. J. Nownes, "Primaries, General Elections, and Voter Turnout: A Multinomial Logit Model of the Decision to Vote," *American Politics Quarterly* 20 (1992): 205–26.

[71] L. Ragsdale and J. G. Rusk, "Who Are Nonvoters? Profiles from the 1990 Senate Elections," *American Journal of Political Science* 37 (1993): 721–46.

[72] M. Henn, M. Weinstein, and D. Wring, "A Generation Apart? Youth and Political Participation in Britain," *British Journal of Politics and International Relations* 4 (2002): 167–92; M. Henn, M. Weinstein, and S. Forrest, "Uninterested Youth? Young People's Attitudes towards Party Politics in Britain," *Political Studies* 53 (2005):

attribute their civic withdrawal to negative perceptions of politicians, government, and candidates,[73] whereas cynicism about politicians is a major predictor of nonvoting in Norway.[74] Aggregate-level studies yield similar results: Grönlund and Setälä's cross-national study of the effect of political trust on election turnout in twenty-two European democracies found that perceived legitimacy or "diffuse support" for the democratic system (i.e., trust in parliament and satisfaction with the democratic system) has a significant positive effect on turnout.[75]

Because disadvantage is a major predictor of abstention, there is clearly more to explaining low turnout than the exercise of "principled deference"; autonomy; "free, equal and reasoned collective action"; self-government; and democratic choice. It is no coincidence that declining turnout is correlated with declining feelings of trust in government, politicians, and democratic institutions in general. As Declan Bannon has observed with regard to declining levels of political trust in Britain, "If politics were a commercial product, the Marketing Director would be replaced."[76]

6.9 Is Abstention Necessarily a Positive Choice? Abstention as a Norm

It might be said that abstention is an individual decision and consistent with democracy even if it runs counter to an individual's best interests; "since democracy is grounded in self-government, in individual liberty, the freedom to make mistakes would seem to be part

556–78; J. Dermody, S. Hammer-Lloyd, and R. Scullion, "Young People and Voting Behaviour: Alienated Youth and(or) an Interested and Critical Citizenry?" *European Journal of Marketing* 44 (2010): 421–35.

[73] J. H. Pammet and L. LeDuc, *Explaining the Turnout Decline in Canadian Federal Elections: A New Survey of Non-Voters* (Ottawa: Elections Canada, 2003): 6.

[74] Pettersen, "Comparing Non-Voters in the USA and Norway": 354–5.

[75] They also found that trust in politicians enhances turnout, although less dramatically, and that satisfaction with the incumbent government does not affect turnout. K. Grönlund and M. Setälä, "Political Trust, Satisfaction and Voter Turnout," *Comparative European Politics* 5 (4) (2007):400–22. See also K. Lundell, "Compulsory Voting, Civic Participation and Political Trust," *Representation* 48 (2) (2012): 221–34.

[76] Declan B. Bannon, "Electoral Participation and Non-Voter Segmentation," *Journal of Nonprofit and Public Sector Marketing* 14 (2010): 109–27.

of a democratic society."[77] But is abstention – and its self-defeating consequences – really a positive choice? And if it is, why is it a "choice" favored predominantly by the disadvantaged? The answer to this question seems to have little to do with either choice or alleged contentment with the political status quo. In voluntary-voting systems, the disadvantaged are subject to a paralyzing coordination problem at election time because the norm of voting that prevails among educated, prosperous, white, and older populations has failed to become firmly established among poorer, less well-educated, and younger populations. Here it is normal *not* to vote. Where social norms discourage a particular form of behavior, it may be irrational to conflict with the norm, even where the norm has maladaptive long-term consequences for members of the nonvoting group. Members of nonvoting minorities may indeed make the quite reasonable calculation that it would be irrational to be the only member of their social group to bother voting, and even if they do not make this calculation, it would still be true. The coordination problem that besets habitual nonvoters is exacerbated by the fact that they are less likely to be targeted by the mobilization efforts of parties.[78] For example, parties are more likely to contact citizens from higher socioeconomic status (SES) groups[79] and less likely to contact the young.[80] Political advertising at election times is also "overwhelmingly" targeted at older audiences.[81]

That voting is at least partly norm-driven is confirmed by research on voting behavior and attitudes. According to results generated by polling in Britain, "civic duty" and "habit" are the primary reasons why "three in five adults vote in a general election even

[77] Keith Dowding, Robert E. Goodin, and Carole Pateman, "Introduction," in K. Dowding, R. E. Goodin, and C. Pateman (eds.), *Justice and Democracy: Essays for Brian Barry* (Cambridge, UK: Cambridge University Press, 2004): 9. This is not their position necessarily. They are just stating the position rhetorically.

[78] P. W. Wielhouwer, "Releasing the Fetters: Parties and Mobilization of the African-American Electorate," *Journal of Politics* 62 (2000): 206–22; P. W. Wielhouwer, "Strategic Canvassing by the Political Parties," *American Review of Politics* 16 (1995): 213–38; Highton and Wolfinger, "The Political Implications of Higher Turnout."

[79] J. Gershtenson, "Mobilization Strategies of the Democrats and Republicans, 1956–2000," *Political Research Quarterly* 56 (2003): 293–308.

[80] Wattenberg, *Is Voting for Young People?* 113–15.

[81] Martin Wattenberg, *Where Have All the Voters Gone?* (Cambridge, MA: Harvard University Press, 2002): 99.

in the worst of cases."[82] Similarly, in their study of American and Dutch absenteeism, Smeenk and colleagues found that the decision to vote depended "on the norms of the social group" to which the person belonged.[83]

For Richard Hasen, low turnout and its attendant dysfunctions are best thought of as a case of "social failure." Social failure occurs when a social norm that would otherwise maximize a group's welfare fails to emerge.[84] Because compulsory voting ensures full turnout, it is able to overcome two of the most common causes of "rational abstention": informational uncertainty about other potential voters' intentions, on the one hand, and the transaction and opportunity costs of voting, on the other. Compulsion enables voters to overcome the problem of insufficient information not only about the real value of an individual vote but also about the intentions of other voters. When a poor, unemployed, lone parent abstains from voting in American elections, she is behaving both rationally and irrationally. Whereas it would be rational in one sense for her to vote (because doing so would protect her interests and those of others like her), at the same time, it will only be rational for her to vote if she can be sure that everyone else in similar circumstances to hers will have the same idea (in fact, she knows they probably won't). Because the voluntary system evokes irrationality, in this case, the mass abstention of those most in need of the protection voting can afford, it will be rational for her to stay at home and preserve her scarce resources, knowing as she does that others like her will most likely make the same calculation. So she *rationally abstains*.[85]

[82] Market and Opinion Research International (MORI), "What Does the Election Tell Us about Consumers" (2001); available at: www.mori.com/pubinfo/rmm-res2001.shtml.

[83] W. Smeenk, N. de Graaf, and W. Ultee, "Thuisblijven bij Verkiezingen in Nederland en de Verenigde Staten [Non-Voting in the Netherlands and the United States]," *Mens en Maatschappij* 70 (1995): 220–241. See also Market and Opinion Research International (MORI), "Survey of Attitudes during the 2001 General Election Campaign" (2001); available at: http://www.mori.com/polls/2001/elec_comm_rep.shtml (last accessed January 7, 2004).

[84] Hasen, "Voting without Law?" 2135, 2167.

[85] According to some rational choice theory, even if the subject in question *did* know that large numbers of those in her social group were intending to vote, it would still be rational for her to abstain in order to free ride. I am conflicted about whether free riding, strictly understood, is the best way of understanding voting abstention, particularly among minority groups (see Chapter 8); nevertheless, even were it possible

Mandatory voting takes this "prisoner's dilemma" factor out of the decision about whether or not to bother voting, thereby resolving a key collective-action problem. Compulsion removes the problem of insufficient information simply by virtue of its existence; knowing that other voters with similar interests to mine are going to vote overcomes any uncertainty about the value of my vote and frees me from having to weigh "opportunity costs" against benefits in an environment where resources and information are scarce. Rather than perceiving the compulsion as yet another unwelcome form of state coercion, compulsory voting may be better understood as a coordination necessity in mass societies of individuated strangers unable to communicate and coordinate their preferences. The single votes of traditional nonvoters are no longer isolated drops in oceans; they now have much greater value because such voters are already organized into meaningful blocs of electoral power. (I explore this issue further in Chapter 8).

It might be retorted that some nonvoting groups are so small and marginalized that it would make no difference if they bothered to vote. But the interests of such groups can be (and usually are) protected by the compelled enfranchisement of other, larger groups of disadvantaged, habitual abstainers such as the young, who tend to be more sympathetic to the plight of other disadvantaged (numerically smaller) minorities such as the unemployed, single parents, or indigenous people.[86]

Compulsion also has a tendency to remove many of the opportunity and transaction costs that normally discourage voters. This is not because of any inherent properties of compulsion but because in well-administered regimes (the only kind I am endorsing here), governments have recognized that they have an obligation to ensure that this imposed duty is not difficult or impossible to perform, in much the same way that governments provide public schools in order to ensure

for her to free ride in this situation, compulsory voting would prevent this from happening. Further, a great number of people who are fairly sure that others in their social group intend to vote still *do* vote. Rational choice theorists sometimes associate this behavior with the "expressive" function of voting. This pleasure or benefit is alleged to be similar to the pleasure we get from cheering on our favorite football team. It doesn't really do much to affect outcomes, but it feels good; it is "cheering for its own sake" or having your say (Loren Lomasky, "The Booth and Consequences: Do Voters Get What They Want?" *Reason* 24 [6] [1992]: 30–4).

[86] Wattenberg, "Why Don't More Americans Vote?"

that the obligation of compulsory school attendance does not place an undue burden on parents (see Chapter 8 for further elaboration of this point). In compulsory systems such as Australia and Belgium, electoral commissions usually take on most of the work associated with registration and voting so that voting is a relatively easy process.[87] The state assumes a high degree of responsibility for making feasible what it requires of voters. It thus makes little sense to use the concept of rational abstention in compulsory settings because compulsion automatically removes the problem of insufficient information simply by virtue of its existence; meanwhile, the opportunity and transaction costs are almost all offset by the state. In fact, it would be *irrational* (although obviously possible) to abstain in compulsory systems because it is much easier to vote than to provide letters of excuse in them.

In any case, the poor not only have a coordination problem at election time: they also have a resources problem. They are poor "in the resources most useful in politics – time, money, connections" and "sophisticated communication skills." This is why education is such a good predictor of turnout. The relationship between education and an ability to coordinate politically is quite important. According to Sidney Verba, education makes people more informed and "more efficacious." It makes "it easier for them to see connections between their values/preferences and governmental action" and engenders the norm that one ought to participate. Education increases "the store of resources that people have," including "skills that make one an effective participant" and income for campaign contributions. It also puts "individuals into networks" of others "who are active and who can help them act effectively."[88] The socially disadvantaged face more challenges in gathering information about politics and voting and are typically less "knowledgeable about politics"; this has an impact on their electoral participation.[89]

[87] Voters don't have to forego too much in terms of opportunities for work or leisure. Also, opportunity and transaction costs (relative to benefits) are lowered in a compulsory setting because voting has more value. Under a system of guaranteed universal participation, it is (both long and short term) rational for the unemployed single parent to vote. Informational certainty about the voting or nonvoting intentions of others with similar interests means that foregoing a day at home will be worthwhile.

[88] Verba, "Would the Dream of Political Equality": 668.

[89] Gallego, "Understanding Unequal Turnout": 241.

Voting is clearly more costly for the disadvantaged, and these costs come in all shapes and sizes. This is vividly demonstrated when considering something as simple as the effect of bad weather on turnout. In the American context, Gomez and colleagues have found "that when compared to normal conditions, rain significantly reduces voter participation by a rate of just less than 1 percent per inch, while an inch of snowfall decreases turnout by almost 0.5 percent."[90] Bad weather has also been shown to affect election results, and this has benefited the vote share of the Republican Party in Electoral College outcomes (such as the 1960 and 2000 presidential elections). Disadvantaged voters (who are more typically Democrats)[91] are more sensitive to the costs of voting; bad weather seems to be "the last straw" for these marginal voters,[92] who are already less predisposed to vote in the first place. This is why voting is notoriously low among the homeless, who, even when they have the formal opportunity (i.e., legal right) to vote, lack almost all the resources needed to realize that opportunity, such as, an education, a home for registration purposes, private transportation to attend polls in bad weather, resources to stay in the media loop, and social networks of habitual voters. Therefore, simple legal entitlement to vote does not satisfy Dahl's "effective participation" criterion, which requires that procedures "be evaluated according to the adequacy of the opportunities they provide for, and the relative costs they impose on, expression and participation by the *demos* in making binding decisions."[93]

6.10 Concluding Remarks

Low turnout is not a neutral, benign, or self-equilibrating phenomenon, and it does not appear to serve any positive democratic function. It does not necessarily denote consent or satisfaction with government, and neither is it always and obviously a sign of citizens exercising

[90] B. T. Gomez, T. G. Hansford, and G. A. Krause, "The Republicans Should Pray for Rain: Weather, Turnout and Voting in U.S. Presidential Elections," *Journal of Politics* 69 (2007): 649–63.

[91] Sides et al., "If Everyone Had Voted."

[92] Because the poor are less likely to have private transportation (as well as many other resources that make it easier to vote), bad weather makes it too costly for many of them to vote.

[93] Dahl, *After the Revolution*: 102–3.

self-government and democratic choice. It does, however, perpetuate elite dominance, social inequality, and unrepresentativeness. It therefore impedes the ability of democratic governments to do what they are supposed to do: to be "of the people, by the people, and for the people."

Low turnout invariably means that individual citizens are marginalized by virtue of their membership in the broader marginalized social group to which they belong. This, in turn, undermines the legitimacy of the democracy in question not only because turnout is low but also because it is *biased*. Turnout levels affect government behavior in a manner that favors voters over nonvoters. But, even if low turnout did not have this effect, because it invariably means socially uneven and incomplete participation, it will always fail to satisfy the criteria of equality, inclusiveness, effective participation, and final control of the agenda that are required to make electoral systems fully procedurally democratic.

Some defenders of low turnout believe that we can determine (or at least confirm) what the *demos* wants electorally by means other than elections, be they polls, postelection surveys, voting lotteries, or random samples. But none of these mechanisms is the recognized, authoritative procedure for making binding decisions in representative democracies: rather, it is voting in elections that represents the "decisive stage." This is the real world, and these mooted alternatives are just fantasies that will never be adopted as alternative mechanisms.

Because turnout matters and demonstrably affects political outputs, and because compulsory voting is the only reliable means by which to achieve consistently high and socially even voter turnout, requiring people to vote is justified.

7

Is Compulsory Voting an Unjustified Burden on Personal Autonomy?

Is There a Right Not to Vote?

7.1 Introduction

A common criticism of compulsory voting is that it represents an unwarranted burden on individual liberty. In making this argument, some critics claim that it violates an assumed right not to vote. Obviously, if there is such thing as a right not to vote, compulsory voting is an illegitimate practice.

While there is no doubt that compulsory voting violates the principle of democratic choice, I argue in this chapter that requiring people to vote is a justified burden on personal liberty. I give both rights- and consequence-based reasons for this position while acknowledging that the rights- and consequence-based reasons are somewhat related.

I make three broad arguments from the rights perspective: the first is that because the right to vote partly defines the structure of democratic government, it cannot be waived; in other words, there is no right not to vote. Second, I argue that because voting is the *master* right that protects all other rights, it should be exercised. Third, although requiring people to vote might violate one interpretation of liberty – negative liberty – it can serve and strengthen a number of other interpretations of liberty, among them nondomination, autonomy, and positive liberty, because of its demonstrated capacity to empower the politically and economically weak. Compulsory voting can therefore be justified as a reasonable infringement of autonomy.

But there are also consequentialist justifications for denying a right not to vote. I offer a number of broad arguments here: the first is that because failure to vote has bad consequences for both democracy and the welfare of certain social groups, we owe it to others to vote. Voting is not, as is commonly thought, a waivable privilege but an inalienable duty-right. In order to promote overall the values of liberty, autonomy, and democratic self-government, sacrificing the freedom to abstain from voting is justified. The second consequentialist justification offered is that voluntary voting generates a collective-action problem that compulsory voting is able to solve; it is thereby better able to serve democratic *desiderata*.

It should be reiterated before proceeding that the following argument applies only to voting within properly functioning and authentic democracies.

7.2 A Right Not to Vote?

When people refer to the right to vote, they generally speak of it as something both highly desirable and, in most cases, hard won; as a result, despite the fact that the existence of a right not to vote is frequently asserted, the issue has not attracted much sustained scholarly attention. But there are some who not only object to the expectation that citizens should vote but go so far as to claim that there is a right not to vote and that it is deserving of the same respect and legal protection as the right *to* vote. For example, Anthony Ciccone has argued that "[t]he hallmark of a free society is that citizens are free to make their own choices including whether or not to vote in a given election contest." He insists that "[t]he logical inverse of the right to vote is a right not to vote" and that because it is "just as important as the right to vote," it should attract the same levels of "strict [legal] scrutiny" when threatened.[1] Others agree that the alleged right "to abstain" is not only important but just as "precious as the right to vote."[2] Jeffrey Blomberg's assertion of the existence of a right to abstain rests on the

[1] Ciccone, "The Constitutional Right to Vote": 347–8.

[2] Lever, "Compulsory Voting": 15–16; A. Lever, "Is Compulsory Voting Justified?" *Public Reason* 1 (2009): 57–74.

belief that "abstention involves a form of political expression"[3]; like Ciccone, he also demands that it be afforded legal protection equal to that of the right to vote.[4] Relatedly, for Jonas Lerman, requiring people to vote "is proscribed by international rights law" insofar as it interferes with political "free expression" and the right to "hold opinions."[5]

Apathy notwithstanding, there are a number of good reasons why people may not wish to vote: for example, some electors may wish to boycott the polls as a form of political protest. Others lament the poor quality of candidates and therefore the lack of real choice at election time (e.g., Judd in *Judd* v. *McKeon* [1926] 38 CLR 380). Some, finding that none of the candidates are worth voting for, consider the compulsion to choose as tantamount to a compulsion to lie (e.g., *Faderson* v. *Bridger* [1971] 126 CLR 271). Nevertheless, to others it may seem perverse to want to waive such an important right as the right to vote. Presumably, those who argue for the right not to vote do not want to waive their voting rights absolutely and permanently. They seem to want either the right to drop in and out of electoral participation as it suits them or else retain their voting rights without ever exercising them.[6]

Because Australia is a signatory to the International Covenant on Civil and Political Rights (ICCPR), Jonas Lerman is surprised that "anti-compulsion groups in Australia and elsewhere have not challenged compulsory voting laws on this basis."[7] But perhaps this is not really so surprising given that the provisions in international law could be equally interpreted as *endorsing* any electoral institution

[3] Thomas Hoffman and Timothy Ulrich, the plaintiffs in *Hoffman* v. *Maryland* (928 F.2d 646, 648–49, 4th Cir. 1991), have also argued (albeit unsuccessfully) that the right not to vote is fundamental because it is a form of political expression. Whether or not abstention is a form of political expression is discussed in Chapter 6, especially note 63.

[4] J. A. Blomberg, "Protecting the Right Not to Vote from Voter Purge Statutes," *Fordham Law Review* 64 (1995): 1015–50.

[5] J. Lerman, "Voting Rites: Deliberative Democracy and Compulsory Voting in the United States" (unpublished paper, 2009): 26; available at: http://papers.ssrn.com/sol3/papers.cfm?abstract_id=1600929 (last accessed November 21, 2010).

[6] For example, Thomas Hoffman and Timothy Ulrich, the plaintiffs in *Hoffman* v. *Maryland* (928 F.2d 646, 648–49, 4th Cir., 1991), had stopped voting altogether, but they wanted to remain registered as voters and asked the court to recognize their right not to vote.

[7] Lerman, "Voting Rites": 26.

that achieves high and socially even levels of voting inclusion under authentically democratic conditions.

The right to vote is set out in the Universal Declaration on Human Rights (Article 21); it is also set out in the International Covenant on the Elimination of Racial Discrimination (Article 5[c]). Most mature democracies are signatories to the International Covenant on Civil and Political Rights (ICCPR), Article 25 of which states that every citizen "shall have the right and the opportunity" without "distinctions" to vote and that elections should be "genuine" and characterized by "universal and equal suffrage." The ICCPR is silent on the right to waive rights (this is hardly surprising given that the ICCPR was intended as a corrective to a *lack* of recognized rights); it is, however, highly suggestive of duties on the part of states and their citizens to actively create congenial conditions for their exercise.[8] Nevertheless, in most industrialized democracies, many categories of persons are not entitled to vote, and although challenges to suffrage disentitlement generally result in courts determining that voting is a fundamental right that should be hard to defease, such courts have never said that it cannot be defeased at all.[9]

Even in a setting such as Australia, where voting is compulsory, the requirement to vote is not absolute. The Commonwealth Electoral Act of 1918 (Section 245) exempts from voting those who are "itinerant," living abroad, or based in the Antarctic at the time of the election (the secrecy of the ballot cannot be assured for those living in the Antarctic, hence the exemption). There is also the rather cautiously worded caveat found in Subsection 14 that electors may abstain if

[8] According to the Preamble, "the individual, having duties to other individuals and to the community to which he belongs, is under a responsibility to strive for the promotion and observance of the rights recognized in the present Covenant." Article 25 provides that "[e]very citizen shall have the right and the opportunity, ... without unreasonable restrictions, ... [t]o vote ... at genuine periodic elections." Similarly, under the Universal Declaration of Human Rights (Article 29, Sections 1 and 2), "Everyone has duties to the community in which alone the free and full development of his personality is possible" and "[i]n the exercise of his rights and freedoms, everyone shall be subject only to such limitations as are determined by law solely for the purpose of securing due recognition and respect for the rights and freedoms of others and of meeting the just requirements of morality, public order and the general welfare in a democratic society."

[9] Lisa Hill and Cornelia Koch, "The Voting Rights of Incarcerated Australian Citizens," *Australian Journal of Political Science* 42 (2011): 2013–228.

voting conflicts with a "religious duty." The reasoning behind these exemptions is a little opaque (and has nowhere been clarified), but it seems to be that the compulsion is void where the burden on voters to conform to the law is unreasonable. The violation of religious belief, for example, is taken to be too burdensome to justify the compulsion (religious freedom is protected under the Australian constitution). Practical difficulties associated with voting attendance are also recognized: for example, itinerant workers obviously find it difficult to meet the residency requirement that would keep their enrollment up to date and valid. Where certain voters are unable to be afforded the same rights as other citizens (such as the right to vote in secret), the compulsion is also suspended.[10] Significantly, though, Australian law does not specifically concede that it is permitting voters to waive rights. Instead, voters are apparently being released from a *duty* either because of the practical difficulties of performing the duty or because other competing duties are found to be more compelling.[11]

So, while electoral law seems to recognize that the *requirement* to vote can be waived and that the right to vote can be defeased, this is not the same as admitting that the *right* to vote is "waivable," alienable, or "invertible."

7.3 Legal Tests So Far of the "Right Not to Vote"

Does the right to vote imply the right not to vote? What do the courts say? There have been few cases of voters alleging a right not to vote, but

[10] Albeit inconsistently: those living in the Antarctic are not required to vote because the secrecy of their vote cannot be assured, whereas the blind and visually impaired *are* required to vote, even though their necessary dependence on assistance in voting makes secrecy impossible.

[11] I would also suggest that Australian citizens living in the Antarctic (who are not required to vote) are not released from the duty because the right to vote in secrecy trumps the duty to vote but rather because the state, due to factors outside its control, has not been able to universalize voting conditions, and it is the consciousness of this failure that triggers the release from the obligation. This is just a surmise based on the fact that the blind and visually impaired are required to vote despite the fact that they have never been able to vote in secret (although they now have this opportunity with recently introduced innovations in e-voting in Australia). My point is that talk of rights is carefully avoided, with a focus instead on the responsibility on the part of the state to provide uniform voting access. When that responsibility is unmet, the obligation on citizens is relaxed.

in all that I have been able to detect, courts have denied its existence. Such a right has been tested most often in Australian courts.[12] The most important test case was *Judd* v. *McKeon*.[13] In 1926 Mr. Judd, a socialist, challenged the validity of Section 245 of the Commonwealth Electoral Act of 1918 that makes failure to vote an offense. He said that he did not want to vote because all the candidates on offer were implicated in the perpetuation of capitalism, "unemployment," "prostitution," and "exploitation of the working class" and that he and other members of the Socialist Labour Party were "prohibited from voting" for any of the candidates.[14] The court rejected this argument, and Mr. Judd was fined ten shillings by the Central Police Court in Sydney. The judgment in *Judd* v. *McKeon* that there is no right not to vote has been endorsed in all subsequent cases.[15] In fact, there are dicta in the recent case of *Rowe* v. *Electoral Commissioner*[16] suggesting that because there "is a form of irreversible evolution in the development of electoral laws toward maximum participation in elections," any law that rendered voting voluntary would be constitutionally invalid due to its negative effect on maximizing participation.[17]

Even in countries that do not have compulsory voting and yet do (arguably) have constitutional protection for suffrage rights,[18] no right not to vote has been found to exist. In the United States, the right not to vote has been indirectly challenged a number of times via constitutional

[12] This is despite the fact that it is fairly easy to abstain in Australia. Further, people are automatically exempt from the requirement to vote if they reside more than eight kilometers from a polling place or are "itinerant, living abroad, or based in the Antarctic at the time of the election." Electors may also abstain if voting conflicts with a religious duty, and they can avoid fines in the case of illness or misadventure.

[13] *Judd* v. *McKeon*, 1926, 38 CLR 380.

[14] Australian Electoral Commission (AEC), "Compulsory Voting," *Electoral Backgrounder No. 8* (Canberra, June 1, 1999); available at: http://www.aec.gov.au/pubs/ backgrounders/vol_8/main.htm (last accessed August 6, 2003).

[15] See, e.g., *Lubke* v. *Little* (1970, VR 807); *Krosch* v. *Springell*; ex parte Krosch (1974), QdR 107; *O'Brien* v. *Warden* (1981, 37 ACTR 13); AEC, "Compulsory Voting."

[16] *Rowe* v. *Electoral Commissioner* (2010, 234, CLR 1).

[17] Anne Twomey, "Deliberative Democracy, Compulsory Voting and the Will of the People," Law of Deliberative Democracy Workshop, New York University, April 6, 2013.

[18] The U.S. Constitution does not explicitly guarantee a right to vote, but it does proscribe abridgements of the "right to vote" (Amendments XV and XIX). In addition, the constitutional guarantee of a republican form of government has sometimes been cited as evidence of such a right (Abraham, *Compulsory Voting*: 5).

challenges to voter purge statutes. All have been unsuccessful,[19] including one that explicitly argued that voter purge statutes violate the right *not* to vote and thereby express political dissatisfaction.[20]

In 1971, the European Court of Human Rights heard a case in which the litigant claimed that compulsory voting violated an express right not to vote.[21] Citing Article 9 of the European Convention on Human Rights ("freedom of thought, conscience and religion"), an Austrian citizen (X) argued that in any free election, "freedom of conscience and freedom to manifest one's beliefs in public" ought not to "be limited by coercive measures and threats of punishment." He noted that the ballot paper only listed two candidates, neither of whom he considered "a suitable Federal President." Having to choose, he suggested, was "even worse than being denied the right to vote."[22] The court dismissed the case as "manifestly ill-founded" within the meaning of the Convention, ruling that, provided there was no compulsion to mark the ballot formally and that the voter was free to "hand in either a blank or spoiled ballot," compulsory voting does not violate Article 9 of the European Convention on Human Rights.[23]

So no court has recognized an explicit "right not to vote." But *should* such a right be recognized? The fact that it has gone unrecognized does not mean that it is undeserving of it.

7.4 Can the Right to Vote Be Inverted or Waived? Perpetuating Democracy

As mentioned, many voting libertarians seem to assume that the existence of any right automatically implies the right to invert it. The

[19] Blomberg, "Protecting the Right Not to Vote": 1017. There are three cases where state courts did find voter purges unconstitutional, but not as violations of an alleged right not to vote. In one case, the statute purging inactive voter registration was found to be "a severe impediment on the right to vote for a substantial number of citizens" [*Michigan State UAW Community Action Program Council* v. *Austin*, 198 N.W. 2d 388, 385, 390 (Mich. 1972)]. In another, the court found that the law requiring annual registration in order to vote was an unconstitutional violation of equal protection under the Texas constitution [*Beare* v. *Briscoe*, 498 F.2d, 244, 248 (5th Cir. 1974)]. See also *Beare* v. *Smith*, 321, F.Supp. 1100, 1108 (S.D. Tex. 1971) (Blomberg, "Protecting the Right Not to Vote": 1017, n. 18).

[20] *Hoffman* v. *Maryland*, 928 F.2d 646, 648–49 (4th Cir. 1991).

[21] See *X* v. *Austria*, Appn. No. 4982/71.

[22] European Court of Human Rights, *Yearbook*: 468–72.

[23] *Ibid.*: 473–4.

assertion that the right to vote implies the right not to vote seems intuitively plausible and uncontroversial; after all, millions of citizens worldwide routinely fail to vote with impunity.[24] Whereas many people do fail to vote, it is unclear whether doing so is the same as exercising a particular right. Simply inverting the positive right with a bit of lexical adjustment does not automatically yield an unassailable negative right. For example, it would be nonsensical to argue that because I have a right to be free from physical assault, I also have a right *not* to be free from physical assault. Are all or any rights "invertible," "waivable," or alienable?

The assumption that rights can be waived is problematic, and this has been shown repeatedly in landmark American legal cases. It has been found, for example, that there is no right to waive the rights to workplace safety, to a minimum wage, to equal employment opportunities, and to the right of a criminal defendant to be tried only when competent. Some cases have also confirmed that an individual's ability to waive constitutional rights in exchange for government benefits is limited.[25] Some rights (such as the right to bear arms) can be waived, but this does not mean that *all* rights can be waived; neither does it prove the general existence of inverse rights. The U.S. Supreme Court observed this in *Singer* v. *United States*, in which it upheld a federal rule that requires government consent for a criminal defendant to waive her right to a jury trial.[26] According to the Court, "[t]he ability to waive a constitutional right does not ordinarily carry with it the right to insist upon the opposite of that right."[27] So even if the right to vote were waivable, this would not mean that it is also invertible, meaning that it would not yield a right not to vote.

Apart from conceiving rights as invertible and waivable, right-not-to-vote advocates also seem to take for granted that rights are

[24] This looks like waiving the right to vote, but I would suggest that it is more like failing to exercise it, for reasons that are made clearer later.

[25] For example, the court in *Perry* v. *Sinderman*, 408 U.S. 593, 597–98 (1972), found that "government employees may not waive their right to free speech as a condition of employment," whereas *Sherbert* v. *Verner*, 374 U.S. 398 (1963), held that "a state cannot condition the availability of unemployment benefits on a beneficiary's waiving her right to the free exercise of religion" (HLR, "The Case for Compulsory Voting": 599).

[26] *Singer* v. *United States*, 380 US 24 (1965).

[27] HLR, "The Case for Compulsory Voting": 599.

individuated and divisible, existing only to serve personal ends. But the right to vote is also a social right intended to serve the social *condition* of democracy. It is "made *possible* only by the existence of organized political communities" and is possessed by individuals by virtue of their membership in communities.[28] Rights do not exist to protect individual liberty alone; therefore, a right does not always imply its inverse. Individual rights often serve public as well as private interests. For example, while the (U.S.) right to a trial by jury protects individuals from the state, it also performs an important collective function by ensuring the legitimacy and accuracy of criminal trials.[29]

If a particular right defines the structure of government or even the structure of a decent society, then any individual's desire to waive it is irrelevant. The example Seth Kreimer gives in making this point is the right to be free from involuntary servitude. The Thirteenth Amendment of the United States Constitution was designed not just to protect individual liberty but also to eradicate a practice that violently conflicted with the ideals of a free society.[30] Should any citizen wish to assent to a life of slavery, the state would not recognize her attempt to waive her right to equal protection because that state has an interest in maintaining a society free from slavery. The same would be true of many other rights, such as a right to education and the right to vote. The right to vote is not just an individual right; it also exists for the purpose of constituting and perpetuating representative democracy, which is a collective benefit.[31]

Therefore, requiring that people vote is not justified merely because of its good consequences because this could justify all manner of unreasonable compulsions. Requiring people to vote is justified because voting is central to the existence and perpetuation of a cherished way of life on which so much else depends. Indeed, representative democracy is substantially *constituted* by voting.

[28] Jones, "In Defense of Apathy": 89.

[29] HLR, "The Case for Compulsory Voting": 599–600; S. F. Kreimer, "Allocation Sanctions: The Problem of Negative Rights in a Positive State," *University of Pennsylvania Law Review* 132 (6) (1984): 1293–1397.

[30] Kreimer, "The Problem of Negative Rights": 1387–8.

[31] HLR, "The Case for Compulsory Voting": 600.

7.5 Does the Harm of Failure to Vote Justify Compelling People to Vote?

Those who insist on the right not to vote are inclined to the view that failure to vote is either not harmful or is a positive service to democracy. A typical argument is that failure to vote, especially in systems where this is easy, is rarely universal and so democracy is able to survive.[32] As H. B. Mayo puts it, we can rely on the fact that there are always enough people interested "in politics and voting to work the political machinery."[33] But, while the "machinery" of democracy might still seem to be working in low-turnout settings, it is debatable whether it is actually working properly.

As shown in Chapter 6, failure to vote harms the interests of members of nonvoting groups. But even if I conceded that the self-harm caused by nonvoting does not justify forcing people to vote,[34] there are still "harm" grounds for insisting that people should vote. Because failure to vote is not randomly distributed, and because it affects government behavior in ways that objectively hurt the interests of the disadvantaged, it impugns a number of fundamental democratic *desiderata* such as representativeness, popular sovereignty, inclusiveness, and political equality. It also distorts some of the primary functions of elections. The functions I have in mind are giving citizens influence over policy makers via the communication of preferences[35]; maximizing gains, minimizing losses, and directing resource allocation toward one's social group[36]; enabling individuals to exercise their interests in self-protection, self-government, and self-development[37]; legitimizing the political system by the communication of either consent or

[32] See, e.g., Saunders, "Increasing Turnout": 71; Ciccone, "The Constitutional Right to Vote": 351; Lomasky and Brennan, "Duty to Vote?"

[33] Mayo, "A Note": 319–22.

[34] I argue that compulsory voting is a form of self-paternalism in Chapter 8.

[35] G. B. Powell Jr., *Elections as Instruments of Democracy: Majoritarian and Proportional Visions* (New Haven, CT: Yale University Press, 2000): 3.

[36] Anthony Downs, *An Economic Theory of Democracy* (New York: Harper and Row, 1957): 45–6.

[37] John Stuart Mill wrote that suffrage is vital to protect individuals "from the abuse of … authority" and "in order that they may not be misgoverned" (J. S. Mill, "Considerations on Representative Government," in J. Gray (ed., intro.), *On Liberty and Other Essays* (Oxford, UK: Oxford University Press, 1991): 342; chaps. 8–10, *passim*).

dissent[38]; expressing identification and alignment with the greater community[39]; and expressing oneself politically.[40]

Jean-Jacques Rousseau famously wrote that "[a]s soon as any man says of the State *What does it matter to me?* The State may be given up for lost."[41] Being enabled to enjoy the benefits of democratic life, of living in a democracy instead of, say, a dictatorship, requires participatory effort. But participating in the mutually advantageous cooperative enterprise of democracy often requires a willingness to give up some freedom, a willingness that, in the name of fairness, should be reciprocal.[42] Note that for Bhikhu Parekh, such obligations do not require everyone to be active all the time, only that "enough" people are engaged.[43] Parekh posits political obligation as analogous to the obligation to report an accident in that although I am obliged to act, I need not if someone has already reported it.[44] Although it is agreed that in a democracy *all* are not obliged to be active *all* the time, in the case of voting, Parekh's analogy is misleading. The obligation to vote is nothing like reporting an accident because an accident only has to be reported by one person for the obligation to be properly fulfilled; further, it doesn't matter who the person is in order for the act to be performed properly. It is different with voting because it matters vitally who and how many actually vote when, in fact, participation is low and socially unrepresentative. So, while we don't all need to be active all the time, all of us need to be politically active on one day every three or so years.

7.6 Voting Rights and Voting Classes

It was noted in Chapter 6 that habitual nonvoters are subject to a disabling coordination problem that makes it irrational for them to

[38] For example, Katz, *Democracy and Elections*; Gans, "The Empty Ballot Box."

[39] A. Winkler, "Expressive Voting," New York University, Vol. 68 (1993) (Los Angeles: UCLA School of Law Research Paper No. 09–14, April 1, 2009); available at: http://ssrn.com/abstract=1371799.

[40] G. Brennan and L. Lomasky, *Democracy and Decision: The Pure Theory of Electoral Preference* (Cambridge, UK: Cambridge University Press, 1993): 25.

[41] Jean-Jacques Rousseau, "The Social Contract," in G. D. H. Cole (trans., intro.), *The Social Contract and Discourses* (London: Everyman's Library, 1973 [1762]): 266.

[42] Hart, "Are There Any Natural Rights?" 61; Rawls, *Theory of Justice*: 111–12.

[43] B. Parekh, "A Misconceived Discourse on Political Obligation," *Political Studies* 41 (2) (1993): 236–51.

[44] Weale, *Democracy*: 192–3.

vote, even though it would be rational to vote if they could be sure that others in their social and economic circumstances were also planning to vote. The inability of the disadvantaged to coordinate voting so as to protect their interests as a class justifies the requirement that everyone entitled to vote should, in fact, vote. As a member of a disadvantaged group or just a concerned egalitarian democrat, I may welcome being required to vote as a solution to this maladaptive collective-action problem. And even if I belong to a disadvantaged group too small to make any difference to an election outcome, compulsory voting can ensure that larger disadvantaged groups sympathetic to my plight can be mobilized to help protect my interests. For example, we know that the young favor social spending for the unemployed.[45]

For Russell Hardin, rights are inalienable when they "protect the interests of relevant *classes* of individuals by changing, in their favor, the terms on which they face other classes." Drawing on J. S. Mill's work here, he gives as his example the collective-action problem that arises when attempting to reduce the legal workday from ten to nine hours:

> Because factory workers as a class face a difficult collective action problem, in which the logic is for all to favor the nine-hour day as a general rule but to work ten hours in their particular cases, they will wind up working ten hours for a day's pay if they are not prevented from doing so. Hence, what they need is not the simple right to a nine-hour day as a general rule but the inalienable right to a nine-hour day. In all of these cases, the members of the relevant class are potentially pitted against each other to their collective harm, and the only way to secure them against that collective harm is to deny them singly the right to free ride on the abstinence of other members of the class.[46]

Although the right not to work ten hours exists for the benefit of the right-holder, it ends up being invoked to prevent the right-holder from acting in a certain way. Therefore, it is not incoherent for a libertarian to argue that inalienable rights are not so much rights as "the denial of rights" because they impose a duty on the right-holder (in this case, the duty not to allow herself to be exploited). On this view, it is contradictory to conceive inalienable rights as individual rights because they only make sense at the group level: the benefits conferred on individu-

[45] Wattenberg, "Why Don't More Americans Vote?"
[46] Hardin, "Utilitarian Logic": 58–9.

als by the right derive indirectly from its effects on the larger class of which she is a member.[47]

Hardin's argument can be usefully applied to the case of the alleged right not to vote because denying the existence of such a right permits democratic systems to resolve the coordination problem faced by the disadvantaged at election time. If the right of any citizen to alienate her vote is denied, then not only will everyone vote, but it will now no longer be irrational for members of disadvantaged classes to vote. Hardin agrees that people should be prevented from alienating their right to vote in the strong sense of selling it,[48] but I would go further and suggest that abstention is also effectively – though unintentionally – *alienation* in the strong sense because of the fact that when the disadvantaged fail to vote, they are transferring their voting power to an already more powerful voter. They are not, of course, literally selling it, but they might as well be[49] given the bad effects of their abstention.

It could be retorted that giving away (or selling) one's vote is not the same as simply choosing to abstain. There are two responses to this objection: first, as was shown in Chapter 6, the persistent failure of certain classes to vote has been shown to affect the distribution of government benefits postelection (*indirect effects*). This is a distortion of the democratic process comparable (though obviously not identical) to the distortions generated by vote buying. After all, democratic governments are supposed to serve the interests of everyone within the electorate, not just those who voted and not just those who voted for the party that wins government. Second, as has been argued in Chapter 6, it is far from clear that failure to vote is a conscious or even desired choice.

So, although democracy is able to survive – to the extent that it still nominally *exists* where turnout is low and socially uneven – it cannot be said to thrive under conditions where a significant proportion of the citizenry fails to vote, and in many cases, it becomes seriously ill, assuming that it is agreed that political inequality, electoral exclusion,

[47] *Ibid.*: 59.
[48] *Ibid.*: 59–60.
[49] At the very least, they are giving it away. This might sound more benign because it is less venal, but it is arguably worse because abstainers aren't getting anything in return for what turns out to be a substantial loss.

elite dominance, unrepresentativeness, exclusiveness, and lack of control of the agenda by the *demos* are inimical to democracy.

7.7 Liberty versus Democracy?

The question of whether compelling people to vote is a violation of individual rights is often framed in terms of two competing sets of values. The first is the set concerned with personal liberty, whereas the second is about democratic legitimacy and vitality. In the compulsory-voting debate, it is generally assumed that you can either serve democracy at the cost of freedom or else sacrifice democratic to liberal *desiderata*. But this may be a false dichotomy because the enjoyment of rights largely depends on democratic conditions; therefore, the strongest argument for denying a right not to vote may actually be one based on the importance of liberty. The U.S. Supreme Court has repeatedly asserted that the right to vote is fundamental because it is the "preservative of all rights"[50] and "the citizen's link to his laws and government."[51] According to the Court, "Other rights, even the most basic, are illusory if the right to vote is undermined."[52] The European Court of Human Rights has also determined that the right to vote is fundamental.[53]

It is unlikely that the determination of these courts to protect the right to vote was motivated by a faith in the *potential* of voting to protect rights: rather, they were operating on the belief that citizens would, in fact, be using suffrage rights for the purposes of self-government and self-protection. As with any other right – and as the empirical evidence cited in Chapter 6 demonstrates – when the right to vote goes unexercised, it only has "formal" existence. But it acquires "material" existence when it is actually exercised.[54] Compulsory voting ensures

[50] See *Yick Wo* v. *Hopkins*, 118 U.S. 356, 370 (1886) and *Smiley* v. *Holm*, 285 U.S. 355, 366 (1932); *Evans* v. *Cornman*, 398 U.S. 419, 422 (1970) and *Cook* v. *Gralike*, 531 U.S. 510, 524 (2001).

[51] *Evans* v. *Cornman*, 398 U.S. 419, 422 (1970).

[52] *Wesberry* v. *Sanders*, 376 U.S. 1, 17 (1964).

[53] *Hirst* v. *United Kingdom (No. 2)* [GC], no. 74025/01, ECHR 2005-IX (Grand Chamber, 2nd instance), (43) 59 (2006).

[54] As Dowding and Van Hees have argued with respect to rights in general [K. Dowding and M. Van Hees, "The Construction of Rights," *American Political Science Review* 97 (2003): 281–93]. Contrast this with Brennan's view that while "people should

that the formal right to vote becomes a material right that is able to do its job of protecting and serving the bearer.

Were people to fail persistently and ubiquitously to express the right to vote, there would be no check against the potential tyranny of those in power, especially those seeking to trespass on realms of individual autonomy. This is why courts tend to regard voting as a "preferred" right.[55] Democratic participation preserves rights; failure to exercise our voting rights imperils all our rights, including the right to vote itself. Voting is one of those rights that, when it goes unexercised too often and for too long, causes other rights (such as the right to equal treatment before the law and the right to equality of opportunity) to be undermined. As has been shown, compared with groups of habitual voters, failure to vote results in demonstrably poorer outcomes for nonvoters in terms of government attention and spending. By contrast, in (compulsory-voting) systems where voting is universal and socially even, government attention and spending are more evenly distributed.

Therefore, although requiring people to vote might violate one's interpretation of liberty – negative liberty – it tends to serve and strengthen a number of other interpretations of liberty, among them nondomination,[56] autonomy,[57] and positive liberty,[58] because of its demonstrated capacity to enfranchise and empower the politically and economically weak.

7.8 "Right" versus "Duty" to Vote

Most voting libertarians assume that voting is a personal right and a personal right only. They also tend to see voting as a *privilege* devoid

have equal voting power ... many should not *exercise* the power they have" (Brennan, "Polluting the Polls": 545).

55 J. A. Douglas, "Is the Right to Vote Really Fundamental?" *Cornell Journal of Law and Public Policy* 18 (2008): 143–201.

56 Pettit, *Republicanism*.

57 S. Lackoff, *Democracy: History, Theory, Practice* (Boulder, CO: Westview Press, 1996): 163; D. Beetham, "Liberal Democracy and the Limits of Democratization," in D. Held (ed.), *Prospects for Democracy* (Cambridge, UK: Polity Press, 1993): 55–73.

58 Isaiah Berlin, "Two Concepts of Liberty," in *Four Essays on Liberty* (London: Oxford University Press, 1969).

of – or even antithetical to – duties.[59] But what if voting is not just a privilege but some other kind of right? Further, what if voting is not only an entitlement but a duty?

In Wesley Hohfeld's classic analytical typology of legal rights, a *privilege* (sometimes referred to as a "liberty right") denotes "absence of duty." In fact, in his scheme of jural relations, "a privilege is the opposite of a duty," a "negation of legal duty"[60] that affords its bearer a right not to be under a duty to act in certain ways[61] and to be free from the claims of others. Hence, if voting is indeed a privilege, citizens are under no obligation to vote. However, within Hohfeld's scheme, the entitlement to vote is not actually a privilege; rather, it is better characterized as a combination of a "claim-right" and a "power-right." A *claim-right* entitles me to make a claim on others so that I am owed a duty by them. In the case of voting, others have a duty not to interfere with the exercise of my right to vote and may even be under duty to afford me the conditions of its exercise. Thus there can be both *positive* and *negative* claim rights. The jural opposite of a claim-right is a "no-right" or "no-claim."[62] Meanwhile, a *power-right* is a legal "ability" whose jural opposite is legal "disability" rather than absence of duty.[63] When a person is disenfranchised, it is not that she legally ought not to vote but that she legally *cannot* vote.[64] My claim/power-right to vote means that not only am I legally entitled to vote but also others have a duty not to interfere with my voting and may even be obliged to facilitate it.

[59] For example, without elaborating, for Saunders, the franchise is a right only, "a benefit, rather … than a potentially onerous duty" ("Increasing Turnout": 74), whereas for Lever, "it is hard to justify a general duty to vote simply because one is a citizen and has a right to vote" (Lever, "Is Compulsory Voting Justified?" 68).

[60] W. N. Hohfeld, *Fundamental Legal Conceptions: As Applied in Judicial Reasoning* (New Haven, CT: Yale University Press, 1964): 38, 45; W. W. Cook, "Introduction," in W. N. Hohfeld (ed.), *Fundamental Legal Conceptions: As Applied in Judicial Reasoning* (New Haven, CT: Yale University Press, 1964): 5–7.

[61] P. Jones, *Rights* (London: Macmillan, 1994): 12–13.

[62] Hohfeld, *Fundamental Legal Conceptions*: 36.

[63] *Ibid.*: 51.

[64] Jones, *Rights*: 23. "Having the right to vote is not just to be free to vote (under no duty not to vote) but to have the power to perform a specific legally recognized action. The difference is that removing a liberty right (privilege) is imposing a duty not to act in certain ways, whereas removing a power right disables the power to establish a particular legal relation" (L. Beckman, *The Frontiers of Democracy: The Right to Vote and Its Limits* [Houndsmills, UK: Palgrave MacMillan, 2009]: 130–1).

So, in terms of Hohfeld's rights scheme, voting is a "claim/power-right." Yet (at the risk of overcomplicating things for the sake of precision) a claim/power-right can also be a duty. There is nothing in democratic (or Hohfeldian[65]) theory that obviously precludes the possibility of conceiving voting as a duty or of conceiving it as *both* a right *and* a duty. This is true even when the duty plays no role in the justification of voting rights.[66] A *duty-right* exists where one has both a duty to do *A* (because others have a claim-right that I perform it) and a claim that protects this duty. If I have a duty to vote, I also have a claim that I not be interfered with in the performance of this duty. There are many duty-rights: there is a duty-right to pay one's debts, judges have duty-rights to impose sentences, teachers have a duty-right to grade the work of their pupils, and police officers have both a right and a duty to arrest criminals. A duty-right exists even when we would prefer not to have it, such as in the case of the duty-right to pay our debts.[67] The concept of a duty-right has been explicitly recognized by courts. For example, in *Albertson* v. *Kirkingburg* (527 U.S. 555, 1999), the court found that Albertson's (a grocery store chain) had a duty-right to dismiss one of its delivery van drivers once the chain discovered that his vision did not meet federally specified vision standards.[68]

Voting can be plausibly characterized as a duty as well as a right not only because others have a claim-right that I vote (see below) but also because the justification for voting rights is only partly rights-based: there are powerful consequentialist arguments for the importance of democracy and voting rights. For example, voting rights have been defended as the best means for self-protection, for achieving utility maximization,[69] and as a practice that promotes and protects "the common interests of the members of a political community."[70] Therefore,

[65] Because the Hohfeldian scheme is about legal rights and duties, it has limitations in any discussion of moral rights. Accordingly, my argument is not bound by the Hohfeldian framework.

[66] This is conceded in principle by Lever ("Compulsory Voting": 9, n. 32), even though she denies that voting is, in fact, a duty.

[67] G. W. Rainbolt, *The Concept of Rights* (Dordrecht, Netherlands: Springer, 2006): 37.

[68] Rainbolt, *Concept of Rights*: 37.

[69] For Anthony Downs, the purpose of voting is purely instrumental, a means of obtaining power, maximizing gains, and minimizing losses.

[70] Weale, *Democracy*: 41–2.

there are consequentialist grounds for a duty to vote insofar as I have a duty to promote certain values or desirable ends (as distinct from my duty to meet the claim-rights of others).

Voting is thus best characterized as both a duty- and a claim/power-right. It is a duty(claim/power)-right not only because of the bad consequences for democracy that flow from failure to vote (which, in turn, generates a universal obligation to act to promote the values and social condition of democracy) but also because (relatedly) other people have a claim-right to have me perform that duty. There are two sets of people with a claim-right on me to vote: first, I owe it to other members of my social class to cooperate so that we are enabled to shape, in our favor, the terms on which we face other classes and thereby derive the liberty and equality-enhancing benefits of voting; and second, I have a reciprocal obligation to all other citizens to vote so that, together, we can constitute and perpetuate the system of representative democracy and collectively enjoy the benefits of living in a properly functioning democracy where elections perform their desired functions.

Thus, on the one hand, voting must be seen as a *duty* because of (1) its special place in serving democratic *desiderata* and in perpetuating democracy as a form of government and (2) because others have a claim-right that I should vote. On the other hand, though, voting must also be a legally recognized *right* (claim/power-right) so as to prevent its erosion and ensure that the claims of the disentitled have purchase (this is largely why I am reluctant to see voting as a duty only).

If voting is a duty as well as a right, it is not unreasonable to refuse to legally recognize a right not to vote or to require voting by law. Under Australian law, for example, according to Subsection 245 (1) of the Commonwealth Electoral Act, it is indeed "the duty of every elector to vote at each election." While there are many duties that we would not consider it right to legally compel, voting is not just any duty – it is a special duty because the existence and proper functioning of representative democracy depend on its performance; further, our welfare and rights depend on its performance.

Arguably, the state in this context is a benign coordinating mechanism for the joint enterprise of democratic community rather than a violator of any alleged right not to vote. If we accept that the state is "a special kind of association … an ethical order, the embodiment of the common life of its members," as Carole Pateman has argued,[71] its role in elections can be seen as that of a coordinating mechanism for horizontal obligation between members of a political community rather than an aggressive imposer of restrictions on freedom.

While it may be true, as Lever has pointed out, that "[c]itizens do not owe their government electoral support or legitimacy,"[72] they do owe it to each other to ensure that their government is as legitimate, representative, and democratically fair[73] as possible.[74] As John Rawls has suggested, people have a "natural duty ... to support and further just institutions."[75]

7.9 Concluding Remarks

In a representative democracy, while *all* need not be politically active *all* the time, nevertheless, for both rights- and consequence-based reasons, we should all participate in periodic elections. Voting is a duty-right, not a personal, divisible, alienable privilege. Not only does the life of democracy depend on the denial of a right not to vote, so too does the life of liberty, broadly understood. The posited right not to vote cannot be recognized because it cannot be universalized – doing so could potentially destroy the form of government for which it exists: democracy, which is a collective benefit. Requiring people to vote is not justified simply because of its good consequences: it is justified because the right to vote defines the very structure of democratic government; further, its universal exercise confers legitimacy on both the electoral process and the government that wins office. Therefore, there should be no legal recognition of a right not to vote.

71 Carole Pateman, *The Problem of Political Obligation* (Cambridge, UK: Polity/Blackwell, 1985): 173.

72 Lever, "Is Compulsory Voting Justified?" 66–72.

73 By "democratically fair," I mean serving the interests of all members of the electorate, not just those of the privileged.

74 For Lever, "it is unclear why support for just institutions should take the form of 'electoral participation' rather than anything else" (Lever, "Is Compulsory Voting Justified?" 67). The reason, as canvassed in Chapter 6, is that legislatures play a privileged role in determining the rights and benefits enjoyed by citizens, including those that determine their ability to participate in other democratic spheres.

75 Rawls, *Theory of Justice*.

Insisting on a right not to vote constitutes a refusal to participate in what appears to be the best form of government for the preservation of rights, namely, representative democracy. Further, people have a duty to support just institutions, especially those that protect rights and welfare. The right to vote is therefore not just a (power/claim) right but also a duty, that is, a duty(power/claim)-right.

The right to vote cannot be inverted, waived, or alienated because other interests are at stake; any individual person's determination to waive such a right is negated by the interests of social classes in self-protection and self-government and the collective interest in perpetuating a democratic form of government. Requiring citizens to vote is therefore a justified liberal democratic practice: in other words, it can be reconciled with both liberal and democratic values.

8

Is Requiring People to Vote Contrary to Democratic Values?

The question of whether compulsory voting is inimical to democratic ideals has been partly dealt with in earlier chapters, where I argued that while it infringed on personal liberty, it enhances the democratic values of legitimacy, representativeness, political equality, inclusiveness, minimization of elite power, and final control of the agenda by the *demos*. In this chapter, I argue that compulsory voting also serves the value of *substantive* equality of political opportunity (as opposed to either political equality or formal equality of opportunity). I also explore a number of other issues relating to the effect on democratic values of compulsory voting. The first concerns the argument that compulsory voting is *over-inclusive* and therefore introduces distortions into the electoral process that undermine good governance. On this view, not only is compulsory voting a bad idea, but there also is a duty for some people – such as those who vote "badly," are indifferent to the outcome of an election, or are "unaffected" by the outcome of an election – *not* to vote in order to protect democratic values. I then argue that although compulsory voting seems to violate the democratic values of voluntarism and autonomy, because of its tendency to empower and protect people politically, it ultimately serves these values. Sometimes we need to reduce a value in order to promote it: specifically, in order to promote overall the values of voluntarism and autonomy, we should compel people to vote. Finally, I argue that compulsory voting is something that we would retrospectively impose on ourselves once we see its good effects, including its ability to solve the voting coordination problem.

8.1 Overinclusiveness, Nonaffected Interests, and "Bad" Voting

The so-called problem of overinclusiveness is sometimes invoked as an argument against compulsory voting. There are different variants of this argument, but in this context, it denotes the idea that higher levels of voting participation can harm rather than serve democratic values by compelling otherwise "reluctant" citizens to vote. Such voters are assumed to be either less affected by, less interested in, or less informed about the election process; therefore, both the electoral outcomes and the process itself would function better without their input. But is overinclusiveness really a problem? And is it really a problem for democratic values?

8.1.1 Overinclusiveness: The "Nonaffected"

It has been suggested that electoral democracy works better when those either indifferent to or unaffected by election outcomes refrain from voting. Compelling all eligible citizens to vote, says Saunders, is a bad idea because some are less affected by the outcome of elections than others. On this view, many people already do this: the reason why abstainers forego voting is that they "are more principled than others." "[B]ecause the issues involved do not concern them greatly," it is either "apathy" or "principled deference" that causes them to abstain. When this leads to low and unequal turnout, it "is not necessarily undemocratic" and may even "serve democratic values by ... making it more likely that decisions really are made by the relevant constituency, with those most affected getting more say."[1]

This characterization of abstention as a principled, altruistic, and conscious choice made to prevent distortions in electoral outcomes is questionable. We should be suspicious of it prima facie because, first of all, it is doubtful that there is really any such entity as an *unaffected interest* where elections are concerned.

I mentioned at the outset that I subscribe to the "all-affected interests" principle, which holds that "everyone who is affected by the decisions of a government should have the right to participate in that government."[2] According to Robert Goodin, this "requires us to

[1] Saunders, "Increasing Turnout": 70–4

[2] See Robert Dahl, *After the Revolution: Authority in a Good Society* (New Haven, CT: Yale University Press, 1971): 64.

include in the *demos* every interest that might possibly be affected by any possible decision arising out of any possible agenda"[3] because once we start to reflect on the direct and ripple effects of election outcomes and the decisions made by our representatives, it soon becomes clear that there is no one in the society who is entirely immune from the effects of those decisions.[4] For Goodin, when taken to its logical (i.e., expansive and "possibilistic") conclusion, this would mean "giving virtually everyone everywhere a vote on virtually everything decided anywhere."[5] For example, because citizens of Iraq are significantly affected by the foreign policy of the United States, they should be allowed to vote in U.S. elections. Similarly, because we are all affected by the extent to which the Chinese state allows its citizens to pollute the earth's atmosphere, we should all be part of the Chinese electorate. I do not, however, take the principle this far: I am only suggesting that everyone within the boundaries of a sovereign state be included in the *demos*. Because no one within a given state is immune from the effects of election outcomes, everyone should be enfranchised. But, in another sense, take the all-affected-interests principle one step further: everyone within a given territory not only should have the right to vote, but they also should actually use their vote. They should be *substantively* – and not just formally – enfranchised.

[3] See Robert E. Goodin, "Enfranchising All Affected Interests, and Its Alternatives," *Philosophy and Public Affairs* 35 (2007): 40–68. Ben Saunders' argument about affected interests also seems to rest on a fictional conception of the nature of elections. He suggests that there are "some particular issue[s] that only affec[t] a subset of the electorate" and that under such conditions there is actually "a duty *not* to vote" (Saunders, "Increasing Turnout": 74). It is hard to imagine what kind of election Saunders has in mind here because, apart from referenda, elections are never single-issue events; rather, they are typically fought on broad platforms with implications for all members of the electorate. Saunders seems to concede that, unlike referenda, election results are more likely to "somehow" affect everyone within an electorate, but he insists that "it is still quite possible" that some will remain unaffected, namely, "isolationist groups" and "those who will soon die or emigrate" (Saunders, "Increasing Turnout": 76, n. 3). Apart from the fact that these groups will still be affected by electoral outcomes (e.g., the nation to which the fictional citizen emigrates may still be affected by the foreign policy of the nation she has left behind; the dying have an interest in the world they leave to their loved ones), these groups do not constitute the majority of people who fail to vote (actually, older citizens are more likely to vote than younger citizens).

[4] Goodin, "All Affected Interests": 68.

[5] *Ibid.*: 64.

We should also suspect the preceding characterization of abstention as a function of being unaffected because, as was shown in Chapter 6, the more socially and economically marginalized a person is, the less likely she is to vote.[6] Can it really be the case that the disadvantaged regard electoral results as having less impact on their interests than the well-off? And even if the disadvantaged do think this way, it isn't objectively true because, relatively speaking (or in terms of marginal utility), the worse off a person is, arguably the more affected she is by government policy. The assumption that electoral decisions are "actually made by the relevant constituency" is problematic because it takes as given that objective interests are closely tied to turnout patterns.[7] This can't be true given that low turnout is concentrated among the young, poor, and marginalized.

8.1.2 Overinclusiveness: The "Indifferent"

In a similar – although not identical – vein, Paul Sheehy proposes that those who are "indifferent about the outcome of an election" are duty-bound to "refrain from voting."[8] At first sight, this sounds reasonable and advisable, but who exactly are these "indifferent" voters? On Sheehy's account, an indifferent voter is someone who "is as happy with any one outcome as another"; therefore, in abstaining, he endures no "disadvantage" or "loss." But there is a logical error here: subjective indifference to an electoral outcome (which does exist) is not the same as being objectively unaffected by an electoral outcome (which seems not to be possible). As mentioned, no one is really unaffected by an electoral outcome, and whether or not a potential voter is aware of this, it is still true.[9] Put simply, a feeling is not a fact. Further, a person's indifference – if it translates into abstention – affects the welfare of others (see Chapter 6). Therefore, the subjectively indifferent person's failure to vote is not only unneutral but also a bad thing

[6] We also know that the younger a person is, the less likely he is to vote. In any case, youth is a surrogate for other forms of disadvantage.

[7] Saunders, "Increasing Turnout": 72.

[8] Paul Sheehy, "A Duty Not to Vote," *Ratio* 15 (2002): 46–57.

[9] However, Sheehy admits that there is a difference between a person who is informed and still indifferent, on the one hand, and uninformed, ignorant, and still indifferent, on the other. But, because the well informed are more likely to vote, I would suggest that well-informed indifferents are quite rare. See Sheehy, "A Duty Not to Vote."

for both herself and others, particularly other members of the same social group.

8.1.3 Overinclusiveness: "Bad" Voting and Bad Government

Another genre of the overinclusiveness argument has to do with the alleged lack of political competence of habitual voters. According to this argument, it is not only unnecessary but a bad idea to preach political activism to those who rarely vote and "would do it badly if compelled."[10] Low turnout has even been described as "a blessing" because those more strongly inclined to vote are seen as more competent to perform the mandate and accountability functions of elections than those less inclined.[11] For Jason Brennan, not only are "[c]itizens of modern democracies ... not obligated to vote, but if they do vote, they are obligated not to vote badly." Therefore, there are many who should "abstain rather than impose bad governance on everyone" through their bad voting. Although Brennan concedes that "it's hard to take democracy seriously when most voters abstain from voting," he prefers the low-turnout scenario to one where "a large percentage of bad voters vote." Hence "opposing universal voting" is not "inherently undemocratic."[12]

For Brennan, the facts "regarding how well or badly actual voters vote" are beside the point because his avowed goal is merely "to establish a normative conclusion" that is "one should not vote badly."[13] Such a goal is surely uncontroversial and welcome (unless, of course, it ends up being used cynically for electoral advantage to exclude minority voters with low literacy, numeracy, and majority-language competence). Yet the implicit agenda of this argument (that only the best-informed and best-motivated people should vote) embodies several empirical assumptions: first, that "bad voting" does occur; second, that it increases with higher turnout; and third, that it has negative effects, namely, "that citizens have to live with racist and sexist laws, unnecessary wars, lower economic opportunities, lower levels of welfare, and so on."[14] All these assumptions are controvertible.

[10] Mayo, "A Note": 319–21.
[11] For example, Rosema, "Low Turnout"; Abraham, *Compulsory Voting*.
[12] Brennan, "Polluting the Polls": 542, 548.
[13] *Ibid.*: 546.
[14] *Ibid.*: 542; Brennan, *Ethics of Voting*. Incidentally, all these outcomes seem more likely to result from *low*-turnout elections.

It is hard to disagree with the position that competent voting is preferable to incompetent voting. Of course, if one can avoid it, one should not vote badly,[15] by which Brennan means without "sufficient moral or epistemic justification."[16] A vote is a precious thing, and ideally, it should not be squandered or used to bad effect. And yet there is no real evidence that we get either worse governance or more distortions in the electoral process when voting is high or compelled, regardless of what survey data might tell us about the political competence of habitual abstainers. In fact, the reverse seems to be the case with respect to the character of governance under high-turnout elections (I deal with distortions in the electoral *process* later). As discussed in Chapter 6, there is a more even distribution of government attention in high-turnout elections. In addition, settings with compulsory voting have less income inequality than voluntary systems.[17] Furthermore, something I did not point out previously is that citizens in compulsory-voting settings feel more positive about their democracy than do citizens in voluntary regimes. As Sarah Birch has demonstrated, compulsory voting "has a strong and significant impact on satisfaction" with the way democracy is working.[18] Australians, for example, exhibit fairly high levels of trust in government compared with citizens in other advanced democracies. They also report "very low levels of perceived political corruption."[19] This perception is grounded in reality: compulsory-voting regimes do, in fact, experience lower levels of corruption.[20] It turns out that the higher levels of trust in compulsory-voting systems are not just a subjective perception: the trust is, in fact, deserved. Finally, as mentioned in Chapter 5, compulsory voting can be an impetus to high standards of electoral management, something that is both a form of good government and an aid to it. Therefore, it is far from clear that compulsory voting does, in fact, lead to worse governance. Instead, it seems to give us more representative government,

[15] However, I would qualify this position by reiterating that competent voting is learned, and so abstention is hardly the solution to the mooted problem of bad voting.

[16] Brennan, "Polluting the Polls": 538.

[17] Birch, *Full Participation*: 131.

[18] *Ibid.*: 132–3.

[19] T. Donovan, D. Denemark, and S. Bowler, "Trust, Citizenship and Participation: Australia in Comparative Perspective," in D. Denemark, G. Meagher, S. Wilson, M. Western, and T. Phillips (eds.), *Australian Social Attitudes 2: Citizenship, Work and Aspirations* (Sydney: University of New South Wales Press, 2007): 102.

[20] Birch, *Full Participation*: 132–3.

less corruption, more citizen satisfaction, and therefore higher levels of legitimacy than voluntary-voting democracies. Therefore, we should be wary of assuming that "bad voting," even where detectable, has a significant effect on how governments function. For example, Selb and Lachat suggest that because compulsory voting brings to the Belgian polls "a substantial share of uninterested and less knowledgeable voters," such voters will be more likely to "cast votes that are clearly less consistent with their own political preferences than those of the more informed and motivated voluntary voters." I am not suggesting that the researchers were mistaken in finding that in Belgium there are fewer voters able to vote in their own interests, only that if this is true, the problem is not big enough to make much difference because, in the end, we know that higher turnout leads to governments that better serve the objective interests of these apparently uninformed voters. As the authors themselves admit, the detected increase in arbitrary voting by reluctant voters did not affect electoral outcomes to any "outstanding" degree.[21]

8.1.4 Overinclusiveness, "Bad" Voting, and Electoral Distortions

It has been suggested that compulsory voting is a bad idea because it "runs the risk of distorting electoral outcomes." The main concern here is that were habitual nonvoters suddenly required to vote – as would happen under a compulsory-voting regime – they would be less likely than habitual voters to "use their votes wisely"[22] and therefore would tend to vote randomly. Again, this gives rise to an alleged "duty *not* to vote." For Jakee and Sun, encouraging high turnout through compulsory voting distorts electoral outcomes because the result will approximate a coin toss. The first problem here is that their argument is based on the assumption of a first-past-the-post system, which no compulsory-voting regime uses.[23] In any case, they demonstrate their point via a formal proof that is based on the "assumption that at least some of those who we compel are more likely to be less interested in or less informed about politics."[24] Is this probable?

[21] Selb and Lachat, "The More, the Better": 591.
[22] Saunders, "Increasing Turnout": 71, 74.
[23] Birch, *Full Participation*: 111.
[24] Jakee and Sun, "Is Compulsory Voting More Democratic?" 63.

According to Robert Goodin, the answer is "probably not": the problem of overinclusiveness is overrated because any random voting will be spread equally across all options and so will cancel each other out.[25] But, as Saunders points out, this "is not obviously true: such votes won't necessarily be spread equally because of 'donkey voting,' which is the most common form of random voting."[26] Although I dispute that there is any such thing as a "nonaffected" person, it is indeed possible that the sudden inclusion of habitual abstainers might distort electoral outcomes because at least some of them – due to factors such as inexperience and lack of interest – will be random voters[27] whose votes will introduce an unintended ballot-order bias. But what is the real extent of *random* voting in compulsory-voting settings?

Let's examine more closely the figures for random voting in one of the few compulsory-voting settings where they have been well documented: Australia. In Australia, true random voting – *donkey voting* – accounts for only around 1 percent of total votes cast.[28] More important, this figure is actually lower than in many systems where voting is voluntary,[29] such as the United States, where the random ballot figure has been estimated between 2 and 4 percent.[30]

It turns out that none of the aggregate empirical evidence strongly points to a dynamic whereby the voting participation of habitual or likely abstainers distorts election outcomes even where a degree of "bad" voting seems to have taken place (I take *distortion* to mean electoral outcomes that do not reflect the true preferences or interests of

[25] Goodin, "Enfranchising All Affected Interests": 58.

[26] *Donkey voting* denotes when voters mindlessly number their ballots from top to bottom or in reverse (Saunders, "Increasing Turnout": 73).

[27] For example, candidates do seem to derive some advantage from ballot position (Orr et al., "Australian Electoral Law"; Birch, *Full Participation*: 111).

[28] Amy King and Andrew Leigh, "Are Ballot Order Effects Heterogeneous?," *Social Science Quarterly* 90 (2009): 71–87.

[29] Birch, *Full Participation*: 111

[30] J. M. Miller and J. A. Krosnick, "The Impact of Candidate Name Order on Election Outcomes," *Public Opinion Quarterly* 62 (1998): 291–330; D. E. Ho and K. Imai, "Estimating Causal Effects of Ballot Order from a Randomized Natural Experiment: The California Alphabet Lottery, 1978–2002," *Public Opinion Quarterly* 72 (2): 216–40. But see also Selb and Lachat ("The More the Better?"), who, writing of the Belgian case, found an increase in arbitrary voting by reluctant voters that probably affected electoral outcomes *but not to any "outstanding" degree* (*ibid.*: 591; emphasis added).

the people casting votes).[31] This may be because when habitual voters start voting, they have already begun to be better informed and more politically competent in the way J. S. Mill would have anticipated. As is well known, Mill saw voting as educative and as something that takes practice: he wrote that one of the "foremost benefits" of electoral participation is the "education of the intelligence and of the sentiments which is carried down to the lowest rank of the people when they are called to take part in acts which directly affect the great interests of the country."[32] Mill's belief seems to be borne out by recent work on the effect of compulsory-voting laws on political sophistication (i.e., political awareness and information). Although some studies have found that compulsory voting has no effect on levels of political sophistication,[33] Victoria Shineman's more recent research concludes that compulsory-voting laws can cause "citizens to increase their political interest and attention to political news as well as their level of information about party platforms." Rather than giving us voters who are more uninformed, compulsory voting has a tendency to "increase the informedness of the active electorate."[34]

But what about invalid voting?[35] After all, informal or invalid voting is comparatively higher in compulsory-voting regimes,[36] and surely it rates as a form of "bad voting." The first thing to note is that, because such votes are not counted, they are incapable of distorting outcomes. But we might still call informality "bad voting" because the

[31] Birch, *Full Participation*: 111

[32] Mill, *Representative Government*: 321.

[33] See Birch, *Full Participation*: 140; Loewen, Milner, and Hicks, "Does Compulsory Voting Lead."

[34] Victoria Shineman, "Compulsory Voting as Compulsory Balloting: How Mandatory Balloting Laws Increase Informed Voting without Increasing Uninformed Voting," paper presented at the Annual Meeting of the American Political Science Association, Toronto, 2010; Victoria Shineman, "Isolating the Effects of Compulsory Voting on Political Sophistication: Exploiting Intra-national Variation in Mandatory Voting Laws Across the Austrian Provinces," paper presented at the Annual Meeting of the American Political Science Association, Chicago, 2009.

[35] A vote is deemed invalid if the voter leaves the ballot paper blank or marks it in a manner otherwise in accordance with the prescribed method (e.g., records only a number "1"; uses ticks or crosses instead of numbers; writes slogans, words, or other marks on the paper without recording a valid preference; defaces the paper so that the vote is unreadable; omits to record any preferences or uses nonsequential numbers).

[36] Hirczy, "Explaining Near-Universal Turnout."

vote is wasted insofar as it does not end up being used for expressing preferences and gaining representation: it appears to lack "sufficient moral or epistemic justification." At this point, adversaries of compulsory voting might suggest that the fact that informal votes don't count only shows that compelling people to vote is a waste of time because informality ends up being the functional equivalent of abstention. But it should be noted that only a small proportion of typical abstainers deliberately cast invalid votes; the vast majority (around 75 percent) sincerely attempt to cast valid votes. In other words, the elector is trying to cast a formal vote but failing. In these cases, the problem is not rooted in apathy or indifference to the outcome (although this is obviously part of the story) but is related to the fact that compulsory voting tends to bring to the polls voters otherwise inhibited from voting not so much by apathy as by low levels of education, poor dominant-language proficiency, and lack of community integration and familiarity with the political system.[37]

Assuming that high turnout is preferable to low turnout and that political inclusion is preferable to political exclusion, the advocacy of voluntary voting as a "cure" for the informal vote seems far from appropriate, especially because, arguably, the poorer and more socially marginal a citizen is, the greater is the need for the protection that voting can afford. Further, learning to vote properly takes practice, and we know from experience that educating people who might otherwise abstain about voting can decrease informality.[38] Given that compulsory voting can increase turnout by as much as 30+ percentage points, a small increase in intentionally invalid votes (in Australia's case, this amounts to around 1 percentage point) and no discernible increase in donkey (random) votes[39] seem to be a tolerable cost of enfranchising the disadvantaged.

[37] S. Young and L. Hill, "Uncounted Votes: Informal Voting in the House of Representatives as a Marker of Political Exclusion in Australia," *Australian Journal of History and Politics* 55 (2009): 64–79.

[38] For example, information and education drives designed to reduce the rate of informal voting have shown some success (Gina Dario and Rod Medew, "Pilot Project on Informality in Port Adelaide," Research Report Number 9 [Canberra: Australian Electoral Commission, 2009]); available at: http://www.aec.gov.au/pdf/research/papers/paper9/research_paper9.pdf (last accessed September 2, 2009).

[39] Compared with the number cast in voluntary systems.

Overinclusiveness thus seems to be a far less serious problem than underinclusiveness. Even if it could be proved empirically that random voting significantly distorts electoral outcomes in high-turnout elections (it hasn't been),[40] it would still need to be shown that this distortion is worse than that caused by the mass abstention of the disadvantaged and the young. The distortion I have in mind is the undemocratic bias in government policy and spending away from nonvoters and toward habitual voters that happens in low-turnout settings. After all, as I have already mentioned, we expect democratic governments to serve the interests of everyone within the electorate, not just those who voted and not just those who happened to vote for the party that wins office.

In any case, it is not obvious that we should tolerate low and unequal turnout (and all its attendant problems) for the sake of an alleged problem that can be substantially resolved by mechanical means: for example, distortions caused by donkey voting in high-turnout electorates can be readily addressed by ballot labeling of party affiliation,[41] by offering "none-of-the-above" type options, or else by randomization of ballot ordering.[42] Therefore, if we really want to have elections free from distortions that impugn democratic values such as representativeness and the inclusion of "all affected interests," we would tend to embrace rather than reject compulsory voting.

8.2 Competence, Exclusion, and the Democratic Ideal

Even if it were true that compulsory voting had no effect on the political sophistication of the electorate, there are some serious flaws in the suggestion that we should make the presence of an informed public the necessary condition for their universal inclusion. First, whereas compulsory voting certainly brings the poor and disadvantaged into the voting process, it has yet to be determined that this necessarily

[40] Birch, *Full Participation*: 140.

[41] This ensures that "voters had the most important piece of information they required at the point of choice. In doing so, it rendered these choices more meaningful for those who cared about voting but were motivated more by party ideology and image than local, personality politics" (Orr et al., "Australian Electoral Law": 575).

[42] This strategy is used in the Australian jurisdiction of Tasmania and is referred to as the *Robson rotation*.

overloads the system with people unable to reflect competently enough on the business at hand. But, even if this did happen, it would not be grounds for welcoming the exclusion of less informed voters because this would adversely affect the poor (whose levels of political competence tend to be lower than better-off citizens; see earlier discussion) in a manner inimical to democratic values. We ought not to forget that the competence argument has historically been used to exclude citizens from minority groups. Accordingly, the U.S. Supreme Court has repeatedly rejected attempts to restrict the franchise in order to promote "intelligent or responsible voting."[43] In the 1970s, the U.S. Congress instituted a federal statute that permanently banned the use of literacy tests nationwide as a precondition for voting, partly on the grounds that they disenfranchised minority citizens.[44] Similarly, according to international human rights law, it is unreasonable to restrict the right to vote "on the ground of physical disability, literacy standards, educational standards or property requirements."[45] While we all agree in principle that informed and competent voting is preferable to the alternative, the reasoning of the courts here is that the franchise is just too important to be conditional on the quality of the reasoning behind a person's vote. Of course, voting libertarians aren't suggesting that we *legally* exclude the less politically informed from the electoral process, but wishing away inclusive mechanisms such as compulsory voting is certainly a good way to arrive at the same effect.

It should also be pointed out that the amelioration of the disadvantage that gives rise to lower levels of political sophistication in the first place is correlated with the presence of compulsory voting (as noted earlier, there is more even wealth distribution in compulsory-voting systems). Because "poverty can inhibit communicative capacity,"[46] those worried about low levels of political sophistication would do better to take a long view of the situation and embrace rather than reject compulsory voting.

[43] See *Dunn* v. *Blumstein*, (1972) 405 U.S. 330, 343; Pamela S. Karlan, "Convictions and Doubts: Retribution, Representation, and the Debate Over Felon Disenfranchisement," *Stanford Law Review* 56 (5)(2004): 1147–70.

[44] See Rep. No. 94–295 (1975), at 23–24; reprinted in 1975 U.S.C.C.A.N. 774 and cited in Karlan, "Convictions and Doubts": 1152.

[45] United Nations Human Rights Committee, General Comment 25, paragraphs 4, 10.

[46] J. Dryzek, *Deliberative Democracy and Beyond: Liberals, Critics, Contestations* (Oxford, UK: Oxford University Press, 2000): 172.

Another serious underlying flaw of the competence argument for electoral inclusion is its misconception of the whole point of democracy. The centuries-old battle to wrest political control from elites and into the hands of the people has always been about *power*, whereas the epistemic considerations have always been secondary (and even sometimes beside the point). Suffragists didn't argue that the disenfranchised knew best: what they wanted was a voice, a say, an equal share in *power*. As Thomas Paine put the case, "The right of voting for representatives is the primary right by which other rights are protected. To take away this right is to reduce a man to slavery, for slavery consists in being subject to the will of another, and he that has not a vote in the election of representatives is in this case."[47] Similarly, there was no mention of epistemic considerations when Susan B. Anthony demanded voting rights for women after her arrest on charges of voting illegally in the 1872 federal election. Who knew best or worst was beside the point; the real point was that voting meant equality and power.

> One-half of the people of this nation to-day are utterly powerless to blot from the statute books an unjust law, or to write there a new and a just one. The women, dissatisfied as they are with this form of government, that enforces taxation without representation, that compels them to obey laws to which they have never given their consent, – that imprisons and hangs them without a trial by a jury of their peers, that robs them, in marriage, of the custody of their own persons, wages and children, – are this half of the people left wholly at the mercy of the other half, in direct violation of the spirit and letter of the declarations of the framers of this government, every one of which was based on the immutable principle of equal rights to all. By those declarations, kings, priests, popes, aristocrats, were all alike dethroned, and placed on a common level politically, with the lowliest born subject or serf. By them, too, me, as such, were deprived of their divine right to rule, and placed on a political level with women. By the practice of those declarations all class and caste distinction will be abolished; and slave, serf, plebeian, wife, woman, all alike, bound from their subject position to the proud platform of equality.[48]

[47] Thomas Paine, "Dissertation on First Principles of Government," in T. Paine (ed.), *The Writings of Thomas Paine, Collected and Edited by Moncure Daniel Conway* (New York: G.P. Putnam's Sons 1894 [1791]): vol. 3, xxiv.

[48] Susan. B. Anthony, "Is It a Crime for a Citizen of the United States to Vote" (1872); available at: http://law2.umkc.edu/faculty/projects/ftrials/anthony/anthonyaddress.html (last accessed May 7, 2013).

For Henry Sidgwick, democratic equality means not only that "everyone should be treated equally"; it also means "that everyone should have a place in the exercise of political authority." The basis for this belief is "that each citizen is as well qualified as any other to contribute to political decision-making."[49] This does not necessarily mean that everyone is equally good at thinking like an economist; only that, in general, we are all safer[50] when we take account of the fact that when elites rule on our behalf, they may not necessarily be ruling in our interests.

8.3 Must All Self-Governing Activities Be Voluntary? Honoring or Promoting Democratic Freedom

A common criticism of compulsory voting is that it "undercuts the idea that voluntary political participation is a distinctive human good, and that democracies are justified in part by their ability to realize that good."[51] For Jason Brennan, "[O]ne reason liberal democracy is such a great gift is that it does not require us to be political animals."[52]

While it is agreed that voluntary political participation is a distinctive human good, it is not clear that liberal democracy is not entitled to make any participatory demands on its citizens. I am also wary of arguments that seem to take voluntarism as the defining feature of democracy because if there is *a* defining feature of democracy, it is that citizens determine who will represent and govern them. Is liberal democracy all about freedom and nothing about responsibility? Obviously, freedom is extremely important in liberal democratic orders, and this is why I (and millions of others) like living in them. But does this mean that the means for securing the framework for freedom has to be achieved voluntarily? Of course, it would be preferable if it could be. But *can* it be? After all, liberal democracy didn't just emerge spontaneously. It was fought for over many centuries in

[49] H. Sidgwick, *The Elements of Politics* (London: Macmillan, 1891): 587.

[50] D. F. Thompson, *The Democratic Citizen* (Cambridge, UK: Cambridge University Press, 1970): 13–19.

[51] Lever, "Is Compulsory Voting Justified?" 14.

[52] Brennan, "Polluting the Polls": 543.

protracted and often violent campaigns, and we shouldn't assume that its survival and good health are automatically assured just because the formal framework is in place. Rather, people need to persistently work it and defend it. An analogous case is a war of defense: people are justifiably conscripted to protect a society from foreign tyranny so that its people can live free. It is not unreasonable to expect people to be willing voter conscripts in order to enjoy the freedom of living in a reasonably well-functioning democracy, given the relatively low costs involved. They can be asked to do this precisely for the sake of freedom and self-government. Voting may be the one democratic activity that can be justifiably compelled so that all the other voluntary forms can exist.

At first sight, this seems undemocratic, but it isn't. There are times when one has to reduce a value in order to promote it. The distinction between honoring and promoting a value is apposite here. This distinction is a version of the analytic distinction between a consequentialist and a deontological attitude toward a particular value. Under a consequentialist strategy, we can design institutions so that the value is *promoted* by them, whereas under a deontological strategy, we can design them so as to *honor* the value.[53] A consequentialist will honor values only insofar "as honoring them is part of promoting them, or is necessary in order to promote them."[54] She will, for example, approve affirmative-action programs that temporarily reduce the value of equality of opportunity in order to promote it in the long term. In order to promote, overall, the values of freedom and democratic self-government, sacrificing the freedom to abstain from voting may be warranted. Therefore, although I agree that people should have the right to limit the extent of their participation in politics, I do not agree that such a right necessarily encompasses a right not to vote. Despite the intuitive appeal of the assumption that democratic participation is, by definition, voluntary, not all democratic action must – or can – be voluntary.

53 Philip Pettit, "Analytical Philosophy," in R. E. Goodin and P. Pettit (eds.), *A Companion to Contemporary Political Philosophy* (London: Wiley-Blackwell: 1995): 7–38.

54 Philip Pettit, "Consequentialism," in P. Singer (ed.), *A Companion to Ethics* (Oxford, UK: Blackwell, 1991): 230–40.

8.4 Voting as a Problem of Collective Action: Individual "Rationality" versus System Rationality

The problem of nonvoting cannot be understood as an abstract problem to be resolved using methodologic individualism. Voting is, by its nature, a social activity, a problem of collective, not individual, action. The question is not whether individual voting is rational or even a duty but rather, "Under what conditions does my individual vote serve me best?" That is to say, "What type of *system* makes voting rational?"

We have seen that the disadvantaged are less likely to vote than advantaged citizens because of the irrationality of doing so in a voluntary system. It has also been noted that compulsory voting takes "prisoner's dilemma" scenarios out of voting. It coordinates democracy by getting it to work as a social activity engaged in by group interests (admittedly this is not everyone's democratic ideal because most of us would prefer it if we all voted in the common interest or according to principles of justice. This is unlikely to occur, however). Voluntary voting, on the other hand, makes rational behavior seem irrational and irrational behavior seem rational. Compulsion is both economical and efficient because it frees me from (1) having to overcome uncertainty about the value of my vote and (2) having to weigh "opportunity costs" against benefits in an environment where resources and information are scarce. Mandatory voting makes elections operate as a *system*, and only in a system that treats voting as a problem of collective action as well as a problem of liberty and private choice does voting really work as a way of registering preferences and achieving representativeness.

Compulsion makes many of the irrationalities of voting and abstaining that plague voluntary systems disappear. It reduces opportunity, transaction, and information costs (see Chapter 6), prevents free riding (such as it exists; see later discussion), and makes voting meaningful by (inadvertently) organizing individual preferences into blocs of interests. This is not to say that voting isn't a bloc-interest business in voluntary systems; it is, however, here that the blocs tend to resolve into the privileged who vote and the disadvantaged who don't, hardly ideal for the democratic pluralist. But, under a compulsory system, the notion of electoral "rationality" undergoes a radical change. It is not now a question of whether or not the individual behavior is "rational" but whether the *system* evokes rational behavior. Voluntary systems evoke "irrational" behavior (i.e., the mass abstention of the poorly off, especially during crises) because they inevitably give rise to obstacles, uncertainties, and disincentives. In such systems, asking the question, "Is it rational to vote?" is just as silly as asking, "Is it rational to pay taxes in a voluntary system?" because free riding and prisoner's dilemmas give rise to irrationalities regardless of what I do and thereby prevent the system from working properly.[55] Voluntary systems convert short-term rationalities into long-term irrationalities and long-term rationalities into short-term irrationalities. Compelling people to vote is thus reasonable to the extent that state coercion is acceptable in resolving problems of coordination in order to improve or generate system utility and provided, of course, that the system utility is characterized by desired and desirable properties. In this case, the desired and desirable properties are representativeness, legitimacy, political equality, inclusiveness, minimization of elite power, control of the agenda by the people, and doing our bit to perpetuate democracy as a system for self-government and self-protection.

Voting is a practice that cannot be understood simply as an agglomeration of individual acts of utility. It only has system rationality (this is a bit like the distinction between system and act utilitarianism). Voting is a problem of collective action rather than individual choice because politics is fundamentally a competitive team sport with gains and losses, regardless of whether we would prefer it to be otherwise, with all participants altruistically acting in favor of the common good.

8.5 Compulsory-Voting Laws as Self-Paternalism

Compulsory voting reverses the norm of nonvoting that exists among certain (usually low-status) social groups, a norm that is perpetuated by the irrationality of their voting under a voluntary regime. It also ameliorates the harm of government policies that distribute costs and benefits

[55] That is to say, while it is rational for me to pay taxes so that I can enjoy the benefits of a properly working infrastructure, it is also irrational for me to pay taxes if others do not.

unequally. In this light, compulsory voting might be best understood as a form of *self*-paternalism.

Self-paternalism is not true paternalism; in fact, it's a form of autonomy. There are certain transactions or decisions that are usually regretted, for example, selling oneself into slavery or failure to wear a seatbelt that leads to injury. These are decisions that a rational citizen might, retrospectively, wish she had not been in a position to make; accordingly, people will generally agree to laws that will prevent them from yielding to actions "which they deem harmful to themselves."[56] In contrast to the standard liberal model of individuals being at all times the sole and best judge of their own interests, this model of *retrospective rationality* anticipates "many occasions on which the individual concerned might mistake [her] future interests and, hence, on which legal compulsion could help protect a person from [her]self." Individuals cannot always "adequately anticipate their future preferences," but retrospective rationality can "save them from this fate."[57] The case of Ulysses and the Sirens offers a useful analogy, one that also underlines the important distinction between our imperfectly informed – and often irrational – *desires* and preferences, on the one hand, and *reasons* informed by objective interests, on the other. Compulsory voting serves reasons rather than desires and preferences. The case of Australia exemplifies this point very well. Although compulsory voting was a government rather than popular initiative, once in operation, the public readily embraced it as a good idea. Extensive survey data show steady support of around 70+ percent for compulsory voting for at least the last five decades, whereas compliance with the law has always been high. Well below 1 percent of the Australian electorate is ever faced with a fine or court attendance in any given election period.[58] Similarly, in Belgium, fewer than 0.25 percent of nonvoters are ever prosecuted.[59]

[56] G. Calabresi and A. D. Melamed, "Property Rules, Liability Rules and Inalienability: One View of the Cathedral," *Harvard Law Review* 85 (April 1972): 1089–1128.

[57] Robert Goodin, *Political Theory and Public Policy* (Chicago: University of Chicago Press, 1982): 49.

[58] Mackerras and McAllister, "Compulsory Voting, Party Stability": 224.

[59] Hasen, "Voting without Law."

8.6 Doing One's Fair Share of the Democratic Work: Is Abstaining Free Riding?

If voting abstention is a form of free riding, it makes it easier to insist that people should vote. But I am conflicted about whether failure to vote really is a form of free riding. In order to free ride, it has to be shown that voting entails costs as well as benefits that free riders can take advantage of without actually contributing. I argued in Chapter 7 that democracy requires participatory effort and that there is a universal duty to vote so that we can all enjoy the benefits of living in a democracy as opposed to a less desirable form of government. From this perspective, individual abstainers could be seen as free riders, but, as was shown in Chapter 6, voting benefits participators. Whether or not individual voters rationalize their voting efforts in this way is unclear (partly because voting seems to be a habit or norm, just as abstention is also a habit or norm); however, we do know that voters tend to benefit, whereas abstainers tend to suffer; therefore, abstainers don't seem to gain too much at the expense of participators – quite the reverse. In general, people don't abstain to avoid doing their "fair share"; they do so because of perceived and real obstacles,[60] high opportunity and transaction costs, and/or because they have insufficient information not only about the real value of their vote but also about the intentions of other voters.[61] It seems that abstainers are free riders in terms of the maintenance and perpetuation of the democratic system but not free riders in terms of the economic and social consequences of habitual failure to vote (these things are not mutually exclusive). Both are undesirable outcomes, democratically speaking, that compulsory voting can readily resolve.

[60] U.S. Census Bureau data indicate, for example, that inability to take time off from work, illness, forgetfulness, and transportation and registration problems were other major obstacles to voting. Of course, there are always some who fail to vote due to apathy.

[61] Insufficient information includes underestimating real political clout, underestimating the adverse effect of abstention on welfare, and finally, the uncertainties that give rise to prisoner's dilemmas.

8.7 Compulsory Voting as *Substantive* Equality of Political Opportunity

I argued in Chapter 6 that actual participation is superior to the mere opportunity to vote and that legal entitlement to vote is not as desirable as actually voting because casting a formal vote tends to protect the material interests of the social group to which the elector belongs. I would like to refine that view here by suggesting that compulsory voting offers something else that is located halfway between *actual* voting and the *formal* opportunity to vote: *substantive* equality of opportunity.

In a properly administered compulsory-voting system such as Australia's, where failure to mark the ballot in a formal manner is possible and permissible, the state is not forcing people to choose between equally undesirable candidates (a common objection to compulsory voting), but it *is* compelling them to engage in the realization of a key liberal democratic value: *equality of political opportunity*. By this I mean that the state provides more than just a universal, formal entitlement to vote and makes sure that everyone is present on election day. In fact, in well-regulated systems such as Australia's, the state operates a kind of elaborate affirmative-action system to ensure that everyone, regardless of contingent status and obstacles experienced, is enabled to realize this capacity. Compulsion in a system such as Australia's brings with it a complex raft of measures designed to ensure that all the obstacles normally experienced by abstainers are removed so that every Australian, regardless, is enabled to vote. Compulsory registration and voting brought with them innovations to ensure that everyone can record a vote regardless of barriers such as being incarcerated, hospitalized, housebound, residing in a remote area, or having conflicting (especially religious) commitments (see Chapter 5).

Under well-functioning compulsory-voting regimes, the opportunity on offer is no mere symbolic value. The state is not simply obliging voters with an opportunity to expressively blow off steam; it is also inviting them to engage in activity that materially affects their lives and economic interests. Mandatory voting thus may be viewed as a positive freedom provided by the state in the same way that a (compulsory) basic level of education is a positive freedom enjoyed by all.

The view in places such as Australia and The Netherlands (before 1970) is that if a person decides to spoil or leave blank her ballot once inside the polling booth, that is her business; the most the state can do – and indeed seeks to do – is provide equality of access to the opportunity of expressing a preference. The nature of this compulsion is analogous to the state requirement that everyone should receive a basic education. Although not everyone who turns up to school necessarily wants to learn, nevertheless, the state is offering substantive educational opportunity by providing schools and requiring attendance. Just as being uneducated vastly limits a person's choices and her capacity for human flourishing, so too does abstention only permit a person to communicate a silence that is ambiguous in every way except for one: its ability to convey the simple message: "Feel free to ignore me." Attendance at a booth gives voters a far greater range of options than abstention, among them a formal vote, a protest vote, a punishment vote, a reward vote, a scribbled-on ballot, and even, in some cases, positive abstention. Even blank votes communicate something.[62] But, in fact, most of those who would normally abstain in voluntary systems do end up using their votes to protect their interests. Each, in one way or another, is participating in self-protection, self-government, and the joint project of constituting and perpetuating democracy.

8.8 Concluding Remarks

Because of its coercive aspects and alleged tendency to enfranchise apathetic and incompetent voters, it is sometimes said that compulsory voting is either inimical to – or generates outcomes that are inimical to – democratic ideals. In this chapter, I have argued that although compulsory voting must inevitably enfranchise some indifferent and incompetent voters, on the whole, near-universal participation does not appear to introduce any significant distortions into the voting process, nor does it appear to lead to bad governance. In fact, it seems to produce governments that are better able to act "for the people." The

[62] In compulsory-voting systems, the incidence of blank votes rises in electorates where there is a lack of perceived choice between candidates on offer, so it is a form of protest about that lack of choice (L. Hill, "Informal Voting under a System of Compulsory Voting," in B. Costar, G. Orr, and J. Tham [eds.], *Electoral Democracy: Australian Prospects* [Melbourne, Australia: Melbourne University Press, 2011]).

so-called problem of overinclusiveness is exaggerated, and its effects are far less egregious than underinclusiveness.

But, even if universal participation did introduce some disagreeable distortions to the electoral process, this would not be grounds for excluding the less competent. I say this not just because it would have an adverse impact on the poor in a way that is inimical to democratic *desiderata* but also because even a democracy with a degree of epistemic distortion is still doing its main job, that is, providing "government of the people, by the people, and for the people." In enfranchising all affected interests, compulsory voting offers not only political equality but also substantive equality of political opportunity. Although, at first sight, requiring people to vote looks like a violation of the democratic values of voluntarism and autonomy, under the right conditions, it is better understood as a form of self-paternalism that indirectly serves both these values while preventing democratic *system* failure.

9

Conclusion

9.1 Summary of Argument

Before moving on to my general conclusion, I offer first a broad summary of the various steps and components of the rather dense argument I have given in the preceding chapters.

1. Compulsory voting is the only really reliable and decisive means by which to raise turnout.
2. Elections and the way they operate are important because voting is the agreed procedure for legitimizing governments.
3. High turnout is preferable to low turnout because low-turnout elections are less legitimate. Low-turnout elections are less legitimate because they are less procedurally legitimate: they only give a partial and biased picture of the priorities of the electorate. This makes the governments of low-turnout election less *substantively* legitimate because government attention is directed only to those sections of the population who vote. Because such people also happen to be better off than nonvoters, this exacerbates political inequality and results in unrepresentative government. Universal, socially even voting confers legitimacy on both the electoral process and the government that wins office.
4. There is no such thing as a right not to vote. The right to vote is fundamental: it is protective of all other rights, and its existence defines the very structure of representative democracy. It

cannot, therefore, be legally waived, and any state's refusal to allow citizens to waive it is justified.

5. Voting is not a privilege right: it is a claim-power-right. Further, it is not just a (claim-power) right: it is also a duty. Voting is a duty-right. Voting is a duty we owe to other voters so that (a) together we can constitute and perpetuate representative democracy so that (b) we can meet other classes of voters on equal terms for the purposes of self-protection and self-government.
6. Voting is not just *any* duty; it is a *special* duty because the existence and proper functioning of representative democracy depend on its performance. So too do our welfare and rights. When democracy functions well, rights are more secure.
7. Compulsory voting seems illiberal because it violates one conception of liberty: negative liberty. But, because it enhances other conceptions of liberty such as nondomination, autonomy, and positive liberty, it can be reconciled with liberal values.
8. Compulsory voting seems undemocratic, but it isn't: sometimes it is necessary to reduce a value in order to promote it. By compelling people to vote, democracy as a system for self-government and self-protection is strengthened.
9. Compulsory voting makes democracy work better, enabling it to function as a social activity engaged in by all affected interests, not just a privileged elite. When managed properly, it is something we would retrospectively wish for because of its ability to solve the collective-action problem that contributes to the mass abstention of the disadvantaged in voluntary systems.
10. Compulsory voting does not seem to give us a less competent electorate, but even if it did, its capacity to deliver political equality – which is more important than political competence – justifies its use.
11. Compulsory voting does not lead to worse government; in fact, it correlates with better government that is more responsive to the needs and priorities of the entire electorate with lower levels of corruption and higher levels of citizen satisfaction and trust.
12. So, in light of the above, compulsory voting is justified.

9.2 Concluding Remarks

It would be preferable if we could find a less coercive means by which to raise turnout. But the fact is that compulsory voting is the *only* reliable way to provide high and socially even voter turnout. In turn, high and socially even turnout gives us government that is better able to serve the interests of everyone and not just the well-off. So, regardless of what survey data might tell us about the political competence of habitual abstainers, when such citizens do start voting, government starts to work not only by and of them but also *for* them. It converts their formal right to vote into a substantive one. But requiring people to vote is not justified just because it makes things better. It is justified because voting makes things better in a way that is fundamental to preserving a cherished way of life. It serves a vital social function: the maintenance and perpetuation of democracy, a collective benefit.

9.2.1 *The End of Voting?*

If the alleged right not to vote were recognized and universally exercised, democracy would soon come to an end[1]; such a right cannot, therefore, be universalized. It might be retorted (and often is) that such a fear is exaggerated because "not everyone will fail to vote." While it is true that not everyone fails to vote in voluntary systems, turnout decline is a near-universal phenomenon in voluntary-voting industrialized democracies worldwide,[2] so complacency here is probably imprudent. Worse still, turnout decline is increasingly concentrated among the disadvantaged so that the *character* of democratic participation is degenerating in a manner inimical to democratic ideals. Turnout decline means greater political inequality and the escalating political exclusion of the young, poor, and disadvantaged. But, even if turnout weren't in decline, the fact that it is low and socially uneven is still

[1] For Anthony Downs, "[T]he consequences of universal failure to vote are both obvious and disastrous" (Downs, *An Economic Theory*: 269). By contrast, Lomasky and Brennan are more complacent: "So no-one bothers to vote. Is this a woeful world in which to find oneself? To our eyes it has more the aspect of a paradise!" In the end, though, they say that they are "agnostic concerning the badness of universal abstention" (Lomasky and Brennan, "Duty to Vote?": 75–6).

[2] Whereas in compulsory-voting regimes such as Belgium and Australia, turnout has remained steady in the 90–95 percent (registered voter) range for decades. The same occurred in The Netherlands while compulsory voting was in force.

a significant concern for egalitarian democrats. In any case, the idea of a right not to vote cannot be admitted because it cannot be universalized; neither can the right to vote be waived because there is a collective interest at stake, namely, maintaining a democratic form of government.

Arresting the problem of declining turnout is more urgent than it ever was because it is being led by the young, particularly the disadvantaged young.[3] In other words, not only do the young vote at lower rates than older generations, but their rate of voting is also declining at a faster rate than that of older citizens.[4] Failure to vote among young people is not, as is commonly assumed, driven primarily by apathy, indifference to the election outcome, or even political ignorance (although these factors obviously must figure in some cases). Rather, it seems to be a function of the fact that recent generations have different political values.[5] It is now widely accepted that young people are losing touch with mainstream politics.[6] Conventional, and increasingly centrist, political agendas no longer resonate with them, and they tend to define politics differently from older generations.[7] Political parties are failing to respond to this state of affairs because they don't have to; after all, young people don't vote. Instead, parties quite rationally cater to the older constituencies that do vote. But, if the young were compelled to turn up, this would have to change, and democracy would be enriched and deepened.

[3] However, being young and disadvantaged is often one and the same thing. Young people are generally poorer; now, more than ever, being young is likely to mean being a renter, being unemployed (including long-term unemployed), being underpaid, and being homeless. We also know that economic deprivation and social exclusion are correlated with higher than average levels of political inefficacy, disillusionment, and cynicism (see Hill, "Compulsory Voting, Political Shyness"). Such states are known to give rise to civic withdrawal.

[4] According to one British survey, whereas 75 percent of registered voters aged sixty-five plus voted, only 37 percent of young people did so (Keaney and Rogers, 2006: 5).

[5] Blais and Rubenson, "Turnout Decline."

[6] *Ibid.*; R. Jowell and A. Park, *Young People, Politics and Citizenship: A Disengaged Generation* (London: Citizenship Foundation, 1998); Wattenberg, *Where Have All the Voters Gone?*

[7] The young were more likely to define politics in terms of "localized," "immediate," and often "postmaterial" issues (M. Henn and M. Weinstein, "Youth and Voting Behaviour in Britain," American Political Science Association Annual Meeting, San Francisco, September 3–4, 2001: 19–20). Young people express interest in issues that do not always figure in mainstream debates. Environmental politics and animal rights are two examples (Jowell and Park, *Young People*: 6).

The dispositions of the young would not bode ill for the future of Western democracies if they were merely life-cycle phenomena, as has been assumed (correctly) in the past. Now, however, the civic disengagement of the young signals a pattern of disengagement that is likely to endure so that turnout will become lower and more socially uneven as time passes.[8] As Jonathan Freedland remarked in the aftermath of the 2001 British election: "[W]hat used to be an under 25 problem a decade ago is now an under 35 problem and fast becoming an under 45 problem; once turned off, these people are staying turned off, perhaps for life."[9] The fact that young people now seem less disposed to adopt the *habit* of voting seems to be signaling a long-term shift in voting behavior. Low-turnout elections – such as are now routine in most Western democracies – leave an indelible mark on the voting habits of young citizens:

> [Those] who first vote in a low turnout election will retain a profile of lower turnout in subsequent elections, even elections in which yet new cohorts vote at a higher rate; so the past leaves a "footprint" in subsequent elections reflecting the low turnout of an earlier era. The same sort of footprint is left by abnormally high turnout eras.[10]

It might be retorted that young people are getting politically involved in other ways, such as mobilizing online to sign petitions and organize other forms of protest. This is true, and it can be very effective, but voting is still the agreed procedure for legitimizing governments and putting into power those who decide whether or not we will go to war, what levels of taxation we will have to pay, whether we are eligible for welfare benefits, and whether it is legal for us to march in a political demonstration.

9.2.2 *Compulsory Voting as the Solution*

The fact that low-turnout elections are now the norm in most industrialized democracies underlines the need for a blanket solution to the turnout problem that is able to target not only the young but *all* social

[8] For a detailed discussion here, see Franklin, *Voter Turnout*.

[9] J. Freedland, "Rise of the Non-Voter," *The Guardian*, Wednesday December 12, 2001.

[10] M. A. Fotos and M. M. Franklin, "Naive Political Science and the Paradox of Voting," paper prepared for the Annual Meeting of the Midwest Political Science Association, Palmer House Hilton, Chicago, April 25–28, 2002: 26.

groups. Like any ingrained habit, voting behavior is quite hard to change. However, laws are very good at changing habits because they not only alter behavior but also can effect shifts in attitudes, enabling people to internalize new preferences.[11] A good historical example is any law instituted for the purpose of granting suffrage rights to previously excluded categories of people, despite prevailing (i.e., hostile) social norms. Such laws, though initially opposed by many (and often the majority) of the public, soon came to be accepted as normal, and eventually, people were able to take their voting rights for granted. Similarly, compulsory-voting legislation, despite any initial (and probably inevitable) resistance, can become an accepted and effective means for establishing or reestablishing the adaptive norm of voting among habitual abstainers[12] and for arresting decline in turnout.

Apart from being the most decisive means for maintaining high and socially even turnout, under the right conditions, compulsory voting can be very well tolerated by the public. Those who object to compulsion tend to conceive the citizen's obligation to vote as an essentially vertical relationship between the individual and the state, whereas the obligation is really an obligation between citizens, with the state acting as "a special kind of association … an ethical order, the embodiment of the common life of its members."[13] On this interpretation, compulsory voting is a form of self-paternalism for the ultimate purpose of enhancing autonomy.

Some who have considered compulsory voting as a solution to low turnout have rejected it according to the rationale that compulsory voting only addresses the *symptom* rather than root causes of nonparticipation. Apart from the potentially misplaced assumption that low turnout is only a *symptom* of something rather than a problem in itself, this type of argument fails to consider the effects of voting participation on the nature of politics and voters and on the relationship of citizens to representatives. Compulsory voting can get to some of the root causes of voting abstention by providing a circuit breaker to the cycle of neglect, mistrust, cynicism, and nonparticipation that occurs in voluntary settings. Political science has known for some time

[11] Hasen, "Voting without Law": 2135, 2167.
[12] *Ibid.*: 2170; Hill, "Compulsory Voting in Australia."
[13] Pateman, *Political Obligation.*

that abstainers tend to perceive government as unresponsive; believing that their vote will be ignored, they abstain.[14] Not surprisingly, as we saw in Chapter 6, relative to voters, nonvoters *are*, in fact, ignored. Abstainers thus become locked into a self-fulfilling cycle of quiescence, alienation, and government neglect. But when everyone votes, the cycle breaks down. At the risk of waxing tautological (this is a *cycle* I'm talking about), pork-barreling becomes less rewarding for politicians because universal voting participation encourages incumbent governments to protect everybody's interests regardless. This, in turn, enhances satisfaction with democracy, as has been shown.

9.2.3 *Illiberal and Undemocratic?*

Because of its coercive aspects and the apparent contradiction of requiring people to exercise a fundamental right, it is often said that compulsory voting is inimical to either liberal or democratic values (or both). I have argued that it can be reconciled with both sets but concede that, from the liberal perspective, mandatory voting does undoubtedly infringe on one interpretation of liberty: negative liberty. At the same time, it tends to serve a number of other interpretations, namely, positive liberty, nondomination, and autonomy. Further, the right to vote cannot be inverted or waived because it exists to serve more than personal ends. I should stress here, however, that the distinction between liberal and democratic values is not always stable where voting is concerned: indeed, liberal democratic values tend to support and reinforce one another, operating in a kind of mutually reinforcing feedback dynamic. For example, the right to free speech is a liberty, but it is also a precondition for democracy; democracy, in turn (via the possession and exercise of the vote), provides support and protection for such a right.

It is also admitted that compulsory voting violates the democratic principle of choice insofar as it denies choice about whether or not to attend a polling place. But this objection is only fatal if it is agreed that choice in this matter is more important than a whole range of other important democratic values that compulsory voting can serve very well, among them legitimacy, representativeness, political equality,

[14] See, e.g., M. Parenti, *Democracy for the Few* (New York: St Martin's Press, 1974): 160; P. Kimball, *The Disconnected* (New York: Columbia University Press, 1972): 17.

substantive equality of political opportunity, minimization of elite power, protection of minority interests, inclusiveness, and final control of the agenda by the *demos*. Further, as I have also argued, restricting choice in this matter enhances choice in other spheres of democratic activity. In order to discredit compulsory voting, it would need to be shown that democracy is worse off when people are required to vote. Because the reverse seems to be the case, under the right conditions, compelling people to vote is a good idea.

Bibliography

Abraham, H. J., *Compulsory Voting* (Washington, DC: Public Affairs Press, 1955).

Althaus, Scott, "Information Effects in Collective Preferences," *American Political Science Review* 92 (1998), 545–58.

Collective Preferences in Democratic Politics (New York: Cambridge University Press, 2003).

Alvarez, Michael, *Information and Elections* (Ann Arbor: University of Michigan Press, 1997).

Amato, Paul, and Bruce, Keith, "Parental Divorce and the Well-Being of Children: A Meta-Analysis," *Psychological Bulletin* 110 (1991): 26–46.

Ansolabehere, Stephen, and Stewart, Charles, III, "Residual Votes Attributable to Technology," *Journal of Politics* 67 (2005): 365–89.

Apps, Alfred, Speech to the Empire Club of Canada, May 2, 2011; available at: http://pdopav2.blogspot.com/2011/06/alfred-apps-speech-empire-club-of.html.

Argyle, M., "Causes and Correlates of Happiness," in D. Kahneman, E. Diener, and N. Schwarz (eds.), *Well-Being: The Foundations of Hedonic Psychology* (New York: Sage, 1999): 353–73.

The Psychology of Happiness (London: Routledge, 2002).

Arnold, D. R., *The Logic of Congressional Action* (New Haven, CT: Yale University Press, 1990).

Aronson, Stacey, and Huston, Aletha C., "The Mother-Infant Relationship in Single, Cohabitating, and Married Families: A Case for Marriage?" *Journal of Family Psychology* 18 (2004): 5–18.

Australian Electoral Commission (AEC), "Compulsory Voting," *Electoral Backgrounder No. 8* (Canberra, June 1, 1999); available at: http://www.aec.gov.au/pubs/ backgrounders/vol_8/main.htm (last accessed August 6, 2003).

Frequently Asked Questions (Canberra, 2013); available at: http://www.aec.gov.au/faqs/ voting_australia.htm#not-vote.

Bagnoli, Mark, and Lipman, Barton, "Provision of Public Goods: Fully Implementing the Core through Private Contributions," *Review of Economic Studies* 56 (1989): 583–601.

Ballinger, Chris, "Compulsory Voting: Palliative Care for Democracy in the UK?" paper presented at the European Consortium for Political Research Joint Sessions workshop "Compulsory Voting: Principles and Practice," Helsinki, Finland, May 7–12, 2007.

Bannon, D. B., "Electoral Participation and Non-Voter Segmentation," *Journal of Nonprofit and Public Sector Marketing* 14 (1) (2010): 109–27.

Bartels, Larry, "Uninformed Votes: Information Effects in Presidential Elections," *American Political Science Review* 40 (1997): 194–230.

Beckman, L., *The Frontiers of Democracy: The Right to Vote and Its Limits* (Houndsmills, UK: Palgrave Macmillan, 2009).

Beetham, D., "Liberal Democracy and the Limits of Democratization," in D. Held (ed.), *Prospects for Democracy* (Cambridge, UK: Polity Press, 1993): 55–73.

Benn, Stanley, *A Theory of Freedom* (New York: Cambridge University Press, 1988).

Bennett, S. E., and Resnick, D., "The Implications of Nonvoting for Democracy in the United States," *American Journal of Political Science* 34 (3) (1990): 771–802.

Beramendi, P., and Anderson, C. J., "Income Inequality and Democratic Representation," in P. Beramendi and C. J. Anderson (eds.), *Democracy, Inequality and Representation* (New York: Sage, 2008): 3–25.

Berlin, I., "Two Concepts of Liberty," in *Four Essays on Liberty* (London: Oxford University Press, 1969).

Besley, Timothy, *Principled Agents? The Political Economy of Good Government* (New York: Oxford University Press, 2006).

Birch, Sarah, "The Case for Compulsory Voting," *Public Policy Research* 16 (2009): 21–7.

Full Participation: A Comparative Study of Compulsory Voting (Manchester, UK: Manchester University Press, 2009).

Blais, A., "Political Participation," in L. LeDuc, R. G. Niemi, and P. Norris (eds.), *Comparing Democracies 3: Elections and Voting in the 21st Century* (London: Sage, 2010): 165–83.

Blais, A., Gidengil, E., Nevitte, N., and Nadeau, R., "Where Does Turnout Decline Come From?" *European Journal of Political Research* 43 (2) (2004): 221–36.

Blais, A. and Rubenson, D., "The Source of Turnout Decline," *Comparative Political Studies* 46 (1) (2013): 95–117.

Blomberg, J. A., "Protecting the Right Not to Vote from Voter Purge Statutes," *Fordham Law Review* 64 (1995): 1015–50.

Boyd, R., "Decline of U.S. Turnout: Structural Explanations," *American Politics Quarterly* 9 (1981): 133–59.

Brady, H. E., Verba, S., and Schlozman, K., "Beyond SES: A Resource Model of Political Participation," *American Political Science Review* 89 (2) (1995): 271–94.

Brennan, Geoffrey, and Lomasky, Loren, *Democracy and Decision* (New York: Cambridge University Press, 2003).

Brennan, J. "Polluting the Polls: When Citizens Should Not Vote," *Australasian Journal of Philosophy* 87 (4) (2009): 535–49.

The Ethics of Voting (Princeton, NJ: Princeton University Press, 2011).

"Mandatory Voting Would Be a Disaster," *New York Times*, November 7, 2011; available at: http://www.nytimes.com/roomfordebate/2011/11/07/should-voting-in-the-us-be-mandatory-14/mandatory-voting-would-be-a-disaster.

The Ethics of Voting (paperback edition with new afterword by the author) (Princeton, NJ: Princeton University Press, 2012).

Libertarianism: What Everyone Needs to Know (Oxford, UK: Oxford University Press, 2012).

Brighouse, Harry, and Fleurbaey, Marc, "Democracy and Proportionality," *Journal of Political Philosophy* 18 (2010): 137–55.

Brody, R., and Page, B., "Indifference, Alienation and Rational Decisions," *Public Choice* 15 (1973): 1–17.

Bronte-Tinkew, Jacinta, Moore, Kristin A., and Carrano, Jennifer, "The Influence of Father Involvement in Youth Risk Behaviors among Adolescents," *Social Science Research* 35 (2006): 181–209.

Brown, Susan L., "Family Structure and Child Well-Being: The Significance of Parental Cohabitation," *Journal of Marriage and the Family* 66 (2004): 351–67.

"Family Structure Transitions and Adolescent Well-Being," *Demography* 43 (2006): 447–61.

Brown, Susan L. and Manning, Wendy D., "Family Boundary Ambiguity and the Measurement of Family Structure," *Demography* 46 (2009): 85–101.

Brunell, T. L., and Di Nardo, J., "A Propensity Score Reweighting Approach to Estimating the Partisan Effects of Full Turnout in American Presidential Elections," *Political Analysis* 12 (2004): 28–45.

Bullock, C. S., III, "Congressional Voting and the Mobilisation of a Black Electorate in the South," *Journal of Politics* 43 (3) (1981): 662–82.

Bunch, Niels J., "Position-Bias in Multiple Choice Questions," *Journal of Marketing Research* 21 (1984): 216–20.

Burnham, W. D., "The Turnout Problem," in J. Richly (ed.), *Elections American Style* (Washington, DC: Brookings Institution, 1987): 110–121.

Button, J. W., *Blacks and Social Change: Impact of the Civil Rights Movement in Southern Communities* (Princeton, NJ: Princeton University Press, 1989).

Calabresi, G., and Melamed, A. D., "Property Rules, Liability Rules and Inalienability: One View of the Cathedral," *Harvard Law Review* 85 (1972): 1089–128.

Caltech/MIT Voting Project, "Voting: What Is, and What Could Be" (Caltech/MIT, July 2001): 13; available at: http://www.vote.caltech.edu/sites/default/files/voting_what_is_what_could_be.pdf.

Caplan, Bryan, *The Myth of the Rational Voter* (Princeton, NJ: Princeton University Press, 1997).

"What Makes People Think like Economists? Evidence on Economic Cognition from the 'Survey of Americans and Economists on the Economy,'" *Journal of Law and Economics* 44 (2001): 395–426.

The Myth of the Rational Voter: Why Democracies Choose Bad Policies (Princeton, NJ: Princeton University Press, 2008).

"The Myth of the Rational Voter and Political Theory," in Hélène Landemore and John Elster (eds.), *Collective Wisdom: Principles and Mechanisms* (Cambridge, UK: Cambridge University Press, 2012).

Caplan, Bryan, Campton, Eric, Grove, Wayne, and Somin, Ilya, "Systematically Biased Beliefs about Political Influence: Evidence from the Perception of Political Influence on Policy Outcomes Survey," working paper, George Mason University, Fairfax, VA, 2012.

Caplan, Bryan and Miller, Stephen, "Intelligence Makes People Think Like Economists: Evidence from the General Social Survey," *Intelligence* 38 (2010): 636–47.

Carlson, Marcia J., "Family Structure, Father Involvement, and Adolescent Outcomes," *Journal of Marriage and the Family* 68 (2006): 137–54.

Cavenagh, Shannon E., and Huston, Aletha C., "Family Instability and Children's Early Problem Behavior," *Social Forces* 85 (2006): 551–80.

Chong, A., and Olivera, M. "On Compulsory Voting and Income Inequality in a Cross-Section of Countries," Inter-American Development Bank Research Department Working Paper 533, Washington, DC, May 2005.

Christiano, Thomas, "Democracy," in Edward N. Zalta (ed.), *Stanford Encyclopedia of Philosophy*, Fall 2008 ed.; available at: http://plato.stanford.edu/archives/fall2008/entries/democracy/.

Ciccone, A., "The Constitutional Right to Vote Is Not a Duty," *Hamline Journal of Public Law and Policy* 325 (2001–2): 325–57.

Citrin, Jack, and Green, Donald, "The Self-Interest Motive in American Public Opinion," *Research in Micropolitics* 3 (1990): 1–28.

Citrin, J., Schickler, E., and Sides, J., "What if Everyone Voted? Simulating the Impact of Increased Turnout in Senate Elections," *American Journal of Political Science* 47 (1) (2003): 75–90.

Clark, Andrew E., and Oswald, Andrew J., "Unhappiness and Unemployment," *Economic Journal* 104 (1994): 648–59.

Conover, Pamela, Feldman, Stanley, and Knight, Kathleen, "The Personal and Political Underpinnings of Economic Forecasts," *American Journal of Political Science* 31 (1987): 559–83.

Converse, Philip, "Popular Representation and the Distribution of Information," in John A. Ferejohn and James H. Kuklinski (eds.), *Information and Democratic Processes* (Urbana: University of Illinois Press, 1990): 25–52.

Cook, W. W., "Introduction," in W. N. Hohfeld (ed.), *Fundamental Legal Conceptions: As Applied in Judicial Reasoning* (New Haven, CT: Yale University Press, 1964): 87–98.

Coorey, P., "Few Back Minchin on Voluntary Vote," *The Advertiser*, May 2, 2005.

Cox, Michaelene, "When Trust Matters: Explaining Differences in Voter Turnout," *Journal of Common Market Studies* 41 (2003), 757–70.

Dahl, R. A., *After the Revolution: Authority in a Good Society* (New Haven, CT: Yale University Press, 1971).

"Procedural Democracy," in P. Laslett and J. Fishkin (eds.), *Philosophy, Politics and Society*, 5th Series (New Haven, CT: Yale University Press, 1979): 52–68.

"The Myth of the Presidential Mandate," *Political Science Quarterly* 105 (1990): 355–72.

Dario, G., and Medew, R., "*Pilot Project on Informality in Port Adelaide*," Research Report No. 9 (Canberra: Australian Electoral Commission, 2009); available at: http://www.aec.gov.au/pdf/ research/papers/paper9/ research_paper9.pdf (last accessed September 2, 2009).

Delli Carpini, Michael X., and Keeter, Scott, "Stability and Change in the U.S. Public's Knowledge of Politics," *Public Opinion Quarterly* 55 (1991): 583–612.

What Americans Know about Politics and Why It Matters (New Haven, CT: Yale University Press, 1996).

Dermody, J., Hammer-Lloyd, S., and Scullion, R., "Young People and Voting Behaviour: Alienated Youth and (or) an Interested and Critical Citizenry?" *European Journal of Marketing* 44 (3–4) (2010): 421–35.

Donovan, T., Denemark, D. and Bowler, S. "Trust, Citizenship and Participation: Australia in Comparative Perspective," in D. Denemark, G. Meagher, S. Wilson, M. Western, and T. Phillips (eds.), *Australian Social Attitudes 2: Citizenship, Work and Aspirations* (Sydney, Australia: University of New South Wales Press, 2007): 95–115.

Douglas, J. A., "Is the Right to Vote Really Fundamental?" *Cornell Journal of Law and Public Policy* 18 (1) (2008): 143–201.

Dowding, K., Goodin, R. E., and Pateman, C., "Introduction," in K. Dowding, R. E. Goodin, and C. Pateman (eds.), *Justice and Democracy: Essays for Brian Barry* (Cambridge, UK: Cambridge University Press, 2004): 1–24.

Dowding, K. and Van Hees, M., "The Construction of Rights," *American Political Science Review* 97 (2) (2003): 281–93.

Downs, A., *An Economic Theory of Democracy* (New York: Harper and Row, 1957).

Dryzek, J., *Deliberative Democracy and Beyond: Liberals, Critics, Contestations* (Oxford, UK: Oxford University Press, 2000).

Dunning, David, Johnson, Kerri, Ehrlinger, Joyce, and Kruger, Justin, "Why People Fail to Recognize Their Own Incompetence," *Current Directions in Psychological Science* 12 (2003): 83–6.

Edlin, Aaron, Gelman, Andrew, and Kaplan, Noah, "Voting as a Rational Choice: Why and How People Vote to Improve the Well-Being of Others," *Rationality and Society* 19 (2007): 219–314.

Ehrlinger, Joyce, Johnson, Kerri, Banner, Matthew, Dunning, David, and Kruger, Justin, "Why the Unskilled are Unaware: Further Explorations of (Absent) Self-Insight among the Incompetent," *Organizational Behavior and Human Decision Processes* 105 (2008): 98–121.

Engelen, Bart, "Why Compulsory Voting Can Enhance Democracy," *Acta Analytica* 42 (2007): 23–39.

Enns, Peter K., and Wlezien, Christopher (eds.), *Who Gets Represented?* (New York: Sage, 2011).

Estlund, D., *Democratic Authority: A Philosophical Framework* (Princeton, NJ: Princeton University Press, 2008).

European Commission and European Court of Human Rights, *Yearbook of the European Convention on Human Rights* (The Hague, Netherlands: Martinus Nijhoff, 1972).

Evans, Jocelyn, *Voters and Voting: An Introduction* (Thousand Oaks, CA: Sage, 2004).

Feddersen, Timothy, Gailmard, Sean, and Sandroni, Alvaro, "A Bias toward Unselfishness in Large Elections: Theory and Experimental Evidence," *American Political Science Review* 103 (2009): 175–92.

Feeley, M., "A Solution to the 'Voting Dilemma' in Modern Democratic Theory," *Ethics* 84 (1974): 235–42.

Feinberg, Joel, *Social Philosophy* (Englewood Cliffs, NJ: Prentice-Hall, 1979).

Harm to Others (New York: Oxford University Press, 1984).

Fomby, Paula, and Cherlin, Andrew J., "Family Instability and Child Well-Being," *American Sociological Review* 72 (2007): 181–204.

Fotos, M. A., and Franklin, M. M., "Naive Political Science and the Paradox of Voting," paper prepared for the Annual Meeting of the Midwest Political Science Association, Palmer House Hilton, Chicago, April 25–28, 2002.

Fowler, A., "Electoral and Policy Consequences of Voter Turnout: Evidence from Compulsory Voting in Australia," *Quarterly Journal of Political Science* 8 (2) (2011):159–82; available at: http://papers.ssrn.com/sol3/papers.cfm?abstract_id=1816649.

Franklin, Mark N., "Electoral Engineering and Cross-National Turnout Differences: What Role for Compulsory Voting?" *British Journal of Political Science* 29 (1999): 205–24.

Voter Turnout and the Dynamics of Electoral Competition in Established Democracies since 1945 (New York: Cambridge University Press, 2004).
Freedland, J., "Rise of the Non-Voter," *The Guardian*, December 12, 2001.
Friedman, Jeffrey, "Democratic Competence in Normative and Positive Theory: Neglected Implications of 'The Nature of Belief Systems in Mass Publics'," *Critical Review* 18 (2006): i–xliii.
Funk, Carolyn, "The Dual Influence of Self-Interest and Societal Interest in Public Opinion," *Political Research Quarterly* 53 (2000): 37–62.
Funk, Carolyn and Garcia-Monet, Patricia, "The Relationship between Personal and National Concerns in Public Perceptions of the Economy," *Political Research Quarterly* 50 (1997): 317–42.
Gallego, A., "Understanding Unequal Turnout: Education and Voting in Comparative Perspective," *Electoral Studies* 29 (2) (2010): 239–48.
Galston, William, "Telling Americans to Vote, or Else," *New York Times*, November 6, 2011: SR9.
Gans, C. B., "The Empty Ballot Box: Reflections on Non-Voters in America," *Public Opinion* 1 (1978): 54–7.
Gaus, Gerald, *Contemporary Theories of Liberalism* (Thousand Oaks, CA: Sage, 2004).
Gelman, Andrew, Silver, Nate, and Edlin, Aaron, "What Is the Probability that Your Vote Will Make a Difference?," *Economic Inquiry* 50 (2012): 321–6.
Gershtenson, J., "Mobilization Strategies of the Democrats and Republicans, 1956–2000," *Political Research Quarterly* 56 (3) (2003): 293–308.
Gilens, Martin, *Affluence and Influence* (Princeton, NJ: Princeton University Press, 2012).
Goggin, Stephen N., Byrne, Michael D., and Gilbert, Juan E., "Post-Election Auditing: Effects of Procedure and Ballot Type on Manual Counting Accuracy, Efficiency, and Auditor Satisfaction and Confidence," *Election Law Journal* 11 (2012): 36–51.
Gomez, B. T., Hansford, T. G., and Krause, G. A., "The Republicans Should Pray for Rain: Weather, Turnout and Voting in U.S. Presidential Elections," *Journal of Politics* 69 (3) (2007): 649–63.
Goodin, R. E., *Political Theory and Public Policy* (Chicago: University of Chicago Press, 1982).
"Enfranchising All Affected Interests, and Its Alternatives," *Philosophy and Public Affairs* 35 (1) (2007): 40–68.
Green, Donald, and Shapiro, Ian, *Pathologies of Rational Choice Theory* (New Haven, CT: Yale University Press, 1994).
Griffin, J. D., and Newman, B., "Are Voters Better Represented?" *Journal of Politics* 67 (4) (2005): 1206–27.
Grönlund, K., and Setälä, M., "Political Trust, Satisfaction and Voter Turnout," *Comparative European Politics* 5 (4) (2007): 400–22.

Grossback, L. J., Peterson, D. A. M., and Stimson, J. A., *Mandate Politics* (New York: Cambridge University Press, 2006).

"Electoral Mandates in American Politics," *British Journal of Political Science* 37 (2007): 711–30.

Guerra, Claudio Lopez, "The Enfranchisement Lottery," *Politics, Philosophy, and Economics* 26 (2010): 211–33.

Haidt, Jonathan, "The New Science of Morality," *Edge*, September 17, 2010; available at: http://edge.org/conversation/a-new-science-of-morality-part-1.

The Righteous Mind (New York: Vintage, 2013).

Halperin, J. P. W., "Note: A Winner at the Polls: A Proposal for Mandatory Voter Registration," *Journal of Legislation and Public Policy* 69 (1999–2000): 69–117.

Hansford, T. G., and Gomez, B. T., "Estimating the Electoral Effects of Voter Turnout," *American Political Science Review* 104 (2) (2010): 268–88.

Hardin, R., "The Utilitarian Logic of Liberalism," *Ethics* 97 (3) (1986): 47–74.

Hart, H. L. A., "Are There Any Natural Rights?" in A. Quinton (ed.), *Political Philosophy* (Oxford, UK: Oxford University Press, 1967): 53–66.

Hasen, R. L., "Voting without Law," *Pennsylvania Law Review* 144 (5) (1996): 2135–79.

Henn, M., and Weinstein, M., "Youth and Voting Behaviour in Britain," paper presented at the American Political Science Association Annual Meeting, San Francisco, September 3–4, 2001; available at: http://pro.harvard.edu/papers/050/050001HennMattoo.pdf (last accessed April 3, 2006).

Henn, M., Weinstein, M., and Forrest, S., "Uninterested Youth? Young People's Attitudes towards Party Politics in Britain," *Political Studies* 53(4) (2005): 556–78.

Henn, M., Weinstein, M., and Wring, D., "A Generation Apart? Youth and Political Participation in Britain," *British Journal of Politics and International Relations* 4 (2) (2002): 167–92.

Hicks, A. M., and Swank, D. H., "Politics, Institutions, and Welfare Spending in Industrialized Countries, 1960–82," *American Political Science Review* 86 (1992): 658–74.

Highton, B., and Wolfinger, R. E., "The Political Implications of Higher Turnout," *British Journal of Political Science* 31 (1) (2001): 179–223.

Hill, K. Q., and Leighley, J. E., "The Policy Consequences of Class Bias in State Electorates," *American Journal of Political Science* 36 (2) (1992): 351–65.

Hill, K. Q., Leighley, J. E., and Hinton-Anderson, A., "Lower-Class Mobilization and Policy Linkage in the U.S. States," *American Journal of Political Science* 39 (1) (1995): 75–86.

Hill, L., "Compulsory Voting, Political Shyness and Welfare Outcomes," *Journal of Sociology* 36 (1) (2000): 30–49.

"Low Voter Turnout in the United States: Is Compulsory Voting a Viable Solution?" *Journal of Theoretical Politics* 18 (2) (2006): 207–32.

"Public Acceptance of Compulsory Voting: Explaining the Australian Case," *Representation* 46 (4) (2010): 425–38.

"Informal Voting under a System of Compulsory Voting," in B. Costar, G. Orr, and J. Tham (eds.), *Electoral Democracy: Australian Prospects* (Melbourne, Australia: Melbourne University Press, 2011).

Hill, L. and Koch, C., "The Voting Rights of Incarcerated Australian Citizens," *Australian Journal of Political Science* 42 (6) (2011): 2013–228.

Hill, L. and Young, S., "Protest or Error? Informal Voting and Compulsory Voting," *Australian Journal of Political Science* 42 (3) (2007): 515–21.

Hirczy, W., "Explaining Near-Universal Turnout: The Case of Malta," *European Journal of Political Research* 27 (1995): 255–72.

HLR, "The Case for Compulsory Voting in the United States," *Harvard Law Review* 121 (2) (2007): 591–612.

Ho, D. E., and Imai, K., "Estimating Causal Effects of Ballot Order from a Randomized Natural Experiment: The California Alphabet Lottery, 1978–2002," *Public Opinion Quarterly* 72 (2) (2008): 216–40.

Hohfeld, W. N., *Fundamental Legal Conceptions: As Applied in Judicial Reasoning* (New Haven, CT: Yale University Press, 1964).

Holbrook, Thomas, and Garand, James, "Homo Economicus? Economic Information and Economic Voting," *Political Research Quarterly* 49 (1996): 351–75.

Hooghe, M., and Pelleriaux, K., "Compulsory Voting in Belgium: An Application of the Lijphart Thesis," *Electoral Studies* 17 (4) (1998): 419–24.

Huddy, Leonie, Jones, Jeffrey, and Chard, Richard, "Compassion vs. Self-Interest: Support for Old-Age Programs among the Non-Elderly," *Political Psychology* 22 (2001): 443–72.

Huemer, Michael, *The Problem of Political Authority: An Examination of the Right to Coerce and the Duty to Obey* (New York: Macmillan, 2012).

Hughes, Colin, and Costar, Brian, *Limiting Democracy: The Erosion of Electoral Rights in Australia* (Sydney, Australia: University of New South Wales Press, 2006).

International Institute for Democracy and Electoral Assistance (IDEA), http://www.idea.int/vt/countryview.cfm?id=15.

Jackman, S., "Non-Compulsory Voting in Australia?: What Surveys Can (and Can't) Tell Us," *Electoral Studies* 18 (1) (1999): 29–48.

Jakee, K., and Sun, G.-Z., "Is Compulsory Voting More Democratic?," *Public Choice* 129 (2006): 61–75.

Jefferson, J. W., and Thompson, T. D., "Rhinotillexomania: Psychiatric Disorder or Habit," *Journal of Clinical Psychology* 56 (1995): 56–9.

Joint Standing Committee on Electoral matters (JSCEM), "Fact Sheet: Report on the 2007 Election," *Issues* (Canberra: Parliament House, June 23, 2009).

Jones, P., *Rights* (London: Macmillan, 1994).
Jones, W. H. M., "In Defence of Apathy: Some Doubts on the Duty to Vote," *Political Studies* 2 (1) (1954): 25–37.
Jowell R., and Park, A., *Young People, Politics and Citizenship: A Disengaged Generation* (London: Citizenship Foundation, 1998).
Kahneman, Daniel, Krueger, Alan B., Schkade, David A., Schwarz, Norbert, and Stone, Arthur A., "A Survey Method for Characterizing Daily Life Experience: The Day Reconstruction Method," *Science* 306 (2004): 1776–80.
Karlan, Pamela S., "Convictions and Doubts: Retribution, Representation, and the Debate over Felon Disenfranchisement," *Stanford Law Review* 56 (5) (2004): 1147–70.
Katz, R. S., *Democracy and Elections* (New York: Oxford University Press, 1997).
Keany, E., and Rogers, B., *A Citizen's Duty: Voter Inequality and the Case for Compulsory Turnout* (London: Institute for Public Policy Research, 2006); available at: http://www.ippr.org/ecomm/files/a_citizen%27s_duty.pdf.
Keech, W., *The Impact of Negro Voting: The Role of the Vote in the Quest for Equality* (Chicago: Rand McNally, 1968).
Kelly, Jamie Terrence, *Framing Democracy* (Princeton, NJ: Princeton University Press, 2012).
Kelsen, H., "Foundations of Democracy," *Ethics* 66 (1955): 1–101.
Kenworthy, L., and Pontusson, J., "Rising Inequality and the Politics of Redistribution in Affluent Countries," *Perspectives on Politics* 3 (3) (2005): 449–71.
Kimball, D. C., "Summary Table on Voting Technology and Residual Vote Rates," University of Missouri, St Louis, December 14, 2005; available at: http://www.umsl.edu/~kimballd/rtables.pdf.
Kimball, P., *The Disconnected* (New York: Columbia University Press, 1972).
Kinder, D., and Kiewiet, R., "Economic Discontent and Political Behavior: The Role of Personal Grievances and Collective Economic Judgments in Congressional Voting," *American Journal of Political Science* 23 (1979): 495–527.
King, A., and Leigh, A., "Are Ballot Order Effects Heterogeneous?," *Social Science Quarterly* 90 (1) (2009): 71–87.
Kreimer, S. F., "Allocation Sanctions: The Problem of Negative Rights in a Positive State," *University of Pennsylvania Law Review* 132 (6) (1984): 1293–1397.
Kropf, Martha, and Kimball, David C., *Helping America Vote: The Limits of Election Reform* (London: Routledge, 2011).
Kruger, Justin, and Dunning, David, "Unskilled and Unaware of It: How Difficulties in Recognizing One's Own Incompetence Lead to Inflated

Self-Assessments," *Journal of Personality and Social Psychology* 77 (1999): 1121–34.

"Unskilled and Unaware – But Why? A Reply to Krueger and Mueller," *Journal of Personality and Social Psychology* 82 (2002): 189–92.

Lackoff, S., *Democracy: History, Theory, Practice* (Boulder, CO: Westview Press, 1996).

Lacroix, Justine, "A Liberal Defense of Compulsory Voting," *Politics* 27 (2007): 190–5.

Landsburg, Steven, "Don't Vote. It Makes More Sense to Play the Lottery Instead," *Slate*, September 29, 2004; available at: http://www.slate.com/articles/arts/everyday_economics/ 2004/09/dont_vote.html.

Lardy, H., "Is There a Right Not to Vote?" *Oxford Journal of Legal Studies* 24 (2) (2004): 303–21.

Leighley, Jan E., and Nagler, Jonathan, "Individual and Systematic Influences on Voter Turnout: 1984," *Journal of Politics* 54 (1992): 718–40.

Lerman, J., "Voting Rites: Deliberative Democracy and Compulsory Voting in the United States," unpublished paper, 2009; available at: http://papers.ssrn.com/sol3/ papers.cfm?abstract_id=1600929 (last accessed November 21, 2010).

Lever, Annabelle, "'A Liberal Defense of Compulsory Voting': Some Reasons for Skepticism," *Politics* 28 (2008): 61–4.

"Is Compulsory Voting Justified?" *Public Reason* 1 (1) (2009): 57–74.

"Compulsory Voting: A Critical Perspective," *British Journal of Political Science* 40 (4) (2010): 897–915.

Levi, Margaret, and Stocker, Laura, "Political Trust and Trustworthiness," *Annual Review of Political Science* 3 (2000): 475–507.

Lijphart, A., "Compulsory Voting Is the Best Way to Keep Democracy Strong," in R. E. DiClerico and A. S. Hammock (eds.), *Points of View*, 8th ed. (New York: McGraw-Hill, 2001): 74–77.

"Unequal Participation: Democracy's Unresolved Dilemma," *American Political Science Review* 91 (1) (1997): 1–14.

Patterns of Democracy (New Haven, CT: Yale University Press, 1999).

Loewen, Peter John, Milner, Henry, and Hicks, Bruce M., "Does Compulsory Voting Lead to More Informed and Engaged Citizens? An Experimental Test," *Canadian Journal of Political Science* 41 (2008): 655–67.

Lomasky, L., "The Booth and Consequences: Do Voters Get What They Want?," *Reason* 24 (6) (1992): 30–4.

Lomasky, L. and Brennan, G., "Is There a Duty to Vote?," *Social Philosophy and Policy* 17 (1) (2000): 62–86.

Louth, J., and Hill, L., "Compulsory Voting in Australia: Turnout with and without It," *Australian Review of Public Affairs* 6 (1) (2005): 25–37.

Lundell, K., "Compulsory Voting, Civic Participation and Political Trust," *Representation* 48 (2) (2012): 221–34.

Mackerras, M., and McAllister, I., "Compulsory Voting, Party Stability and Electoral Advantage in Australia," *Electoral Studies* 18 (2): 217–33.
Mackie, Gerry, "Why It's Rational to Vote," unpublished manuscript, University of California, San Diego, 2009; available at: http://www.polisci.ucsd.edu/~gmackie/documents/RationalVoting.pdf.
Mahler, V. A., "Electoral Turnout and Income Redistribution by the State: A Cross-National Analysis of the Developed Democracies," *European Journal of Political Research* 47 (2008): 161–83.
Manning, Wendy D., and Lamb, Kathleen, "Adolescent Well-Being in Cohabitating, Married, and Single-Parent Families," *Journal of Marriage and Family* 65 (2003): 876–93.
Mansbridge, Jan, *Beyond Self-Interest* (Chicago: University of Chicago Press, 1990).
Markus, Gregory, "The Impact of Personal and National Economic Conditions on the Presidential Vote: A Pooled Cross-Sectional Analysis," *American Journal of Political Science* 32 (1988): 137–54.
Martin, P. S., "Voting's Rewards: Voter Turnout, Attentive Publics and Congressional Allocation of Federal Money," *American Journal of Political Science* 47 (1) (2003): 110–27.
Martinez, M. D., and Gill, J., "The Effects of Turnout on Partisan Outcomes in U.S. Presidential Elections 1960–2000," *Journal of Politics* 67 (2005): 1248–74.
Matsler, S., "Compulsory Voting in America," *Southern California Law Review* 76 (2002–2003): 953–78.
Mayer, Susan, *What Money Can't Buy: Family Income and Children's Life Chances* (Cambridge, MA: Harvard University Press, 1997).
Mayo, H. B., "A Note on the Alleged Duty to Vote," *Journal of Politics* 21 (2) (1959): 319–23.
McAllister, Ian, "Compulsory Voting, Turnout, and Party Advantage in Australia," *Politics* 21 (1986): 89–93.
McDonald, Michael P., and Popkin, Samuel L., "The Myth of the Vanishing Voter," *American Political Science Review* 95 (2001): 963–74.
McLanahan, Sara, and Sandefur, Gary, *Growing Up with a Single Parent* (Cambridge, MA: Harvard University Press, 1994).
Mendelberg, Tali, "The Deliberative Citizen: Theory and Evidence," in Michael X. Delli Carpini, Leonie Huddy, and Robert Y. Shapiro (eds.), *Research in Micropolitics*, Vol. 6: *Political Decision Making, Deliberation, and Participation* (Amsterdam: Elsevier, 2002): 151–93.
Mercier, Hugo, and Sperber, Dan, "Why Do Humans Reason? Arguments for an Argumentative Theory," *Behavioral and Brain Sciences* 34 (2011): 57–111.
Mill, John Stuart, "Considerations on Representative Government," in J. Gray (ed., intro.), *On Liberty and Other Essays* (Oxford, UK: Oxford University Press, 1991): 205–470.

On Liberty (Indianapolis, IN: Hackett, 1981).

Miller, Dale, "The Norm of Self-Interest," *American Psychologist* 54 (1999): 1053–60.

Miller, J. M., and Krosnick, J. A., "The Impact of Candidate Name Order on Election Outcomes," *Public Opinion Quarterly* 62 (3) (1998): 291–330.

Milner, Henry, Loewen, Peter John, and Hicks, Bruce M., "The Paradox of Compulsory Voting: Participation Does Not Equal Political Knowledge," *IRPP Policy Matters* 8 (2007): 1–48.

Morton, Rebecca, Piovesan, Marco, and Tyran, Jean-Robert, "The Dark Side of the Vote: Biased Voters, Social Information, and Information Aggregation through Majority Voting," working paper, Harvard University, Cambridge, MA, 2012.

Mueller, D. C., and Stratmann, T., "The Economic Effects of Democratic Participation," *Journal of Public Economics* 87 (9–10) (2003): 2129–55.

Murphy, Liam, and Nagel, Thomas, *The Myth of Ownership: Taxes and Justice* (Oxford, UK: Oxford University Press, 2002).

Mutz, Diana, "Mass Media and the Depoliticization of Personal Experience," *American Journal of Political Science* 36 (1992): 483–508.

"Direct and Indirect Routes to Politicizing Personal Experience: Does Knowledge Make a Difference?" *Public Opinion Quarterly* 57(1993): 483–502.

Mutz, Diana and Mondak, Jeffrey, "Dimensions of Sociotropic Behavior: Group-Based Judgments of Fairness and Well-Being," *American Journal of Political Science* 41 (1997): 284–308.

Nagel, J., and McNulty, J. E., "Partisan Effects of Voter Turnout in Senatorial and Gubernatorial Elections," *American Political Science Review* 90 (4) (1996): 780–93.

Nagel, Mato, "A Mathematical Model of Democratic Elections," *Current Research Journal of the Social Sciences* 2 (2010): 255–61

Neuman, W. Russell, *The Paradox of Mass Politics* (Cambridge, MA: Harvard University Press, 1986).

Noel, Hans, "Ten Things Political Scientists Know that You Don't," *The Forum* 8 (2010): 1–19.

Nownes, A. J., "Primaries, General Elections, and Voter Turnout: A Multinomial Logit Model of the Decision to Vote," *American Politics Quarterly* 20 (1992): 205–26.

Nozick, Robert, *Anarchy, State, and Utopia* (New York: Basic Books, 1974).

O'Connor, Thomas G., Caspi, Avshalam, DeFries, John D., and Plomin, Robert, "Are Associations between Parental Divorce and Children's Adjustment Genetically Mediated? An Adoption Study," *Developmental Psychology* 36 (2000): 429–37.

Orr, G., *Australian Electoral Systems: How Well Do They Serve Political Equality?* (Canberra: Democratic Audit of Australia, 2004).

"The Australian Electoral Tradition," in G. Orr, B. Mercurio, and G. Williams (eds.), *Realising Democracy: Electoral Law in Australia* (Leichhardt, UK: Federation Press, 2003): 1–6.

Orr, G., Mercurio, B., and Williams, G., "Australian Electoral Law: A Stocktake," *Election Law Journal* 2 (3) (2002): 383–402.

O'Toole, F., and Strobl, E., "Compulsory Voting and Government Spending," *Economics and Politics*, 7 (3) (1995): 271–280.

Pacek, A., and Radcliff, B., "Turnout and the Vote for Left-of-Centre Parties: A Cross-National Analysis," *British Journal of Political Science* 25 (1995): 137–43.

Palfrey, Thomas, and Poole, Keith, "The Relationship between Information, Ideology, and Voting Behavior," *American Journal of Political Science* 31 (1987): 510–30.

Pammet, J. H., and LeDuc, L., *Explaining the Turnout Decline in Canadian Federal Elections: A New Survey of Non-Voters* (Ottawa: Elections Canada, 2003).

Panagopoulos, Costas, "The Calculus of Voting in Compulsory Voting Systems," *Political Behaviour* 30 (4) (2008): 455–67.

Parekh, B., "A Misconceived Discourse on Political Obligation," *Political Studies* 41 (2) (1993): 236–51.

Parenti, M., *Democracy for the Few* (New York: St. Martin's Press, 1974).

Park, A., "Teenagers and Their Politics," in R. Jowell, J. Curtice, L. Brook, and S. Witherspoon (eds.), *British Social Attitudes: The 12th Report* (Aldershot, UK: Dartmouth, 1998): 42–52.

Pateman, C., *Participation and Democratic Theory* (Cambridge, UK: Cambridge University Press, 1970).

The Problem of Political Obligation (Cambridge, UK: Polity/Blackwell, 1985).

Peter, Fabienne, "Political Legitimacy," in Edward N. Zalta (ed.), *Stanford Encyclopedia of Philosophy*, Summer 2010 ed.; available at: http://plato.stanford.edu/archives/sum2010/ entries/legitimacy/.

Petrocik, J., "Voter Turnout and Electoral Preferences: The Anomalous Reagan Elections," in K. Schlozman (ed.), *Elections in America* (New York: Allen and Unwin, 1987): 121–132.

Pettersen, P. A., "Comparing Non-Voters in the USA and Norway," *European Journal of Political Research* 17 (3) (1989): 351–9.

Pettit, P., "Consequentialism," in P. Singer (ed.), *A Companion to Ethics* (Oxford, UK: Blackwell, 1991): 230–40.

"Analytical Philosophy," in R. E. Goodin and P. Pettit (eds.), *A Companion to Contemporary Political Philosophy* (London: Wiley-Blackwell, 1995): 7–38.

"Liberty as Anti-Power," *Ethics* 106 (1996): 576–604.

Republicanism: A Theory of Government and Freedom (New York: Oxford University Press, 1997).

Pew Research Center, "Are We Happy Yet?" February 13, 2006; available at: http://www.pewsocialtrends.org/2006/02/13/are-we-happy-yet/.

"Public Attitudes toward the War in Iraq: 2003–2008," March 19, 2008; available at: http://pewresearch.org/pubs/770/iraq-war-five-year-anniversary.

"What Voters Know about Campaign 2012," August 10, 2012; available at: http://www.people-press.org/2012/08/10/what-voters-know-about-campaign-2012/#knowledge-differences-between-voters-and-non-voters.

Ponza, Michael, Duncan, Greg, Corcoran, Mary, and Groskind, Fred, "The Guns of Autumn? Age Differences in Support for Income Transfers to the Young and Old," *Public Opinion Quarterly* 52 (1988): 441–66.

Powell Jr, G. B., *Elections as Instruments of Democracy: Majoritarian and Proportional Visions* (New Haven, CT: Yale University Press, 2000).

Power, T., and Roberts, J., "Compulsory Voting, Invalid Ballots and Abstention in Brazil," *Political Research Quarterly* 48 (4) (1995): 795–826.

Putnam, Robert, *Bowling Alone* (New York: Simon and Schuster, 2001).

Ragsdale, L., and Rusk, J. G., "Who Are Nonvoters? Profiles from the 1990 Senate Elections," *American Journal of Political Science* 37 (3) (1993): 721–46.

Rainbolt, G. W., *The Concept of Rights* (Dordrecht, Netherlands: Springer, 2006).

Ranney, A., "Nonvoting Is Not a Social Disease," in R. E. DiClerico and A. S. Hammock (eds.), *Points of View*, 8th ed. (New York: McGraw-Hill, 2001): 78–88.

Rawls, John, *A Theory of Justice* (Cambridge, MA: Harvard University Press, 1971).

Justice as Fairness: A Restatement (Cambridge, MA: Harvard University Press, 2001).

Raz, J., *The Morality of Freedom* (Oxford, UK: Clarendon Press, 1986).

RFE/RL Newsline, "None of the Above Finishes Sixth …, " Radio Free Europe/Radio Liberty, April 6, 2000; available at: http://www.rferl.org/content/article/1142131.html.

Rhodebeck, Laurie, "The Politics of Greed? Political Preferences among the Elderly," *Journal of Politics* 55 (1993): 342–64.

Rose, Richard, "Evaluating Election Turnout," in *Voter Turnout from 1945 to 1997: A Global Report on Political Participation* (Stockholm, Sweden: International IDEA, 1997): 45–6.

Rosema, M., "Low Turnout: Threat to Democracy or Blessing in Disguise? Consequences of Citizens' Varying Tendencies to Vote," *Electoral Studies* 26 (3) (2007): 612–23.

Rosenblum, Nancy, *On the Side of Angels: An Appreciation of Parties and Partisanship* (Princeton, NJ: Princeton University Press, 2010).

Rousseau, J. J., "The Social Contract," in G. D. H. Cole (trans., intro.), *The Social Contract and Discourses* (London: Everyman's Library, 1993 [1762]): 5–124.

Rubenson, D., Blais, A., Gidengil, E., Nevit, N., and Fournier, P., "Does Turnout Matter?" *Electoral Studies* 26 (3) (2007): 589–97.

Salisbury, R. H., "Research on Political Participation," *American Journal of Political Science* 19 (1975): 326–7.

Saunders, Ben, "The Equality of Lotteries," *Philosophy* 83 (2008): 359–72.

"Democracy, Political Equality, and Majority Rule," *Ethics* 121 (2010): 148–77.

"Increasing Turnout: A Compelling Case?," *Politics* 30 (1) (2010): 70–7.

"The Democratic Turnout 'Problem'", *Political Studies* 60 (2) (2012): 306–20.

Schmidtz, David, *The Limits of Government: An Essay on the Public Goods Argument* (Boulder, CO: Westview, 1991).

The Elements of Justice (New York: Cambridge University Press, 2006).

Schmidtz, David and Brennan, Jason, *A Brief History of Liberty* (Oxford, UK: Wiley-Blackwell, 2010).

Sear, C., and Strickland, P., "Compulsory Voting," Standard Note SN/PC/954 for members of the House of Commons (Canberra: Parliament and Constitution Centre, 2001).

Sears, David O., and Funk, Carolyn L., "Self-Interest in Americans' Political Opinions," in Jane Mansbridge (ed.), *Beyond Self-Interest* (Chicago: University of Chicago Press, 1990): 147–70.

Sears, David O., Hensler, Carl, and Speer, Leslie, "Whites' Opposition to 'Busing': Self-Interest or Symbolic Politics?" *American Political Science Review* 73 (1979): 369–84.

Sears, David O. and Lau, Richard, "Inducing Apparently Self-Interested Political Preferences," *American Journal of Political Science* 27 (1983): 223–52.

Sears, David O. Lau, Richard, Tyler, Tom, and Allen, Harris, "Self-Interest vs. Symbolic Politics in Policy Attitudes and Presidential Voting," *American Political Science Review* 74 (1980): 670–84.

Selb, Peter, and Lachat, Romain, "The More the Better: Counterfactual Evidence on the Effect of Compulsory Voting on the Consistency of Party Choice," paper presented at the ECPR Joint Sessions of Workshops, Helsinki, Finland, May 11, 2007.

"The More the Better? Counterfactual Evidence on the Effect of Compulsory Voting on the Consistency of Party Choice," *European Journal of Political Research* 48 (5) (2009): 573–97.

Sheehy, P., "A Duty Not to Vote," *Ratio* 15 (1) (2002): 46–57.

Shineman, V. A., "Compulsory Voting as Compulsory Balloting: How Mandatory Balloting Laws Increase Informed Voting without Increasing Uninformed Voting," paper presented at the Annual Meeting of the American Political Science Association, Toronto, 2010.

"Isolating the Effects of Compulsory Voting on Political Sophistication: Exploiting Intra-National Variation in Mandatory Voting Laws Across the Austrian Provinces," paper presented at the Annual Meeting of the American Political Science Association, Chicago, 2009.

Siaroff, A., and Merer, J., "Parliamentary Election Turnout in Europe since 1990," *Political Studies* 50 (5) (2002): 916–27.

Sides, J., Schickler, E., and Citrin, J., "If Everyone Had Voted, Would Bubba and Dubya Have Won?," *Presidential Studies Quarterly* 38 (3) (2008): 521–39.

Sidgwick, H., *The Elements of Politics* (London: Macmillan, 1891).

Singer, Peter, "Why Vote?" *Project Syndicate*, December 14, 2007; available at: http://www.project-syndicate.org/commentary/why-vote-.

Singh, S., "How Compelling Is Compulsory Voting? A Multilevel Analysis of Turnout," *Political Behavior* 33 (1) (2011): 95–111.

Solomon, J. D., "Even Those Who Don't Vote Should Have to Go to Polls," *USA Today*, October 24, 2002; available at: http://www.usatoday.com/news/opinion/2002-10-24-oped-solomon_x.htm.

Somin, Ilya, "Voter Ignorance and the Democratic Ideal," *Critical Review* 12 (1998): 413–58.

The Problem of Political Ignorance (Palo Alto, CA: Stanford University Press, 2013).

Sourander, A., Elonheimo, H., Niemela, S., et al., "Childhood Predictors of Male Criminality: A Prospective Population-Based Follow-Up Study from Age 8 to Late Adolescence," *Journal of the American Academy of Child and Adolescent Psychiatry* 45 (2006): 578–86.

Southwell, P. L., "The Effect of Political Alienation on Voter Turnout, 1964–2000," *Journal of Political and Military Sociology* 36 (1) (2008): 131–45.

Spooner, Lysande, *No Treason: The Constitution of No Authority* (New York: Free Patriot Press, 2012).

Studlar, D. T., and Welch, S., "The Policy Opinions of British Non-Voters: A Research Note," *European Journal of Political Research* 14 (1986): 139–48.

Swenson, K. M., "Sticks, Carrots, Donkey Votes and True Choice: A Rationale for Abolishing Compulsory Voting in Australia," *Minnesota Journal of International Law* 16 (2) (2007): 525–52.

Tabarrok, Alex, "The Private Provision of Public Goods via Dominant Assurance Contracts," *Public Choice* 96 (1998): 345–62.

Tajfel, Henry, *Human Groups and Social Categories* (New York: Cambridge University Press, 1981).

"Social Psychology of Intergroup Relations," *Annual Review of Psychology* 33 (1982): 1–39.

Tajfel, Henry and Turner, J. C., "An Integrative Theory of Intergroup Conflict," in W. G. Austin and S. Worchel (eds.), *The Social Psychology of Intergroup Relations* (Monterey, CA: Brooks-Cole, 1979): 33–47.

Texeira, R. A., *The Disappearing American Voter* (Washington, DC: Brookings Institution, 1992).
Thompson, D. F., *The Democratic Citizen* (Cambridge, UK: Cambridge University Press, 1970).
Trueman, C., "The Electoral Commission of 2001," *History Learning Site*: http://www.historylearningsite.co.uk/electoral_commission_of_2001.htm.
Twomey, Anne, "Deliberative Democracy, Compulsory Voting and the Will of the People," Law of Deliberative Democracy Workshop, New York University, April 6, 2013.
Verba, S., "Would the Dream of Political Equality Turn Out to Be a Nightmare?" *Perspectives on Politics* 1 (4) (2003): 663–79.
Verba, S. and Nie, N., *Participation in America: Political Democracy and Social Equality* (New York: Harper and Row, 1972).
Verba, S., Schlozman, S. L., Brady, Henry E., and Nie, Norman, "American Citizen Participation Study," 1990 (Ann Arbor, MI: Interuniversity Consortium for Political and Social Research [distributor], 1995); available at: http://dx.doi.org/10.3886/ICPSR06635.v1.
"Citizen Activity: Who Participates? What Do They Say?" *American Political Science Review* 77 (1993): 303–18.
Wall, A., Ayoub, A., Dundas, C. W., Rukambe, J., and Staino, S., *Electoral Management Design: The International IDEA Handbook* (Stockholm, Sweden: International IDEA, 2006).
Walzer, Michael, "Philosophy and Democracy," *Political Theory* 9 (1981): 379–99.
Watson, T., and Tami, M., *Votes for All: Compulsory Participation in Elections* (London: The Fabian Society, 2000).
Wattenberg, M. P., "Where Have All the Voters Gone," paper presented in the Political Science Seminar Series, RSSS, ANU, May 13, 1998.
Where Have All the Voters Gone? (Cambridge, MA: Harvard University Press, 2002).
"Why Don't More Americans Vote?" *Boston Globe*, September 21, 2003.
Is Voting for Young People? (New York: Pearson, 2008).
Weale, A., *Democracy* (New York: St. Martin's Press, 1999).
Wellman, Christopher Heath, *A Theory of Secession* (New York: Cambridge University Press, 2005).
Wellman, Christopher Heath and Simmons, A. John, *Is There a Duty to Obey the Law?* (New York: Cambridge University Press, 2005).
Westen, Drew, *The Political Brain* (New York: Public Affairs, 2008).
Westen, Drew, Blagov, Pavel S., Harenski, Keith, Kilts, Clint, and Hamann, Stephan, "The Neural Basis of Motivated Reasoning: An fMRI Study of Emotional Constraints on Political Judgment during the U.S. Presidential Election of 2004," *The Journal of Cognitive Neuroscience* 18 (2007): 1947–58.

Wielhouwer, P. W., "Strategic Canvassing by the Political Parties," *American Review of Politics* 16 (1995): 213–38.

"Releasing the Fetters: Parties and Mobilization of the African-American Electorate," *Journal of Politics* 62 (2000): 206–22.

Winkelmann, Lilliana, and Winkelmann, Rainer, "Why Are the Unemployed So Unhappy?" *Economica* 65 (1998): 1–15.

Winkler, A., "Expressive Voting," New York University, 1993 (UCLA School of Law Research Paper No. 09–14, Los Angeles, April 1, 2009); available at: http://ssrn.com/abstract=1371799.

Wolchover, Natalie, "People Aren't Smart Enough for Democracy to Flourish, Scientists Say," *Life's Little Mysteries*, February 28, 2012; available at: http://news.yahoo.com/people-arent-smart-enough-democracy-flourish-scientists-185601411.html.

Wolfinger, R. E., and Rosenstone, S. J., *Who Votes?* (New Haven, CT: Yale University Press, 1980).

Young, S., and Hill, L., "Uncounted Votes: Informal Voting in the House of Representatives as a Marker of Political Exclusion in Australia," *Australian Journal of History and Politics* 55 (1) (2009): 64–79.

Zukin, Cliff, Keeter, Scott, Adolina, Molly, Jenkins, Krista, and Delli Carpini, Michael X., *A New Engagement?* (New York: Oxford University Press, 2006).

Index

CPSIA information can be obtained at www.ICGtesting.com
Printed in the USA
BVOW07s0112231014

372012BV00001B/20/P